The
Radical
Renewal

ALSO BY NORMAN BIRNBAUM

The Crisis of Industrial Society
Social Structure and the German Reformation
Toward a Critical Sociology

The
Radical
Renewal

THE POLITICS OF IDEAS
IN MODERN AMERICA

Norman
Birnbaum

Pantheon Books
New York

A portion of this book appeared in a
different form in *The Crisis of Modernity*,
edited by Günter H. Lenz and Kurt L. Shell,
published by Campus Verlag, Frankfurt am Main.
Copyright © 1986 by Campus Verlag.

Library of Congress Cataloging-in-Publication Data

Birnbaum, Norman.
The radical renewal.

Bibliography: p.
Includes index.
1. United States—Intellectual life—20th century.
2. United States—Civilization—1970–.
3. United States—Politics and government—1945–.
4. Politics and culture—United States. I. Title.
E169.12.B55   1988   973.927   87-46065
ISBN 0-394-70659-5

Book design by The Sarabande Press

Manufactured in the United States of America
First Paperback Edition

For S.G.

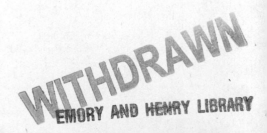

Contents

Acknowledgments

First things first: I record, with pleasure, my gratitude to my colleagues at Georgetown University (President Timothy S. Healy, S.J., Dean Robert Pitofsky, former Dean David J. McCarthy, Jr., Professor Judith Areen) for many things—most especially, a humane setting for reflection.

The International Institute for Environment and Society of the Science Center for Social Research, West Berlin, and its director, Professor Udo Simonis, provided hospitality during the year 1986. My thanks in Berlin also extend to Professors Peter Wapnewski and Wolf Lepenies, former rector and rector, respectively, of the Wissenschaftskolleg (Institute for Advanced Study, Berlin). They were good enough to extend a welcome despite the inability of their administration, for the better part of a year, to settle on a title for me. Was I a guest fellow, a guest scholar, or something else—and how, in any event, translate these terms of art into German? Their unfailing courtesy despite this severe travail demonstrates that minor triumphs of scholarly content over bureaucratic form are possible.

The delight and profit I have derived from membership in the Wellfleet Psychohistory Conference is very great. Its meetings, so benignly convened by our maximum leader, Dr. Robert Jay Lifton, are events against which one can measure one's annual progress. Since this usually has been slow, the meetings mark my calendar like so many medieval days of penitence.

I have worked with Richard Barnet and Marcus Raskin for so long that our common assumptions mark this book. Perhaps that is why their works do not figure in the text, as if I took their precious ideas for granted. I trust that with their characteristic generosity and sense of the essential, they will forgive me and recognize how much they are present in the book.

They also serve who sit and think. Years ago, I had a fellowship from the John Simon Guggenheim Memorial Foundation for a book on the Marxist legacy. My Marxist legacy, in the event, was exhausted: the book was never written. Perhaps this one can serve as a very belated alternative. Let the same be said by way of acknowledgment to the School of Social Sciences of the Institute for Advanced Study (Princeton), for a year's membership.

Much of the matter of the book on the academic disciplines comes from work I did at Amherst College on a grant from the Carnegie Corporation (Carnegie Foundation for the Advancement of Teaching) for a study of the college curriculum. Finally, both the Exxon Education Foundation and the Andrew W. Mellon Foundation were good enough to give assistance to Georgetown University Law Center for our program in Humanities and the Law. A good deal of this book reflects my teaching in that program.

My appreciation goes, as well, to my publisher, André Schiffrin, and my editor, James Peck, for advice and encouragement. Fred Wiemer was of great help as copy editor, Marlene Arnese as bibliographer, and S. W. Cohen and his associates as indexers. Mary Ann DeRosa and her colleagues at Georgetown University Law Center were unfailingly efficient in dealing with the manuscript, as was Inge Boehm with a large segment of it at the Wissenschaftskolleg.

Lastly, I owe a great debt to friends in politics. I have learned much from those in parties, social movements, and unions on both sides of the Atlantic. Whatever of hope and realism this work contains reflects their pedagogy.

Preface

Not so long ago, a Jesuit friend asked me why I had not become a neoconservative. "After all," he said, "You are from New York, you admired Trotsky, and, of course, you are Jewish." These may be necessary conditions for neoconservatism, but they are not sufficient. I have adhered to the tradition of the Enlightenment, and to the effort to construct a more moral society, for three reasons. I am a New Yorker, but I left the city at the age of sixteen to attend Williams College. I was struck at once by something about the larger American society that appears to have escaped the notice of those who later were so pathetically grateful to be allowed to join it. It was, if in its own way and in its own accents, no less distressed than the ethnic province from which we came. I certainly admired Trotsky for his historical vision and his struggle against Stalin: I still do. More, I have always worked in the Marxist tradition and have been active in radical politics. I never belonged to either the American Communist Party or any variety of Trotskyite group. I do not wish, then, to deny or repudiate my past, and I find the curious mélange of authoritarianism, despair, and rootlessness that characterizes the neoconservatives spiritually repugnant. Finally, I have retained enough of my Jewishness to interpret the world as incomplete. We are in this world not to justify it but to fulfill it.

Good intentions are not enough. We need ideas that are complex and deep as well as critical. This book discusses the views of American society developed by my teachers, my contemporaries, and our students. No doubt it bears the mark of my experience. I spent the years 1952 through 1966 in Europe. For many years, I taught a discipline that has lost the central position it once claimed. I trust that the text shows how much can be learned about our culture and society from scholars in American studies, history, law, political economy, and philosophy. It is also evidence that a radical tradition in our intellectual life still has much to teach us.

1

SOCIAL THEORY IN THE UNITED STATES: THE LEGACY OF THE RECENT PAST

I

Introduction

Some time ago I was asked by colleagues at the University of Frankfurt to give a paper on the reception of the Frankfurt School in the United States. I responded that the Frankfurt School had indeed been influential in America. What was most interesting were the intellectual predispositions which led many to take its ideas seriously—and, later, the ways in which these ideas were Americanized. Rephrased in these terms, the reception of the Frankfurt School does give us a useful starting point for a journey which must carry us far from the heart of Europe—to the struggle over the self-definition of our republic.

The Frankfurt School had an important influence in the United States in two distinct and separate periods. From as early as 1934, Adorno, Horkheimer, Lowenthal, Marcuse, Pollock (and Fromm and Neumann and Wittfogel) were in the United States. The Frankfurt School's work had considerable impact on American social science in the subsequent decade and a half, and (no less important in that period) on the thought of those irrepressible generalists, the New York intellectuals. The Frankfurt School émigrés came to a United States caught up in the New Deal, which itself incorporated three decades of critical American social thought. A new historiography skeptical of many aspects of liberal-capitalist ideology, an institutional economics opposed to ideas of the primacy of the market (and derived in no small measure from the *Kathedersozialisten* of Germany), a philosophical pragmatism which entailed a new sense of thought's public responsibilities, and a legal realism which depicted legal institutions and tradition as instruments of class domination rather than repositories of ultimate morality—these were some of the antecedents of the New Deal. Indeed, the New Deal's battalions of innovative bureaucrats were educated on these doctrines—sketched with fine detail in a book by a scholar, Morton White, who himself as a younger student at Columbia knew the Frankfurt émigrés. The New Deal drew as well on large residues of American

3

populism—and some of the most significant social movements activated by the New Deal and the Depression, not least the union-organizing campaigns of the period 1934–37, were directly influenced by American Marxism. There was an American Marxism, a consequence of the amalgam of a native socialist tradition and the impact of the Russian Revolution. That Marxism was essentially economic in its focus, although some of the early writings of Sidney Hook did attend to themes of Marxist humanism never remote from, if not at the center of, the Frankfurt School's work. Interestingly enough, Hook thought of connections between Marxism and pragmatism later adumbrated by Habermas—less surprising when we consider that Hook's teacher, John Dewey, had begun his career with intensive studies of Hegel. The immediate implication of the component of self-generating activity in this version of Marxism was, however, to provide philosophic legitimation for systematic programs for fundamental changes in economic institutions. The social uses of psychoanalytic theory in the United States took the same direction: witness those studies of character and cultural and social milieu initiated by Margaret Mead and others in an effort to falsify the view that aggressive competitiveness was a permanent feature of human nature. It is true that there was a distinctive American idiom, in which a democratic populism and a certain aggressive optimism (derived from Calvinism, no doubt) generated a language quite different than that of Europe. The New York intellectuals, Jewish or not, were sufficiently Europeanized in their thought to serve as bearers of the Frankfurt School's message. That Columbia University in New York and not Harvard in Cambridge offered the Frankfurt Institute of Social Research hospitality was significant. Suffice it to say, then, that the first reception of critical theory in the United States reflected the assumptions and intentions of an engaged American intelligentsia in the New Deal epoch.

The change, when it came, was rapid and total. Nothing illustrates it more effectively than Edward Shils's critique of *The Authoritarian Personality.* Shils, who had been a cotranslator of the works of Karl Mannheim, is exaggeratedly typical in his career. Beginning in the critical atmosphere of the New Deal decade, he displayed an unfailing gift for anticipating the *Zeitgeist.* He was a neoconservative *avant la lettre* and influential as a founder of the Congress for Cultural Freedom and adviser to the Ford Foundation's European programs. In other words, he was a collaborator in the Central Intelligence Agency's disbursements of funds to intellectuals. His rejection of *The Authoritarian Personality* (which was published in 1950) was a rejection of the uncertain synthesis of American progressivism and European social criticism it entailed. In its place, there was already developing that peculiar American amalgam of formal pluralism and insistent technocracy, of a consensus about the necessary connection of a domestic welfare state and a world empire, which was later to be termed corporate liberalism.

The social science that dominated the American universities from 1945 onward, typified by Parsons's consensualism, Hartz's view of a monolithic American equation of liberalism and the market, and the Keynesians' theory of negotiated economic growth, were quite open in declaring the new world the best of all possible ones. Populism and progressivism were derided, indeed depicted as dangerous (McCarthyism and systematic anticommunism were now explained as due to the Stalinist toadying of the intellectuals or to excesses of democracy against which only a responsible elite was protection). A theory of world development advanced the view (not least in the works of one of the architects of the Vietnam War, Walt Rostow) that modernization was a global process in which the United States (the West Europeans limping behind but given good grades for their effort to catch up) served as a very successful and compelling model of what all societies would, or at least should, become. Psychoanalysis itself became a prestigious medical speciality, its tragic aspects ignored, its socially critical implications not forgotten but insistently converted into their opposite. Discussions of the possibilities of another society, or of major changes in the existing one, were dismissed as utopianism or sectarianism, if not psychopathological (or regrettable remnants of a Stalinist mentality, the definition of which was extended to encompass large aspects of American progressivism).

Finally, a special category of thinkers and of thought emerged: social critics and social criticism. Social critics were persons who did not respect what the academy described as rigorous disciplinary discourse (and which was in fact a set of conventions that owed much to guildlike interests and even more to the lack of historical and philosophical cultivation that marked, alas, many American social scientists). These persons, worse yet from the viewpoint of those who looked on them patronizingly, wrote for a general public—not for fellow scholars or client groups. They could be, however, encapsulated or sanitized. It remained only to describe or interpret their work as addressed to society's defects or flaws—but not to an alternative model of social organization or culture. An entire component of the Western tradition was miniaturized, its adherents degraded to the role of court jesters.

This process occurred *pari passu* with another, no less profound in its effects—or rather, with two others. One may be described as the academicization of the avant-garde. The migration of artists and writers to universities; the sponsorship by universities of small-circulation journals of culture and politics; the inclusion, in literary curricula especially, of matters hitherto the concern of intellectuals outside the university; and the recognization of modernism and the disavowal of the genteel (and Protestant) tradition, were components of this phenomenon. The other process may be described as the vending or even commercialization of the avant-garde. A numerically expanded educated public, and the extension of cosmopolitan standards to the provinces—as well as the application to the cultural market of techniques of entrepreneurship and publicity—all contributed to that diffusion of modernism which, of course, also took the edge off it. A contribution, difficult to measure exactly but by no means small, was certainly made by the attainment of middle-class economic standing by the East European immigrant Jewish population of previous decades. It is now difficult to imagine, but in 1946 a Luce weekly, *Life,* could still print an attack on the art of Jean Dubuffet as subversive of Western culture and major university faculties could debate whether to appoint Jewish academics to teach English since it was supposedly not their tradition. The triumph of the New York School in painting, of the Jewish novel in literature, the emergence of *Commentary* (once the *Contemporary Jewish Record*) as a standard of reference for serious cultural discussion, the accession of the *Partisan Review* editors from the status of eccentric bohemians to arbiters of cultural taste—all were so many pieces of evidence for the conclusion that the main body, whatever that was, had hastened to join the avant-garde. It was, however, an avant-garde quite denuded of serious social thought. The work of the Europeans during this period (1945–65) sometimes constituted irritations; rarely was it seen as a stimulus. Sartre was a public figure, but his thought was taken seriously by a small group of philosophers and teachers of literature, not by social scientists. Bloch was unknown, and Gramsci and Lukács were virtually ignored. The Europeans thought worthy of consideration were usually those who crossed the Atlantic to offer reassurance: Raymond Aron from France, and of course Isaiah Berlin and Karl Popper.

What had happened to the legacy of European social thought—including that of the Frankfurt School—in the United States? Weber, his authoritarianism, imperialism, and systematic irrationalism thoroughly ignored, was converted into someone who had had the good fortune to anticipate the work of Talcott Parsons. In another, more serious interpretation, he was depicted as a profound comparativist (rather than as a pure conceptualist). On this reading, indeed, his historical work at least hinted at objections to the enormous complacency and philistine self-congratulation of the votaries of "modernization." Neumann's great work on Nazism, which demonstrated that the term "totalitarian" could not apply to the Third Reich, was elevated to classical status—and ignored. Arendt's *The Origins of Totalitarianism* was received as an instant masterpiece, and its conclusions—that capitalist society could not sustain the values of the bourgeois revolution, indeed systematically destroyed these—was as enthusiastically overlooked. A floodtide of minor work, marked by confessional self-abasement or tedious elaboration of the obvious, quite obscured the problems entailed in the failure of the Russian Revolution. In the narrow areas of social research, Paul Lázarsfeld labored very hard to eliminate a larger social purpose from empirical inquiry—and when pressed, occasionally supplied a vague rationale in terms of the necessity to educate that democratic public opinion which his studies showed existed only in the tracts of those who thought the United States an achieved liberal democracy.

To be sure, there was another American spirit—in a not entirely uncomfortable inner emigration. The quarterly *Dissent* was founded in the Eisenhower years (with a gift from Norman Mailer, whose *Naked and the Dead* had been hugely successful despite, or maybe because of, its antimilitaristic theme). In contributions from the Jewish labor movement and American socialists, from revisionist Marxists and recent graduates from Trotskyism, it kept in touch with the intellectuals in the unions, and derided the pieties and sterilities of the first Cold War and its concomitant, what Irving Howe termed the American Celebration. Michael Harrington synthesized a Catholic social tradition with a Marxist legacy. In a striking instance of collaboration across the generations, it was Dwight Macdonald (whose *Politics* had been the last expression of the radicalism of the decade 1930–40 until it ceased in 1947) who later (1962) in the *New Yorker* called the public's attention to Harrington's study of poverty, *The Other America*. The *Monthly Review* group (Baran, Sweezy, Leo Huberman) persisted in a systematic economic criticism of American capitalism and showed themselves often rather more aware of its international, which is to say imperial, implications than their social democratic contemporaries. That awareness had a negative aspect: it took the group a very long time (stimulated by the Sino-Soviet dispute and by the Eurocommunism of the Italian Communist Party) to arrive at a systematic analysis of Stalinism. We can say that the social democrats, the socialists, and some of the revisionist Marxists suffered from the opposite difficulty. Utterly convinced that the Soviet Revolution had been betrayed and distorted, they had to struggle to arrive at a position independent of the conventional anticommunism then dominating the ideological marketplace. That anticommunism, let it be said, often included a large repudiation (if at times an unavowed one) of the idea of progress. When it was combined with advocacy of social reform, that advocacy was usually hedged. Conservatives who held that progress was an illusion and those who thought it was a useful idea agreed on this—that the Western industrial democracies anno 1955, some regrettable flaws apart, were incarnations of the most that could be hoped for.

The Frankfurt School, however, did live on in the United States. In the first instance, it did so in the work of Herbert Marcuse. His *Soviet Marxism* was a tortuous text—but it did attempt a view of the Soviet Union in terms of its own social development, rather than in the categories of the vacuous "totalitarianism" model institutionalized in American Sovietology. (It was the misfortune of Zbigniew Brzezinski and Carl Joachim Friedrich, who knew enough history to know better, to develop on the eve of the Polish October and the rising in Hungary [1956] an argument on the impossibility of change in Soviet-type states.) Much more importantly, in *Eros and Civilization* he presented a historical account of the development of the Western psyche. The psychoanalytic depiction of repression and of the psyche, generally, was seen not as a capitulation to the constraints of a limited historical setting, but as a profoundly exact statement of the nature of bourgeois culture and society. In controversies, *inter alia* with Fromm in *Dissent,* Marcuse rejected one interpretation of Freud's work as lamentably superficial. The portrait of the social setting in Fromm, Horney, and (by implication) the American anthropologists, assumed that it could be altered in a benign way by a singular combination of insight and social engineering. It ignored, therefore, the tragic dimension in Freud's depiction of the development of Western culture—or rather, the depiction as a statement of the inevitability of repression. Marcuse thought that surplus repression could be ended, if the historical development of the productive forces and their organization allowed it. In effect, he joined anew the realms of freedom and necessity. Marcuse left entirely open the question of historical agency, which was to suffuse (by implication) his later *One Dimensional Man* and to constitute a central preoccupation of the New Left. He opened, however, the way for a renewed sociocultural critique of capitalism in its recent forms.

A more direct attack on those institutional forms came from the great American heir of the Frankfurt School, Charles Wright Mills. A student of Hans Gerth, he met the school's members in New York after joining the Columbia faculty in 1945, and proceeded to unite his own American radicalism with a Marxist sociology. Mills was rather isolated from the official leadership of American sociology and academic social science, but he did enjoy a very large public. His themes, the bureaucratization of culture and society, the moral irresponsibility of American elites, the destruction of citizenship, the necessity of the development of a new political vanguard in the newer sections of the labor force, were exactly those taken up after his premature death (in 1962) by the American New Left. Mills had succeeded not merely in translating European social thought into an American idiom; he had concretized it in the situation of the American empire. No doubt a certain lack of sublety in his thought was the price he paid for sticking obdurately to ideas of citizenship and individuality he took from the American tradition. In his person (a Catholic Texan who had studied in Texas and at the University of Wisconsin), he was quite unlike the eastern Jewish or Protestant intellectuals who were initially receptive to the Frankfurt School's work.

Others may have brooded about alienation; Mills built the houses he lived in. Another father of the New Left also spoke in an American idiom—the historian William Appleman Williams, who held that organization for imperial domination had corrupted, if not destroyed, the American polity. Paul Goodman, whose *Growing Up Absurd* struck a generation as an exact depiction of the spiritual defects of its parents and teachers, was an eclectic who may well have read the writings of the Frankfurt School but who eschewed systematic social thought in favor of an immediate kind of cultural criticism.

The ideas used by the political movement that eventually, in its academicized form, accounted for a second reception of the Frankfurt School already owed something, then, to the school—but the school's ideas came to it in indirect fashion, through Mills, and through the legacy of cultural criticism of the New York intellectuals. Marcuse's *Eros and Civilization* was a text known only in small circles, and if his work *Reason and Revolution* was standard reading on Hegel, it was all the Hegel most American students ever learned. His *One-Dimensional Man* coincided with, and was taken up by, the protest movement of the period 1964 onward, and on no account generated it, even if it expressed in rather more historical and general form what Goodman had been saying.

I have referred to the political and protest movement of the period, and it remains for me to render the characterization more precise. It had several elements, of unequal weight and density, both specific and diffuse. The protest of black students (and of the black population generally) at segregation in the South and discrimination throughout the society evoked sympathy and support among white students and some of the educated middle class. (Those who oppose a supposedly enlightened or liberal middle class to a narrow working class, in cultural-political terms, ignore the unequivocal allegiance of most of the educated in the United States to the Republican Party.) This movement of sympathy was extended as protest also involved Hispanics, American Indians, and Asian-Americans. The designation of these as "Third World" people within the United States led at times to depictions of ethnic relationships in this country as internal colonialism, at others to the belief that these minority segments of the nation would provide a vanguard for an anticapitalist and anti-imperialist movement. More generally, the black protest led to a reconsideration of American history, to a retroactive delegitimation of pious views of American history as a moral progression toward ever greater egalitarianism. The movement protesting the war in Vietnam (which began some years later) followed the same course—for some— from specificity to a more general or systematic view. The protest led to a sustained reconsideration of America's world role since 1945, and to a new view of our imperial history since the end of the last century—since, indeed, the war with Mexico. The Free Speech movement at Berkeley was in this respect exemplary: begun by veterans of the not entirely quiescent left of the late years of the decade 1950–60, and of the movement of sympathy for southern blacks, it initially focused on the university as an institution in league with the centers of power in the larger society. This was generalized to a rejection of bureaucratic careerism and culture, to the kind of analysis of American society found in Mills's *Power Elite* of 1956. What distinguished the movement of the decade 1960–70, no doubt, from the American student movement of the period 1930–40, the New Left from the old one in general, was the emphasis on culture and personal change. This was an uneven or serial phenomenon, made up of fragments of psychoanalytic theory, some drawn from Wilhelm Reich, components of Protestantism and the American search for a true self, and elements utterly remote from Calvinism: the systematic self-indulgence and ego destruction of the drug cult. It is easy enough, now, to be patronizing about the demand for personal authenticity that was expressed in this way. (Lionel Trilling was among the patronizing, but he might not have written his most considerable book had the New Left not seized the theme and forced it upon us.) It did lead tens of thousands to oppose the war and refuse service in it, and it also played a major part in reawakening American feminism. By the time the movement in its political form had run its course, those who had been through it were obliged to rethink the entire history of American radicalism, its roots in (or distance from) our culture, and to devise a new view of the national experience. In particular, the questions of the relationship of democracy to populism, of the American working class to social reform, of nation to empire, were raised anew.

This is, to be sure, not the place to attempt a definitive evaluation of the political consequences of the movement of the decade 1960–70. To see in it only a convulsive and ignorant attack on impregnable cultural traditions and social institutions, which resulted in the disintegration of the New Deal's reformist coalition, the election of Nixon, and then the triumph of the peculiar Reaganite synthesis of ideology and manipulation, is to ignore several things. One is that the movement did constitute the most successful anti-imperial movement in the history of the West, up to and including widespread disaffection in the armed forces. Another is that the impetus it gave to black and feminist consciousness has been permanent—whatever countermovements have been mobilized. The third is that a new awareness of the political dimensions of culture and of cultural issues has seized the public—by no means an awareness that is entirely dominated by the fundamentalism or pseudotraditionalism of the right.

The negative legacy of the movement is, or should be, obvious—its almost systematic disregard of economic questions. That disregard has now been replaced, in important parts of the academy, by a new set of economic analyses that has renewed the tradition of institutional economics (and also, Marxism) in American thought. The difficulty is that whereas the cultural and even the anti-imperial parts of the original program have become projects for social movements, the new economic thought has a rather narrow basis in the unions and various interest groups. The problem is an aspect of two questions that are intrinsic to the disparate sorts of social thought we find in the contemporary United States: the question of agency (which historical groups may be expected to alter the present situation?) and the question of public and rhetoric (to whom, and how, do thinkers speak, or for whom do they write?). So acute, so pervasive are these questions that they suffuse every aspect of theoretical discussion. Indeed, these questions may yet redeem theory— by obliging theorists to consider thought's connection to a world it has most definitely not yet remade.

What, however, is social theory? It is easier to say what it is not. It is clearly not an articulated set of propositions subject to verification or falsification by experiment. No community of social scientists in agreement on the assumptions of their discipline (or disciplines) can be found. Even in those periods in which consensus reigned in one or another discipline, significant groups of dissenters could be found, arguing that the dominant consensus represented the forcible closure of very open questions. The continuing process of self-reflection in social science has been reinforced, in recent decades, by a compelling development in the natural sciences: the analysis of the sociotemporal structure of scientific work. The distinctions between natural and social science may now seem less fixed, but their indistinctness does not support the party which argues that the social sciences must eventually be seen as identical with the natural ones in the latter's rigor. Rather, those elements of cultural and philosophical and political variability, of insertion in a social milieu, that more obviously mark the social sciences are now seen to characterize the natural ones. The argument continues. For the moment we can draw from it a larger, if more open, conception of social theory.

In this conception, experience and sensibility, intuition and purpose—however loosely defined—have their functions. Social theory is the effort of a social group to reflect upon itself, not a record of experience alone but an effort to master it. The questions of historical subject and of public are not ancillary to the enterprise but constitutive of it.

It is true that in the period 1946–64 most American social scientists wrote for each other—indeed, wrote mainly, if not exclusively, for colleagues in their own discipline. It would be a mistake, however, to see this as conclusive evidence of the hermetic status of the social sciences. The quantitative expansion of the social sciences, the domination of each discipline by successive waves of intellectual fashion, the coinage of special languages like so many currencies of small countries, the Byzantine elaboration of internal hierarchies ruled by persons not quite gigantic in intellecutal stature—all of these were (and are) derivative phenomena. The American social sciences constituted a social technology, and a legitimating ideology, for the larger society—more precisely, for many of its elites. Connected to the corporate structure, to the foundations, and to government by intermediaries recruited from the university not despite but because of their utter absence of critical distance from the distribution of power, the social sciences in the end delivered much of what was required of them. Analytical empiricism (termed by Mills "abstracted empiricism") took society as a given—if not immutable, then unlikely to change in major ways or in surprising or unwelcome ones. It therefore extrapolated from the immediate situation to a timeless realm in which insubstantial entities ("actors," "norms," "values," "sentiments," and occasionally—underemphasized and unspecified—"constraints") governed human action. Despite the enormous emphasis placed upon psychoanalysis in the areas of therapy and in certain kinds of social commentary (as in Riesman's typology of personality), a consensual behaviorism devoid of passion ruled the social sciences. Surprisingly, preparation for war and war itself was accompanied by a flattened notion of human nature, in which aggression—innate or induced—had no fundamental part. Depictions of politics were segmented, allocated now to portraits of a liberal and pluralistic domestic system, now to notions of an emerging world order—menaced, to be sure, by historically obtuse forces that employed revolutionary ideology but which failed to see that the last authentic revolution had been the American one.

It would be too simple to declare that the opposition was confined entirely to the margins. At times, its criticisms rendered the proponents of the new orthodoxy somewhat nervous. Given the paucity of Marxist scholarship in the period, a quite extraordinary amount of energy was expended in iterations of Marxism's one-sidedness and its historical obsolescence. The notion of economic classes in American society was converted into that of income groups. For ideas of imperialism, views of modernization were substituted—subject or dominated peoples portrayed as volunteers in a global struggle to turn humanity into a triumphant mass of consumers. Even some decades later, it is not entirely clear why so many had to be persuaded of so little. The technological segments of the social sciences (public-opinion polling, studies of organizational behavior, small-scale conflict resolution) seemed to work on another plane. Perhaps the point was to avert the possibility that these might be connected, intellectually, by their own proponents with other social projects, even with the project of domination of which they were a part.

One sphere in which academic social science in its most conventional form and critical thought met, even coexisted uneasily, was the study of, or rather preoccupation with, mass society. Lazarsfeld's work, a last gasp of his historical awareness, dealt with the reception of mass communications and at least by implication with the destruction of ideas of citizenship. The view that populism could be bent to the service of chauvinism and fundamentalism (heavily charged with ignorance and paranoia) was a beginning point for systematic reflection on the naïveté of American radicalism in its earlier form, a justification for what was later to be termed corporate liberalism—the manipulative rule of an elite engaged in the adjustment of conflicts that were not ever allowed to fully engage public consciousness. It was not, except for a very few thinkers, employed as a beginning point for an inquiry into the conditions for the reactivation of the democratic ideal. That, too, would have been thought naïve. It is true, certainly, that (here Mills was an honorable exception, and Hannah Arendt from quite another perspective refused her assent to a depiction of the United States as a fulfilled eighteenth-century polity) many radicals were embarrassed, indeed disoriented, by the failure of their fellow citizens to show more spiritual independence.

Still, there was an opposition. The academy did provide a protected space for some critical thought, despite the general sterility of the social sciences. Remnants of classical Marxism, increasingly revitalized by attention to themes of Marxist humanism; the legacy of Veblen; legal scholarship that had not accepted the assignment to the law of the status of the primary instrument of a manipulative social technology—these combined in jagged fashion with two themes that were, in the period after 1960, to dominate discussion. One was, simply enough, the anti-Protestant revolt in culture. It was hardly new, and recent scholarship has shown how much of American reform was motivated by the desire for a more expansive, a psychologically freer, existence. Stimulated in the immediate postwar period by sources as diverse as Wilhelm Reich's doctrines and the supposed libidinal freedom of black culture (united in a personal way by Mailer in his influential essay "The White Negro"), this current carried forward an honorable if traditional American theme. Money—in a larger sense, the pursuit of the things of this world—deadened the spirit. Emerson and Thoreau were summoned to join Adorno (known for his studies of popular music and bits of his work on mass communications) in an improbable alliance. The other theme was, again simply enough, refusal of empire. Nineteenth- and early twentieth-century roots were there: think of Thoreau and the Mexican War, the opposition to the conquest of the Philippines, the movement that evoked such repression during the First World War. It was complicated in the period after 1945 by the domination of much of international conflict by the struggle with and over Stalinism, by the confluence of important elements of the New Deal coalition with the new imperial apparatus, by the very internationalism of the anti-imperial party. What was later to become a conservative opposition to unlimited American military and political engagement abroad (voiced by Senator Fulbright and Ambassador Kennan) had no part in this initial anti-imperial response. Rather than the skeptical realism (as they would put it) of these thinkers, it was sustained by a strain of pastoral idealism, by American pacificism.

I conclude this introduction by pointing, again, to a paradox. Systematic criticism of American culture as the culture of capitalism, refusal of the American empire as a system of domination, and a desperate search for lost civic virtue and democratic participation were the most salient themes of the oppositional social theory that preceded the turbulence of the decades beginning in 1960. What was, if not missing, certainly underemphasized was a critique of production; we had, instead, a critique of consumption. There was a literature on work and workers, but an analysis of economic processes (as contrasted with their cultural and social consequences) was almost absent. Baran and Sweezy's *Monopoly Capital* was an exception, but even these resolute Marxists had to deal with the problem of the surplus produced by a capitalism that seemed very successful. A small group of scholars, historical and institutional in their approach, attended to the American labor movement. Change might come, protest might move the nation—but the idea of an anticapitalist movement, of an alternative form of production, exerted no conviction. The conviction has, haltingly, since returned—but in a different intellectual and political context, to which I now turn.

II

Is There
an American Polis?

Every attempt to conceive of an altered American society must struggle against an assumption disguised as a fatality. The social contract in which the nation originated legitimated the market as our central, indeed primordial, institution. Acquisitiveness and individualism, liberty and property, were practically inseparable. It is true that church, community, family, race, and region each bind groups of Americans together. Even our pluralism, however, has much of the market about it, if a political market, in which the commodities traded are power and prestige. Suppose, however, that these assertions were only partially true, or, more precisely, that other principles contended for the American spirit. Suppose, indeed, that before acknowledging the primacy of the market early Americans envisaged a republic of virtue, its citizens united in the cultivation of common terrain—not dispersed to work exclusively on their private gardens. Imagine, too, that this republic were conceived as a political community, a polis—so that public life had its own morality, quite distinct from and even superior to the private sphere. We would possess the elements of a very different sort of American politics, in which rights and responsibilities were in more evident balance, in which civic solidarity counted for as much as the defense of property.

In fact, we do have a past usable in this way. What is still a debate among historians of the eighteenth and early nineteenth centuries, of analysts of the transformation of European politics on American soil, has consequences at least as large as the explication, by other historians, of America as a class society. We need not attempt the impossible, the invention of a future in total rupture with the past. We may be able to draw upon traditions which, if not buried, have been overlaid, to suggest that there are possibilities in our national experience undreamed of by these who think of Locke as a New Englander, Hobbes as a Virginian.

It would be absurd to deny that we inherit a legacy of exploitation and racism, of domination and inequality. It would be absurd to do so because the clarity given us by the newer cultural and social history is so hard-won—and so contested by philistines in eager ideological service to those who have good (or rather, effective) reasons for presenting our history as a tale of unalloyed goodness. I do not say fairy tale: fairy tales are complex structures, full of insight into ambiguity and conflict. The point rather is that inquiry that seems almost antiquarian, joined to abstract reflection that appears at times pedantic and remote (the recent debate in political philosophy), is utterly contemporary.

Here, moreover, a critical or radical party in American thought must defer to others—or at least share the honor of producing a fuller vision. Not so long ago, in a pastoral letter the Catholic archbishop of Denver instructed his Catholic brothers and sisters that they possessed traditions that could serve the nation. They had a conception of community that enabled them to transcend the atomizing individualism of Protestantism. As the nation undertook the twenty-first–century tasks that would demand cooperation and solidarity, certain forms of Protestantism would be found wanting of moral resources. No doubt the archbishop could reread Perry Miller on the Massachusetts Bay Colony (or Walter Rauschenbush on social Protestantism) with profit. But his argument remains a strong one, the more so as he selected the social ethic of the evangelicals for special attention. The archbishop, in the end, attributed Catholicism's political strength to its access to natural law. Those who pride themselves (excessively) on their modernity find this conception obsolete—or embarrassingly naïve. There is, however, a connection— and by no means a tenuous one—between ideas of the naturalness of community and a very radical tradition. The nineteenth-century humanist who wished humanity, as a species being, to live a fuller species life was in that tradition.

We are not able to say the same of those historians who have given such loving attention to the idea of republicanism, of civic virtue, of the public life, in early American history. Most of them are distinctly not radical in their politics and may be described as despairing conservatives or ecumenical skeptics.

That is no less reason, and perhaps more, to take their work on a republican tradition seriously. Repelled by the venality and vulgarity of our politics, they have taken refuge in the academy for the same reasons many radicals have. It offers a chance, at least, of contemplating a better society—if not, alas, of pursuing one.

We are, of course, far from the schematism of the Progressive historians, with their depiction of a people in permanent combat with oligarchies. The Progressives, however, were not backwoods Manicheans. They understood very well that the course of American history constituted a continuing reduction of the idea of popular sovereignty. Were they saying in this respect anything very different than their more reserved contemporary successors who see in the very sobriety of debate over the Constitution the antithesis of the eschatological enthusiasm of the revolutionary years? What is original about recent work is that it sets a context for early American ideas of representation and popular sovereignty. These were not invariably ends in themselves, and most certainly not exclusively intended to secure property rights. They entailed an American distillation of European tradition. Cromwellian ideas of commonwealth, the country party's view of the court in England, were adapted to American circumstance.

What, more precisely, were republican tradition and civic virtue, the Crown and its servants having been expelled? American arguments against British tyranny had been mixed. Some did derive from natural law and from the right to property. Men had property in themselves and so could dispose of their own bodies and spirits. Other arguments came from historical assertions of the particular rights of Englishmen. Ideas of republican virtue moved on a rather different plane. They avoided the antithesis of universal and concrete, abstract and historical, which so agitated the colonists and their English adversaries and supporters. Virtue could be cultivated, or developed—but only in the civic sphere. At the beginning of a national history that encompassed (and encompasses still) a quite extraordinary amount of privatization, one version of the nation insisted on an autonomous and even sublime sphere of politics. Civic rights and civic duties, education and government, the cultivation of character and the public life, were inextricably connected.

Much was confined, no doubt, to rhetoric. Racism and slavery, fear and loathing of the white poor, counted for more. In a work the more shocking for the stolidity of its prose, Morgan suggests that in Virginia, republicanism and slavery made one another possible. Lesser and grander whites could share a franchise they united to deny to blacks (and Indians). The freeholders' republic and the slaveholders' one were, for a long time, identical. Dealing with the contradiction, one reflective conservative, Diggins, has suggested that the language of interests found in *The Federalist Papers* was simultaneously a renunciation of a republican idea of virtue and a tribute to it. Virtue was not always attainable. The good sense and experience of the Federalists gave the nation a workable set of everyday institutions. In crises, however (so Diggins), only the idea of sin could mobilize spiritual energies, and infuse our politics with meaning. Diggins offers the case of Lincoln as the supreme example: only his melancholy Calvinism enabled him to lead the war on the evil of slavery. That fallible humans should believe, religiously, in their own fallibility may or may not be sublime. In most cases, however, it has led to resignation, even cynicism. Diggins's own search for a lost soul of American politics, as he terms it, ends on a pathetic note: it remains lost. Reminiscences of Niebuhr are not entirely faint. In depicting American history as occurring after the Fall, Diggins may believe that he is providing an apology, of sorts, for interest-group politics. In fact, he leaves us almost nothing except a dizzying alternation between the disappointments of the profane and very rare moments of the sublime.

The many students of early American politics have combined, in effect, to secularize our understanding of it. The more open of the authors of the Constitution saw nothing to hide in the avowal of a natural inequality—resulting in differences of property. Their principle of difference, to anticipate Rawls, left no alternative to capitalism. Where, however, did that leave virtue—and what sort of republic could result? There are several possible answers. One is that the idea of virtue is viable only in crises, to be conscripted for moral service when all else fails. Another is that it serves as a permanent standard against which to measure the baseness of ordinary institutions. Yet another is that it constitutes a moral reservoir, upon which movements of renewal can draw. The older Progressives may have envisaged a real republic of toilers, at battle with an inauthentic one of spoilsmen. Hartz and Hofstadter half affirmed, half derided, a democracy of greed. The newer historians imagine a nation ambiguous or irresolute, hopelessly divided as to its whether it rests on discernible social principles at all. Are they, perhaps, reading into the past the burdens of present philosophical disputes? What is surprising about much of the historical literature (often written by scholars quite distant from pure philosophic inquiry) is the closeness with which is reproduces the themes of current argument about our polity.

The argument reminds us that the consensus on capitalism is potentially fragile. It is, indeed, a very long time since fear of a revolution against property moved our elites. Much of the second half of the nineteenth century, and no small part of this one, was marked by just that fear. And did not the Reagan administration initially consider appointing as chairman of the National Endowment for the Humanities a historian who held that the Emancipation Proclamation was an unconstitutional taking of property? Slave society had every reason to fear a rising by the slaves. Not racism alone, but a sense of the dangers of social upheaval, made northern (and western) Americans for decades accomplices in slavery. Indeed, the profound class conflicts of the epoch after the Civil War were interpreted in ways that attest the continuity of fear. The working class was depicted as barbarian; the task of domesticating it was equated to the war against Indians on the frontier. Other figures of speech joined the struggle to a general war on the lesser races; intimations of empire made their appearance. In what was a parody of the past both unwitting and witless, the professorial antiradicals of the decade 1960–70 were quick to denounce their students and colleagues as barbarians. By this time, to be sure, empire had already come; the fear was that it might go. The search for a different past, the debate on first principles—each expresses the shock of recent events. The decade 1960–70 hardly fulfilled standard Marxist prophecies of class conflict, but the threat to an entire system of rule was acute.

As with the inquiry into early American political philosophy, the (very) abstract debate among political and social philosophers on the elements of a good society appears remote from these historical torments. Each debate, however, bears closely upon the present. Indeed, Rawls's *Theory of Justice* was instantly identified as an apologia for the Great Society—correctly. Ronald Dworkin's argument about rights referred explicitly to the civil disobedience so evident in the recent past. The philosophers do argue in their own terminology, the very abstractness of which enables them to question the permanence of our ideas.

Let us begin with Rawls. His work on justice uses the language of analytical philosophy—hardly enlivened by occasional recourse to that of welfare economics—lacks historical references, and is very weak in its psychological dimensions. The humans who populate Rawls's society are curiously disembodied, isolated selves somehow forced into relationship with one another. No doubt there is something enduringly American about their primary concern with position, power, and wealth. More importantly, Rawls raises to universal categories the aims of the liberal welfare state. The principle of difference asserts that no economic or social difference is justified which does not ultimately give the momentarily disadvantaged an equivalent benefit.

The most interesting criticism has come from those sympathetic to Rawls's aims of redistribution and social justice. Sandel argues that Rawls's community of equals is not a community at all, but a collection of isolates. In a painstaking reconstruction of the irreducible social element in ourselves, Sandel shows that Rawls's selves are bundles of needs, thoughts, and wishes—but not persons. The description of humans as having property in themselves (indispensable to the liberal intellectual genealogy) is ultimately unsatisfactory: property (and even more, self) are social ideas that describe social relationships.

The humans bargainings behind Rawls's veil of ignorance (ignorance of their endowments and fate) arrive at the principle of difference to serve their own selfish interests. They agree to justice as systematized fairness because they are quite uncertain that unfairness will work to their advantage. Sandel (and others) insist that Rawls is not quite consistent. His humans also need recognition from others—as if there were a substratum of sociability in human character that precedes the calculated reenactment of the social contract basic to Rawls's society. I have not found in the discussion of Rawls the aphorism from Durkheim's criticism of Spencer's view of contract as the basis of industrial societies: everything in the contract is not contractual. The thought, however, is there—if expressed in different terms. One argument (by Charles Taylor) is that we not only enter into terms of a relationship; we work at the kinds of persons we wish to become. Another (again by Sandel) is that Rawls at times uses the language of knowledge. Knowledge, however, is not choice: it presupposes constants, or processes, to which the contracting parties adapt. Sandel reminds us that there is a great divide in the history of social thought. For most of Western history, ethical knowledge was just that—learning how to behave by learning what sort of person to become, in deference to fixed criteria of right and (even more) set models of humanity. In the modern, or secularized, epoch, voluntarist thought has prevailed: we select among possible systems. Rawls inhabits a modern landscape, but traces of older sorts of moral dwellings can be found in it.

Very different sorts of criticism, then, have been directed at Rawls—a tribute not only to the care and weight of his thought but to its expressive function. Rawls published his *Theory of Justice* in 1971. The Nixon administration, unlike Reagan's, had launched no broad attack on the American welfare state. Indeed, some scholars argue that it even extended the work of its Democratic predecessors. Rawls's book was regarded as a philosophic charter for welfare-state liberalism, for a reconciliation of liberal individualism and equality, personal autonomy and redistribution. Significantly, Rawls (having made of the rights of citizens a postulate of fairness) did not deepen his argument about citizenship—or participation. Social structure did not interest him. His critics concentrated on this lacuna—at least his radical critics did. They insisted that he had ignored the structure of the self, and its most profound motives, the elements in human groups that shaped the terms of agreements about justice (and everything else). The major criticisms, however, condense into two. One regrets that Rawls did not go beyond what Popper might well see as a successful venture in methodological individualism: the solitary self remains the irreducible element of Rawls's society. The second argument restates the first, perhaps, but in political terms. Human historical structures are all we know, and these are political communities, however conflicted or flawed. It is plausible to construct an ideal scheme of allocation, and to measure actual human institutions by this ideal. We are still left with all the problems of agency, belief, and purpose that beset the effort to think of human, rather than divine, justice.

After Rawls, sociophilosophical debate appears to have reverted to its initially fragmented state, with contending camps engaged in a very loud *dialogue des sourds*. Appearances deceive. If we understand Rawls as making a last stand for liberalism, the engagement of some thinkers with his work released their energies for new beginnings—or, at least, more spirited efforts to move in directions they had already charted.

Barber is unusual in that he moves freely between the analysis of ideas and the description of institutions. Indeed, his work on strong democracy is undogmatically prescriptive. It entails a stringent rejection of conventional sorts of analysis in politics—because these derive political action, institutions, and thought from other realms. Barber intends something else than the usual critique of reductionism or scientism in social thought. His point is, rather, that even the derivation of political action and thought from other realms of social existence denies the autonomy, and the potential nobility, of the public sphere. Barber, clearly, has been influenced by Arendt—the Arendt who was an early proponent of the view that the new order of the ages envisaged by the early Americans was to be a republic of virtue. Barber has the honesty to acknowledge that cultural and social institutions undreamed of by Jefferson, Madison, and their contemporaries (and even by Lincoln) make republican virtues very difficult of attainment. His solution is to actualize citizenship by decentralizing democracy, and he treats of the innovations that could accomplish this. The project of restoring the autonomy of politics in practical terms has other antecedents. We are reminded, again, of the realms of necessity and freedom in Marx, who believed that these would coexist even in postrevolutionary society.

Another reminder of the tradition that engendered Marxism has come from Alasdair MacIntyre. Less resolutely optimistic than Barber, he regrets that we live in a world denuded of civic virtue. If much less sanguine about the immediate possibilities of institutional innovation, he puts his hope in the recovery of a view of humans as capable of moral growth—above all, during and through the search for themselves that in other settings (and in other views) confirms contemporary atomization and narcissism. For MacIntyre the search can occur only in a reconstituted public sphere.

Our thinkers, then, have neither abandoned the definition of humans as political beings, nor renounced the possibilities of community and solidarity. We may well ponder the fact that recent emphases on community and sociability are by no means the exclusive work of those seeking large-scale social reform or reconstruction. Bellah and his colleagues, discussing the Americans who spoke in *Habits of the Heart,* assert that they suffer from not being embedded in public life. What difference is there, we may ask, between this diagnosis and the arguments advanced by Berger and Neuhaus, their call for the renewal of intermediate institutions? Berger himself may have given an answer by asserting, not without satisfaction at the discomfiture of the party of enlightenment, that kin, church, neighborhood, even nation, have been ignored or even denigrated by that party. The naturalness he seeks to recover or restore is (or is intended to be) historically specific. The overestimation of our capacity for thinking, and acting, in universal categories strikes him (the argument is not, to be sure, unfamiliar) as evidence for a sin of pride, and perhaps as the characteristic modern sin of pride.

The difference at issue lies, not in terms like "community" and "solidarity," or in the generic assertion that an atomizing individualism is neither an accurate account of human nature nor a viable basis for a social ethos. It lies in the realm of attitudes to the future—whether we deal with a project of recovery that is also one of construction. The insistence that lost treasures can be found again does not necessarily entail enthusiasm for them in their present form. Indeed, it may express energies of a very radical (even revolutionary) kind. Put in another way, we still have ideas of a community which could be not only much improved, but much more nearly ideal. In this nation, philosophers may propose, but lawyers dispose. The actual American social contract is located in constitutional jurisprudence. The work of the legal academy, sometimes taking the form of comment upon or criticism of judicial decision, sometimes anticipating decision, is a continuous exercise in applied social philosophy. It is conducted in a language seemingly precise, but in fact ambiguous—or, perhaps more accurately put, open to differing (and sometimes conflicting) canons of interpretation.

Analyses of legal standards and reasoning, depiction of the functioning of the legal system as an institution, combine in no fixed or uniform fashion with the broadest kind of economic and social (and sometimes psychological) assertion. The law journals are never more philosophical, of course, than when their contributors devote pages to convincing their readers (and, above all, themselves) that their function is solely that of social grammarians. Many lawyers are hardly so unselfconscious, and readily acknowledge that they are pronouncing on, or promulgating, social values, even entire sets of these. Some are honest enough to use the term "ideology." Constitutional debate is a continuous dialogue of American society with itself. One very singular aspect of it is that rival groups of specialists engaged in it each loudly insist that they alone speak for a public interest that might otherwise remain unarticulated—above all, by the public itself.

The debate on interpretive as opposed to noninterpretive constitutional jurisprudence serves the legal academy as a framework, perpetually likely to disintegrate, for other arguments. Pressed, few lawyers will insist that there is any letter of constitutional law. Even strict constructionists will acknowledge that their logic leads to a gigantic deconstructive project, in which they would have to tear down or otherwise efface most of our constitutional history since 1789. A large segment of constitutional rhetoric recurs to a trope of progress. In a nation at least partially committed to the Enlightenment, it could hardly be otherwise. Looking back more modestly, we can say that the movement of legal realism was intellectual progress: it advanced the analysis of law by making lawyers scholars not only *in* but *of* the law, social scientists by some other name. The earlier generations of legal realists have had three schools of successors, whose arguments give our law schools more intellectual vitality than is evident in most other disciplines.

The first of these schools are the votaries of the economic analysis of law. Most of its advocates adhere to modern caricatures of classical economic models. I use the term "caricature" because after Marx, Marshall, and Veblen, after the past one hundred years of social thought, we might expect a decent minimum of reticence about reducing social structures to machines for cost-benefit calculi. Reticence is nowhere visible, but a manic courage is: the scholars in question have liquidated complexity, history, and tradition. The last remaining materialists, they hold that everything (and, by implication, everyone) has a price. Theirs, however, is not a refined system of national accounting, an American version of the Gosplan now under criticism in the USSR. They join their analyses to an unreflective sort of methodological individualism—and their vision of society reminds us of nothing so much as that (quite untrue) depiction of imperial England as a nation of shopkeepers. Humanity as a race of bookkeepers, in the grip of an obsession that obliges us to keep counting: no satiric writer can equal Posner, with his proposals to auction off body parts for the ill and babies to those seeking to adopt them. That these positions are termed "conservative" is quite unintended evidence of how little, in our society, many conservatives think is worth conserving. Their spiritual resources are measured by the capacity of their desktop computers, their vision encompassed by what can be stored on discs. By contrast, the ordinary liberal technocrat appears as a character from Dostoyevski.

The technocrats in question would shrink from the designation: how would it look, after all, on a résumé? (The use of the term "résumé" rather than "curriculum vitae" also tells us something: lives are expected to have a finished narrative structure and on no account represent stages in a moral progression.) The technocrats have put legal realism at the service of the modern administrative state (and extended it, in practice and theory, to the entire pattern of large-scale organization and central-ized decision that unites public and private sectors). In their omnipre-sence, the modern administrative state and the large corporation erase the boundaries between public and private interests, and between legal questions of procedure and social questions of substance. The liberal technocrats—precisely when they claim to represent a public interest in the demarcation and regulation of intersecting jurisdictions—supply both the state and the private sector with legitimation. They do so by describing their function as the resolution of conflicts.

In fact, they occupy mined ground. From the conceptual world of legal realism, they draw, as justification for their powers, the intimation that they are simply resolving already fixed and formed conflicts in the body politic. From their factual integration with the existing structure of power and property, they derive the practical limits upon their intel-lectual capacity to envisage solutions to these conflicts. They present themselves, in dizzying alternation, as simple servants of society and as philosopher-kings with higher powers. A liberal like Alexander Bickel expressed this ambiguity with consummate skill by elevating "ripeness" to a criterion for constitutional decision. The courts did have political functions, but had to be preternaturally cautious in saying so. Theodore Lowi was blunter. The second American republic, as he terms the administrative state, has abandoned the principles of the first one, and ought to return to it. Interestingly, Lowi's work was acclaimed a master-piece of political science—by those of his colleagues who continued, after reading it, to demonstrate that they totally lacked any idea of how to effect the transition.

It was (and is) at this point that the Critical Legal Studies group exploited the inner uncertainty of American liberalism. Roberto Unger, above all, has argued that the technocratic captivity of that liberalism is an inevitable result of the development of an administered capitalism. In confronting it, the Critical Legal Studies group has two faces, as do the other heirs of the decade 1960–70. On the one hand, it takes its distance from its liberal teachers and legal realist predecessors by enunciating a recondite Marxism, replete with citations from authorities of impeccable standing—from contemporaries like Anderson and Habermas to iconic figures like Adorno and Gramsci. Singularly, older Marxist theoreticians of law like Renner are ignored. On the other hand, the group reverts to American radicalism and reads the law as a social text, as a story of domination and exploitation, greed and prejudice. The more subtle in the group see that if the law is a text, it is indeed open to very different readings. The depiction of the law as a system of interpretation provides something more profound than connections to work in philosophy and literature. In a reversal of the field that has added to the bewilderment of their more stolid colleagues, the interpretive segment of the movement casts away the intricate structuralism of even modern Marxism, as well as the more linear causality of a canonical legal realism. It restores political and spiritual openness to the project—by calling for radical social experimentation with the law. Unger has termed the process subversion, and has been understood quite literally by his eminent university president, who has risen (or descended) to the challenge by taking not intellectual but administrative measures to halt the process. Since the subversion in question is the critical reworking of assumption and belief that is characteristic of modern thought, it is difficult to believe that the challenge can be dealt with so crudely.

Implicit support for the position that the law is a (relatively) open text has come from an unexpected quarter. Dworkin is certainly not thought of as associated with the Critical Legal Studies movement. He writes not in the direct style of an American legal brief (or law-review article)—but rather as an Oxford philosopher would speak, anticipating objections, making one hundred fine points, moving toward a conclusion less by constructing a structure of argument than by showing that all other positions constitute so many prefabricated intellectual ruins. Dworkin is even further from the language of deconstruction. The assertion that there is conceptual arbitrariness in the relationship of words to things (or processes or persons), even more the incredible assertion that there are no things, processes, or persons, simply constructions, would strike him as odd. Still, when he insists that judges (and those promulgating the law generally) do pronounce upon, even find, rights, he admits a substantial amount of interpretation into the practice of jurisprudence. Dworkin insists that judges deal with, and in, actual rights. If we accept his picture of jurisprudence as initial image, we may still look behind it. The judges in his texts, the public and polity whom they address, construct rights, fashion practical standards out of common experience and so alter it. Is this a description that can be applied to any group or agency (administrative ones, too) making political decisions? I do not believe so: the method as described by Dworkin entails a good deal of reflectiveness, a certain amount of conflict, and an indispensable minimum of dialogue. In short, it meets the criteria set by the Critical Legal Studies group for a more critical and open sort of legal thought.

Let us return to earlier notions of a republic, of civic virtue. A society in its politics—above all, law—does something other than balance interests or adjudicate rights. Even when we stick to that language: balance and adjudication define (and implicitly create) rights. The ostensibly prosaic routines of administration, upon examination, are no less political than elections—or Supreme Court decisions. Politics is, at its highest point, a continuous scrutiny of society by its members. We know that much of what passes for politics is force unlimited by constraint, fraud untouched by moral rigor, manipulation devoid of reflection, and passivity emptied of self-respect. One thing alone can alter our condition: the continuous self-activation of a conscious citizenry. Marx, writing in the optimistic aftermath of the American and French revolutions, declared that we had to move from the idea of citizenship to the notion of humanity. Sobered by the experience we have endured since, our newer American political philosophy asks how we may become citizens. That seems, for the moment, task enough. Atomized and mechanical notions of citizenship have been questioned. Much of liberalism appears to be an orchestrated illusion, or a gigantic self-deception. It assumes what remains to be proven, that we do have a fully functioning citizenry. A morally inspired and politically noble social science has to begin modestly—by inquiring into the possibilities for the recreation of citizenship. A liberal political philosophy that supposes that the American Revolution was a success has contributed to the ossification of the nation's thought.

III

Empire and
World System

That the United States has an empire is a proposition that some years ago was strenuously denied. We had a system of alliances, we had assumed responsibility for a "free world" (which included Messrs. Franco, Globke, Salazar, Somoza)—but the notion of empire was repugnant to republican taste. Even geopolitical realists disliked the term: empire, after all, implied a commendable inner cohesion in the metropolis, and the difficulty of conducting foreign policy in a democracy was one of their central themes. Two otherwise unimportant, indeed trivial, alterations of rhetoric recently did signify a profound change in attitude. Arthur Schlesinger, Jr., himself a participant in the Kennedy administration, published a book on the concentration of power in the presidency and titled it *The Imperial Presidency*. To be sure, there was a certain discretion about this liberal concession to reality. It was the presidency, not the nation, that was imperial—but, upon reflection, the historian did attribute the hypertrophy of presidential power (and of the hubris of the occupants of the office) to the concentration of power in the area of what is termed national security (but which is more accurately termed national insecurity). More recently, Irving Kristol (who edited *Encounter* when it was under CIA tutelage and who must be numbered among the neoconservatives) has suggested that it would be entirely accurate and appropriate to use the term "empire" to describe the nation's foreign involvements. Kristol, to be sure, is possessed of what in his circles must count as quite disturbing honesty; did he not in the *Wall Street Journal* declare that the Europeans were quite within their wits to be frightened out of them by nuclear weapons on their soil?

The new honesty is, in many respects, a new brutality. For the moment, at least, the center (always more rather than less feeble, its own weight absurdly exaggerated) has collapsed. Advocates of American world domination openly confront their domestic opponents, liken the conflict to a civil war, and make no secret of their willingness, if necessary, to sacrifice liberal ornaments like constitutional rights and the separation of powers to defend their conception of the nation and its mission. The liberal critique of empire suffered from an inner contradiction that tells us much about postwar American society. National Security Directive 68, drafted in 1949 by Paul Nitze, was also the work of Leon Keyserling, chairman of the Council of Economic Advisers and an author of the Full Employment Act. Postwar American prosperity rested on unimpeded access to cheap raw materials, protected markets, and possibilities for investment in much of the world. An American-dominated world system enabled American domestic production to expand, and the American unions were fully integrated into the system. The unions became transmission belts for influencing (where necessary, creating) unions abroad, principally but not exclusively in Europe. American empire, then, rested on rather more than the CIA and the armed forces, on the purchase or submission of foreign elites (usually, elites quite willing to cast their lot with empire for fear of domestic or other enemies). It rested on an ideological and socioeconomic concensus within the United States, whose architects were not recruited from the traditional right but who came from and indeed led the New Deal coalition.

The American liberals, it should be remembered, were also American nationalists. American participation in the Second World War had accomplished what the New Deal could not, or at any rate did not, do: it produced full employment. The vision of a unified and fulfilled nation promulgated by the liberals had a number of elements reinforced by the war and its immediate aftermath. These included the themes of the corruption, or at least debility, of the Old World and the superiority of democracy as an instrument of social equality and economic growth. The immediate postwar period showed how ephemeral and fragile was the alliance with the Soviet Union despite the crude pro-Soviet propaganda of the alliance period. The liberals, however, had other than geopolitical or global economic grounds for unmitigated hostility to Stalin's Russia. Quite apart from the putative dangers posed by Communist internal threats in Germany and western and southern Europe, they were in danger of being outflanked ideologically by the American right. Russia's entry into the war in 1941 had only strengthened much of the right's conviction that the United States should remain out of it. The internationalist sectors of the American elite were of course realistic enough to accept the alliance with Stalin, but after the war they were not too fastidious to refuse the right's help against the possibility of a strenuous resumption of the New Deal. What actually occurred was the construction of a new consensus, in which the elements of a welfare state were accepted in return for the participation of the urban working class and the farmers in the profits of empire. The integration of the immigrant groups from eastern and southern Europe in the society, the opening of access to elite and subelite positions, constituted a social fundament for this process. American Catholics from central and eastern Europe required little prompting to join in systematic anticommunism. The Germans welcomed it (as the Federal Republic was transformed into a model ally) as a convenient device for minimizing the recent past. Jewish groups apparently experienced an inner and outer need to distance themselves from historical connections to radicalism. Moreover, the sympathy of American Protestants in particular for the new state of Israel (a sympathy that in some measure alleviated guilt over the passivity of the United States and the allies during the extermination of European Jewry), and the de facto alliance with Israel, provided yet other grounds for attachment to the United States. Except to blacks, a large amount of egalitarianism was in fact provided by postwar society: we confront something far more substantial than illusion.

In this setting, the liberal academy had an unenviable task: it had to justify empire while criticizing it. The task was made easy by the academy's astonishing capacity for historical forgetfulness, for theoretical and rhetorical neologisms, and by the recruitment to it of thousands of entrants from ethnic and social groups that had not hitherto been represented in the professoriat. The new social sciences in particular tended to attract these recruits. The whole was held together by the one principle that was rigorously adhered to: a strict division of intellectual labor, which fetishized "disciplines." These in turn made fragmented vision, historical ignorance, and ideological bias the concomitants of their reconstructions of social process. Political philosophy and Sovietology dealt with the Soviet threat and the pathologies of Marxism.

Economics and to some extent political science treated of "development." International relations depicted superpower conflict and alliance systems. Anthropology and sociology asked why other populations were unlike Americans, not infrequently suggesting that this was due to unfortunate historical circumstances. A view of "modernization" (along with an unchallenged antirevolutionary assumption) provided a simulacrum of common discourse. Terms like "exploitation" or "imperialism" were exorcised, and "domination" was what happened in Eastern Europe—or in China, which functioned (until Nixon's reconciliation with the People's Republic) as an antisociety of large dimensions.

Criticism, then, took the form of opposing "excesses" (like seeing the hand of Stalin and his successors in every social disturbance at home and abroad). Mixed economies were admitted—provided that they allowed decent amounts of American private investment. Above all, the world's difficulties were attributed to the unequal rate of a process termed "modernization," which, when completed, would complete its pacification. Behind much of this lay, of course, two convictions. One was that the American model of political and social development was canonical, especially the model provided by the New Deal and the Keynesian welfare state. The second was that domination, relationships of power, could be domesticated—no—nullified. This was a projection onto the globe of what was current in academia, a systematic denial of the structure of power in the United States.

In retrospect, what is surprising is that it took so long for these illusions to become apparent for what they were. In part, the determination of any number of scholars who did not think of themselves as ideologues to fortify an ideology of liberal empire was responsible. Theories of the convergence of industrial societies, of the end of ideological conflict, had their function. What destroyed the postwar synthesis, however, were political developments and their cultural refraction. Those who planned and executed the Vietnam War were those who had planned the miserable expedition to the Bay of Pigs. Those who were shocked by the Bay of Pigs as a moral disaster (an attempt to impose a counterrevolution on a nation that had little inclination for it) were later shocked by the Vietnam War—and some of them, at least, began to reconsider the connection between empire and liberalism.

The structural connections were, of course, easiest to establish. The economic, ethnic, and political groupings contributing to the imperial consensus were hardly invisible. The sum of the advantages drawn by the nation from its position of global domination was hardly hidden. Somewhat more difficult to characterize, paradoxically, were the particular groups staffing the imperial apparatus: perhaps the integration of the universities in the imperial system had something to do with the functional blindness of scholarship. The empire required an apparatus: bureaucrats, experts, military. It is surprising how little these were studied in connection with their expanded functions. The economic aspects of empire posed other difficulties: the private sector no doubt profited from them, but those advantages were unevenly distributed. There were, indeed, explicit and implicit conflicts of interest within the private sector. The historian John Lewis Gaddis has shown that a certain kind of conservative was more worried about budgetary deficits and those costs of empire than about the Soviet threat, and named Eisenhower as typical of this attitude. He also urged that the Democrats, as the party of federal spending, were drawn to larger arms budgets and an expansionary foreign policy in every sense.

That large sectors of American industry profited from or constituted themselves as what Seymour Melman termed "Pentagon capitalism" is obvious. Once these have been identified, however, other and more profound questions remain. To what extent does the entire system depend upon the maintenance or expansion of high levels of arms spending? What are the economic and political connections between industries directly engaged in arms production and those dependent upon the raw-material sources protected by imperial engagement, or dependent upon the freedom to move capital across borders without political interference by nationalism or revolutions? To what extent, indeed, can an arms sector in the national economy be clearly distinguished from other sectors? Given the intricate connections of education and research, corporate structures and market organizations, to both military and nonmilitary sectors of the economy, a conceptual separation is a theoretical exercise, sundering what in reality is fused. Vulgar proponents of empire have long recognized this, arguing for public consumption that prosperity and employment depend upon expanding arms production. Most economists have assiduously avoided these questions, possibly because they have avoided questions of the institutionalization of the market in general. A growing set of radical economists have now begun to tackle these, joined by institutionalists who ostensibly eschew a radical perspective but who insist that the political dimensions of economy have been ignored.

In other respects, however, the critique of empire is more advanced. The impact of the Vietnam War, the countercultural revolt in general, have led to a cultural critique of American imperialism—with historical dimensions. A good number of anthropologists, many attracted to the field by their critical distance from their own culture in any event, have studied themes as varied as the supposed war-making or acquisitive propensity of humans and the effects of domination on rulers and the ruled. Historians and students of American culture have expanded upon the dimensions of internal imperialism: the extirpation of the Indians, the legacy of conquest on ideology and psyche. The relationship of Protestantism, and the sense of world mission, to imperial opinion has been explored. Racism, obviously, has been the object of scholarly opprobrium, but the connections between domestic racism and imperial domination have been established only tentatively. Of course, the peculiar character of America's relations to the Oriental nations (China and Japan) has not escaped even the most conventional of historians. The particular American relationship between xenophobia (frequently directed at white Europeans, from eastern and southern Europe, mainly Catholics) and nationalism has had some clarification. The clarification, however, has not quite extended to the recent demonstration of the extraordinary assimilating power of American nationalism, which in a very short period of time made hyperpatriots of those whose ancestors rioted against military service during the Civil War. Perhaps there is a distinction between American xenophobia and a European kind of nationalism. Possibly, a stereotypical anticommunism expresses a revolt against secular culture of a sort analagous to Nazism: the recent recrudescence of a peculiar American combination of militant Protestant fundamentalism and imperialism suggests that it does. These phenomena have been insufficiently studied, and the usual hypotheses on the decline or eclipse of community are clearly inadequate. American fundamentalism develops in communities that may be threatened, but which are quite intact.

Does empire, then, require a counterenlightenment? There is a growing literature on the distortion of production through the misallocation of resources to arms, a distortion that extends to scientific and technological research. Consider, however, the case of the state of Texas. It has a state university, and research centers which, in order to enhance the economic weight of the state, invest in Nobel Prize winners in physics and biology. Its local school boards, or some of them, insist at the same time on instruction in creationism. Perhaps what we are experiencing is not primarily the progressive cretinization of segments of American society (many of which were never touched by the modern currents once assumed to be normative). We are experiencing, instead, its segmentation. The imperial apparatus is able to maintain itself less by ideological persuasion (the opinion polls suggest that the American public fears nuclear war at least as much as it fears the Soviet Union, and it is strikingly unmilitant about figures like Castro and the Sandinistas) than by its sheer presence and weight. It has outgrown its rationale, and instead manufactures rationales to justify its existence: consider the recent shift in rhetoric from "world communism" to "terrorism" to "Islamic fundamentalism."

Historians have increasingly emphasized segmentation as a central characteristic of American society for a long period. Earlier forms of segmentation were, however, often vertical, although vertical, regional differences also contained or enveloped class differences. Work on populism has also focused on the differences between the agrarian South and West and the industrial East, differences that included cultural and religious antagonisms between eastern workers (including many Catholic immigrants) and southern and western farmers. More than some remnants of populism found their way into the antiwar movement of the First World War and into what was later to be termed isolationism, whose domestic components included a large suspicion of the internationalist eastern elites. Despite occasional short-term bursts of chauvinism, we do find evidence of increasing vertical division over empire. Contrary to the stereotype assiduously propagated by the right, the American industrial working class was more opposed to the war in Vietnam than the educated middle class. The Korean War, its costly but little-remembered predecessor, was vastly unpopular with the ordinary families whose sons died in it. To what extent a generalized suspicion of elites is at work, we cannot yet say. The class and cultural divisions evident in the differential incidence of conscription in the Vietnam War

36

have been remarked upon. What has been less remarked upon is the remarkable ability of the American elite, in all recent wars, to avoid much of the fighting by occupying staff and governmental posts. This has not, it appears, gone entirely unnoticed. In the present situation, in which the officer corps of the services are mobility channels for the middle reaches of the middle class and the ranks are filled by blacks, Hispanics, and poorer whites, the rhetorical courage of the elites has to be paid for by the physical sacrifice of the plebs. Other studies (most of them done by military intellectuals) suggest that the American armed forces always relied on material superiority while systematic analyses of the conduct *inter alia* of the Civil War, the Indian campaigns, and the war in the Philippines, suggest that the free-fire zones, village relocations, and defoliation of the Vietnam War are not unique in American history. The American left, however, lacks its own Engels. A systematic critique of American military tradition is conspicuous by its absence: much of the critical literature is at the level of exposure. There is, of course, much to expose, not least the bureaucratic and technical momenta that can lead—ineluctably—to nuclear war.

I have expressed skepticism as to whether there are vast reserves of bellicosity in our nation. The question, however, as the discussion of segmentation suggests, may be rather different. American nationalism is not like European nationalism, rooted in common cultural and historical experiences: it is an acquired taste. The problem is whether, given what we know about low rates of electoral participation in the United States, citizenship is also a taste, but one for which half the population has for one reason or another lost enthusiasm. The bearing on questions of empire is clear enough: half the population endures our politics passively, whether because it does not care enough to vote, or concludes that its voting makes no difference. The role of the media intrudes: consider the extent to which television, in particular, renders events more immediate and at the same time undermines the public's capacity for sustained thought about historical processes more complex than a rapid sequence of discrete events. Much has been made of the supposed effect of the horrors of the Vietnam War on the nation's television public. A good deal less has been said about the decline of literacy in the sense of the ability of the electorate to connect larger social processes to its own lives and interests. It would be fatuous to allege that the

37

electronic media alone are responsible for this decline; many other cultural and social processes are at work. The early inquiries of the Frankfurt School, stimulated by its enforced migration to the United States, may have had more political significance and historical relevance than was at first thought.

The received models, however, clearly do not encompass the imperial dimensions of American society. Divisions within the class owning large-scale property and within the technocratic elites alternately serving it and using it for their own advantage are, perhaps, comprehensible. What is less comprehensible is the way in which, even for the rulers of the world's strongest superpower, domination is so difficult. Notions of an empire directed from the metropolis may be correct, but the structure and content of the process are formless. The singular mixture of political cooperation and resistance manifested in even those parts of empire most domesticated and integrated into American rule (Western Europe and Latin America), the realization that other capitalist econo-mies are in successful competition with the United States, have led to a new type of analysis. The idea of a world system has made its appear-ance.

In its current form, of which the work of Wallerstein is exemplary, it has two sources. One is the Marxist idea of a world market, modified by the contributions of Hilferding on financial capital. The other is the *Annales* school of historiography, with its notions of the long-term, of the interaction of historical structures, with its rootedness in historical geography. Wallerstein has elaborated the concepts of core and periph-ery, has taken seriously the historical mobility of capital. He and those who think like him have moved beyond selective attention to the na-tional state or the bloc system, to deal with phenomena which resemble in the international system nothing so much as the new corporatism that is supposed to have replaced the serial conflicts of class society. That is, congealed or fused economic and political interests endow regions and sectors of world society with corporate interests and, increasingly, ideolo-gies. We are witnesses not merely to the internationalization of class conflict but to the transformation of the structure of class. Without any present prospect of the development of consciousness and political unity across the parts of the world system, the parties seeking changes in the balance of class relations within their own nations are more or less helpless. The structure of these relations is increasingly impervious to national policies, since it is increasingly international. The analogy to the new corporatism has, however, pronounced limits: given political democracy and the setting of the national state, antagonistic classes could find ways to organize their conflicts. However weak and incomplete the practice of citizenship in the industrial democracies, there is no global equivalent of it. A variety of forms of economic and political conflict from oligopolistic control of the world market to revolution have erased the distinction between economics and politics, base and superstructure. For our immediate purposes, what is striking is how little awareness of this situation has penetrated much of the academy, where the separate disciplines categorize the world in ways that were dubious some decades ago, but which are now grotesquely out of date. It cannot be said that the critical party in American social science, with some honorable exceptions, has done much better. Its internationalism is often enough an internationalism of good intentions. It envisages some eventual alteration in the internal relationships of power as a necessary precondition of an international change, while international changes pose new terms of conflict that are ignored. Wallerstein's merit, in the last analysis, is to have insisted that the very notion of society requires rethinking. Few of his contemporaries have risen to the challenge.

However, in a way reminiscent of the nineteenth-century historians, Henry Kissinger *has* risen to the challenge. His works (above all, his memoirs) are a sustained statement of the theoretic position that power is the irreducible element of social existence—within and between nations. His references to values, in his writings as well as in his pronouncements in office, are strained: what excites him is the primordial nature of the struggle for existence. He has (at least before he opened a consulting business with major firms as clients) not hesitated to jest about his lack of interest in economic questions. Perhaps we do him an injustice in ignoring his standing as a social thinker, and should recognize him as the supreme student of empire. In any event, by comparison with Kissinger, the usual academic exponent of American hegemony is a stutterer, inhibited by the need to think up apologia to which Kissinger would not condescend.

An exception to the caution and dullness of the social scientists are the natural scientists—especially those who have experienced the integration of their disciplines in preparation for war. The natural scientists in question are often those engaged in abstract work on the frontiers of knowledge, not those producing applied knowledge. Coming from or descending from the generation that worked on the first nuclear weapons, they seem to have internalized Einstein's warning that the invention of nuclear weaponry has changed everything but our way of thinking. That is, they have worked at changing just that. Similar developments have been evident in areas such as genetic manipulation (or, no less starkly, preparation for biochemical warfare). It is striking that on issues like the structural imperatives to the arms race, the degradation of the environment, the problems of the public control of science, many of the scientists have been far more critical of existing institutions, far more open to new possibilities of social organization, far more historical and even visionary in their outlook than social scientists. Indeed, whereas the theoretical natural scientists have to a visible extent preserved their political independence, by contrast with applied scientists, in the social sciences the specialists in theory (*vide* the long postwar reign of a consensual model of society) have been far more influenced by the constraints upon the application of knowledge. We may put it another way and say that the natural scientists still seem to be seeking a citizenry to address, the social scientists (in their majority) working in bureaucracies or for clients. Perhaps it is not surprising that the work that undermined much of the positivistic scientism of the social sciences, Kuhn's *Structure of Scientific Revolutions,* was written by a physicist turned historian (and sociologist) of science.

We must conclude on a somewhat surprising note. In the heart of empire, there are of course opponents of it. We have no one Treitschke (although some would, absurdly, claim the succession). We have, instead, hundreds if not thousands of small ones, mostly reluctant to avow their nationalism, or presenting it as a higher form of global benevolence. We have, also, no one Mommsen (perhaps Kennan comes close). Our liberals are in one way or another imperial. Our radicalism is, however, relatively unsystematic. Williams's *Empire As a Way of Life* is a depiction of empire and politics, in a large sense, but is in its theoretic structure expressive of nothing so much as Williams's own sense of original (and lost) American values. (Europeans would be surprised to learn that this particular critic of empire is a graduate of our

Naval Academy, and chose to live on a remote part of the Oregon coast.) Like the depiction of our society, the depiction of its imperial role is a matter of lights and shadows, contrasting perspectives. Some ultimate synthesis may connect empire and nation, world politics and our social structure, that structure and our culture. For the moment, the analysis is strongest where not limited, where much of what it says is implied or tentative. We turn to one of its strongest recent components, the depiction of economic institutions.

IV

Economy
and Society

The contemporary heirs of the classical economists and those of Karl Marx have apparently reversed the positions of their spiritual ancestors. The classical economists once argued that the market was (as the triumph of capitalism in the early modern age showed) the fundamental human institution. The demise of feudalism and mercantilism enabled us to experience, directly, the true structure of society. It was what we saw before our eyes. The market was the omnipresent mechanism for expressing wants, satisfying needs, and accumulating wealth. Not only was it omnipresent; it was so deeply rooted as to constitute social nature itself, a replica if not an extension of the rest of nature. (Darwin's biology imitated, rather than inspired, the social thought of the epoch.) It was Marx and his followers who argued that there was another, deeper, structure to human life. The capitalist production and exchange of commodities was a historically specific, and indeed transient, form of human sociability. It would pass—not least because it would conflict with society's inner development, with the necessity of satisfying both basic economic and higher cultural needs, not least political ones.

Consider the present situation. The Marxists, and many who to some degree have absorbed their teaching, insist on the evidence immediately before us. There are no pure markets, and economy, polity, and society are everywhere inextricably connected. Social choices, and often those of the most basic kind, are conveyed by political decisions, through political struggles. It is the classicists who argue that the institutions before us are, in the last analysis, oppressively unreal. The true and profound structure of human social existence is the market. It remains only to free ourselves of our wretched bonds to the illusion that the common life can be organized in other ways. What could ensue, what must ensue, is a gigantic release of energy and productivity—in every sphere.

Occupying, as usual, an ill-defined middle, the disoriented survivors of Keynesianism are close to the Marxists in this. They now proclaim what was once their unavowed assumption, that there are no pure markets, but that the markets they seek to manage can be directed by the state. They have secularized, increasingly, their version of economics, rejecting the theology of the total-market economy. They remain stuck, however, with the language of classical market analysis—since they envisage no other plausible methodological alternatives.

The work of the discipline of economics proceeds, then, in clashing schemes that have in common only their name. A considerable number of neoclassical theorists make of their remoteness from actual economic and social events a point of honor. Their mathematical models are supposed to be utterly abstracted. They are sometimes justified by their putative capacity to generate empirical truths—but that capacity is to be found more in pronouncement than in practice. Others of the neoclassicists do the work of the world. Some offer analyses of the functioning of the highly imperfect markets before us. No small number engage in apologetics. Tacitly, at least, these last acknowledge that economics is a historical or political inquiry. It is perhaps not strange that so many early theorists of nuclear strategy came from economics. They found it easy to abstract from all complexity, from institutional setting. They are as distant from any form of actual warfare as they would be from the actual working of a large firm.

The social science that considers itself the most pure is, then, in utter disarray. The neoclassicists still live in hope of their version of the eschaton—the clearing of the market. We could say that the Marxists still await their version of the Last Judgement, the final crisis, but for the fact that so many of them are preoccupied by what Sweezy grasped five decades ago: the multiple and serial forms of capitalist crises were not foreseen by Marx. They have become historians of economic and social institutions, sometimes moralists. If the neoclassicists are obsessed by the image of a pure market, somewhere, sometime, the Marxists desperately seek for agencies and evidence of a socialist transformation that remains beyond our grasp. The Keynesians, meanwhile, have to struggle with the dismal conviction of having been expelled from their version of Eden—the American version of the welfare state.

For some of them, the experience has been educative. When, in 1963, John Kennedy declared at Yale that there were no longer ideological problems, only technical ones, he was no doubt influenced by his economic advisers, among them Heller and Tobin. Recently, they have declared that economic analysis must begin with the political ends of economic policy, the social choices built into public policy. Ideology has returned—if by another name. Tobin, Nobel Prize notwithstanding, acknowledges that we cannot predict with any accuracy the relationship between employment and inflation. Wasn't it just a few years ago that the Phillips Curve had the (imputed) solidity of a major construct in physics? Each acknowledges that structural changes in the world economy, as well as the preferences actualized in the Reagan budgets, have altered the objects of economic analysis.

Not all the Keynesians will acknowledge reality so straightforwardly. In two works, Olson has made a modest beginning toward reinventing the world. In one, he demonstrates to his own satisfaction that the clash of group interests in society precludes the development of a general welfare. There is, he argues, no economic equivalent of the general will. The difficulty is, he does not put it that way, and so speaks political philosophy without realizing it. In another book, Olson declares that we have to reconstruct the microeconomic foundations of macroeconomics. He finds little else available other than notions of interest already woefully schematic in the nineteenth century, whence they come. His intimations that interests can lead to cooperation are not as sophisticated as those of Rawls, and do not answer the objections raised decades ago by Arrow.

Far more elegant and general critiques of economics come from McCloskey and Thurow. In a work that combines a command of the ordinary instruments of mathematical economics and recourse to the traditions of rhetoric, McCloskey demonstrates that the very structure of economic argument is a singular and unstable synthesis of unexamined assumption, irrelevant evidence, and unreliable method. Insofar as it seems to work, it serves to unite the several disciplinary churches, invariably willing to declare a truce in their own dogmatic struggles to make common cause against the educated laity. Indeed, the principal claim of the economists is that by definition no lay person can be economically educated: theirs is a permanent Counterreformation. Thurow makes many of the same points, in the end, but does so by concentrating on the concrete political and social structures that determine the actual working of the economy.

Thurow, too, belongs to the Keynesian party, if we understand this to mean those in the parliamentary democracies who think that there is a large and plausible role for the state to play in allocating income, stimulating production, and steering the economy generally. If an American reformist coalition organizes in the next decade, it will have to find a common denominator between these late Keynesians and a more radical party. For the moment, much separates them.

The radicals, or the economists influenced by Marx (and Veblen) view the market, in part, as a system of power. They also conceive of it historically, as changing with the rest of society. Intellectual boundaries are, to be sure, increasingly indistinct: there is a political border area in which liberals who see no alternative to state intervention and radicals obliged to settle for minimalist reforms may meet. The conceptual division is still great enough, and that entails precisely the question of aggregate or system. The Keynesians still think of an economy and a polity, the radicals of a process of domination (and exploitation). The Keynesians suppose that they can deal with the connection between economy and polity case by case. Even here (recall Robert Reich's insistence on the interdependence that characterizes all economic relationships, making these social ones) the radicals are increasingly setting the agenda. The conservatives, in their embodiments as neoclassical economists, do not dominate discourse. Hayek may have constructed a system of liberty impervious to the accidents of time and place (and an epigone like Nozick has made of the right to keep previously acquired property the major fundament of human society). The categories of economic thought likely to serve us in the next decades require more of a sense of complexity and history. They will come from Galbraith and Sweezy, from chastened Keynesians and modern Marxists.

Is their Marxism, however, Marxist? Marx was influenced by nineteenth-century doctrines of human self-realization, of historical evolution, and of science. He began with the intent of describing the conditions for the transcendence of human alienation. He continued with a description of the emergence of capitalism. He arrived at a system of political economy in which the deformation of human nature in capitalism was transmuted into the categories of exchange and production. Borrowing from Newtonian mechanics, he wrote of "the laws of motion" of capitalism, and thought of dedicating *Capital* to Darwin. The Newtonian phrase and the image of evolution were intended to convey an ineluctable process. Under Marx's own eyes, however, capitalism was changing, moving toward its modern forms of concentration (and internationalization). Meanwhile, in part under his own leadership, the working class and socialist parties were challenging the domination of the new proprietors and their allies from older social strata. The newer American Marxists have accepted the ambiguities and even the contradictions of the Marxist project. They propound theories of the economy and they also advance proposals to change it. They are a good deal more open about their values than many of their critics. What is less clear is their relationship to the major currents of Marxist thought, which variously assert the disproportion between the amounts produced in the sectors of capital and consumption goods, the inevitability of underconsumption, the falling rate of profit, and competition between the separate sectors of capital (including international competition) as primary causes of crisis. These are, of course, highly abstract ideas. Finding ways to use them to elucidate complex and contradictory historical evidence is not easy, the more so as there is also a Marxist scholasticism to match the neoclassical kind. In it, disembodied entities ("capital," "value," "labor") take on lives of their own, as if Marx in the *Grundrisse* had never demonstrated a grasp of the subtle interplay of observation and theory that would do credit to a contemporary natural scientist. (The literary Marx of *The Eighteenth Brumaire of Louis Napoléon*, the ironic one who in *Capital* described capitalists as Moneybags, makes the scholastics seem especially arid.) That America is not Western Europe we know; making sense of the particular development of our own society in Marxist terms that would avoid schematism is, equally, not easy.

Marx himself seemed to accept a condensed version of the frontier thesis as true of America, was impressed with the expansive character of our capitalism, and placed his hopes for change where he put it, at the end of his life, in both Britain and his native Germany—with a reformist movement engaged in democratic politics.

In any event, the newer American Marxists have had to explain the postwar expansion of capitalism, subsequent stagnation, and the temporarily successful counterattack on the American welfare state under Reagan. The aim of the coalition led by Reagan was, clearly, to reduce the American welfare state to its dimensions of circa 1947. That project has been brought to a stop, but it is exceedingly obscure what will follow. Above all, the internationalization of the capitalist world economy, and a drastic limitation of America's predominance in it, pose difficult questions for a political economy that seeks to be worthy of the name.

The single most important postwar work of Marxist economics in the United States, Baran and Sweezy's *Monopoly Capital*, made striking use of the concept of a socially produced surplus. Capitalism was obliged to produce a surplus, above the wage fund, but could not because of its own organization assure its consumption in ways that would assure either rising general standards of living or a continuation of a high level of production. The surplus was used, instead, in irrational and wasteful ways (when judged by other than narrowly quantitative criteria) whose only value—if a very temporary one—was that they sustained the economy. Baran and Sweezy refocused, in effect, the point of attack of classical Marxism. At the very least, they so enlarged the idea of the process of accumulation and production to encompass much of what in narrower versions of Marxism was considered nonproductive activity. The enlargement, of course, was a response to the changed structure of capitalism. It did, however, pose problems for those who persisted in the belief that laws (or statements of historical tendency) constructed in the nineteenth century were adequate to explain a mid-twentieth-century society. Above all, Baran and Sweezy departed from the belief that there was a hidden and deep productive structure of which all else was but a derivative. They achieved, in terms of political economy, that fusion of

46

base and superstructure already evident in modern Marxist work on culture, history, and politics.

The notion of a surplus has also made a Keynesian appearance in the form of the full employment budget and of hypothetical national income gains from full employment. Shortly before his death, Heller described Kennedy as the first president to set full employment as an aim of economic policy in specific terms. The Keynesians, in other words, now ask under what political conditions a surplus may be enlarged, and managed for the general good. They have also asked, under the pressure of the disintegration of some of their assumptions, why inflation has occurred without full employment. Their answer, that monopolies and oligopolies (sometimes in collaboration with unions) can control their own sectors of the economy, is not very remote from Marxist analyses.

A good deal of Marxist inquiry has been directed to the structure of the labor market, to the processes of work and the organization of the workplace, to the conditions governing class consciousness—and, therefore, politics. Gordon, Edwards, and Michael Reich have offered a condensed economic history of our society with their succession of the stages of the history of work in America. If proletarianization, homogenization, and now differentiation have indeed followed upon one another, perhaps we have a newer and larger version of the old theory of the labor aristocracy. At any rate, newer analyses of dual or multiple labor markets have lent substance to analyses of our knowledge of the structure, and uses, of racial and sexual discrimination. Michael Reich has argued that it is false to depict racial discrimination as invariably successful in protecting whites against blacks: the ostensibly advantaged whites suffer, too, if in more insidious, invisible, and permanent ways, some of them quite economic.

Another sort of radical inquiry concerns the social organization of technology. Edwards and Marglin among others have shown that there is no set path for the development of the division of labor and the organization of work, that criteria of economic efficiency indeed are inextricably fused with the pursuit of power. The domination of the labor force is at least as important to capital as worker productivity, and the kinds of hierarchy we experience correspond not to technological but to political imperatives. David F. Noble has set out on a parallel track in describing in minute detail both the emergence of what was termed scientific management and contemporary technologies. Sabel, on his own and with Piore, has argued that there are social preconditions to the kinds of efficiencies and flexibilities demanded by an advanced market. Indeed, he pictures much of our economy as socially obsolete, insufficiently developed in matters such as the autonomy and education of the labor force. The description follows from his insistence that ideological and social context, the communal and ethnic and familial relationships in which the enterprise is embedded, define and hence determine class conflict. There are, in other words, no pure market relations. Sabel's argument is a severe criticism of what he sees as the reductionism of both the neoclassicists and a form of Marxist orthodoxy. It is part, however, of a broader current of thought that amounts to a demand for the extension of citizenship to the workplace. The Keynesians and neoclassicists still refer to human capital, and so may be deemed monolithic, one-dimensional, in their view of society. They return everything, or nearly everything, to a simple version of economics. The newer Marxists, by contrast, appear decidedly less materialistic: they draw their rhetoric from culture and politics as spheres of value.

The welfare state is, clearly, a compromise formation. It is, in part, the work of elites who calculated that it could lessen social conflict—by socializing costs that, in the end, they might have to bear on their own. It is also, however, the result of continuous effort by those who sought to diminish elite privileges by curbing the working of the market. The welfare state has canalized and contained class conflict. It has also become the locus of it. A good many thinkers (O'Connor the most articulate of them) have attributed the fiscal difficulties of the modern state to the class conflict displaced onto its most ordinary operations. The costs of compensating those disadvantaged by the market, of administering funding for both social services and material infrastructure, falls upon the state. Its revenues depend, however, upon agreements concerning cost-sharing by opposing parties in class conflict—and are subject as well to the fluctuations of the business cycle, through their effects upon state revenue. An economic recession increases costs to the state but diminishes its revenues. The ensuing struggles attest either the integration of the state in the market, or the integration of the market in the state. The formulations are absurdly schematic. When we take note of additional state functions (consumer protection, the several sorts of regulation), the categories of economy and polity lose their distinctiveness. No doubt property—particularly large-scale property—does not. Its own functional boundaries are defined, however, by something like consent. That consent may be the result of apathy or resignation, illusion or manipulation, and it may well legitimate enormous amounts of force, fraud, and theft. Its legitimating function, however, suggests that political economy is also a special case of political philosophy. The economists who flee that conclusion are refugees from the traditions of their own discipline. Proud of their status as masters of one set of instruments in an intellectual division of labor, they do not see that the instruments (and the processes they so imperfectly describe) in fact master them.

Most of the economics taught and practiced in the United States (where there is substantial employment of economists in government and the private sector) is self-consciously ahistorical, devoid of philosophic and above all political self-criticism, and superbly immune to the thought that its finely differentiated categories, its exquisitely developed techniques, may (in ways once ascribed to Dr. Dühring by Engels) measure nothing so much as its own ignorance. There is an American tradition of institutional economics, and as derivative of that, an early Keynesianism (and even a residual classicism) that is political—in the sense of describing the distribution of wealth not in terms of abstractly understood mechanisms or schematically conceived motivations, but as a major part of social organization. Indeed, the American Protestant tradition insisted on the moral component in the economy, and from abolitionism (and free-labor doctrine) to the social-reform movements of the turn of the century denounced the separation of market from moral judgment. No doubt the rise of a discipline of economics ostensibly separated from moral judgment (but which, inevitably, takes the present forms of social organization as given) was part of a larger process of rationalization and secularization. The distribution of ideology (frequently disguised as methodological canon) in economics in our universities has followed, however, the development of our politics. Keynesian-ism had its high point when some state steering (of fiscal policy espe-cially) was a major item on the political agenda. The confusion of recent economic policy represents the inner conflicts of capitalism: extreme Keynesianism in the sphere of military spending is practiced by those who advocate systematic deregulation. One aim of recent policy has been to render the private sector more competitive by reducing its labor and social costs: the pursuit of deregulation is, by any other name, a declaration of class war from above.

The revival of a critical political economy in the United States owes much, curiously, to the relative absence of a challenge to the private sector by the union movement. There are critical sectors of the move-ment (the machinists' union, in particular, mobilized the resources of the academy to develop its program for a conversion of the arms industry and a major reallocation of investment, and the Congressional Black Caucus works with some unions). Mainly, however, it has been con-cerned with the indispensable immediate tasks of protecting the stan-dard of living of unionized workers, dealing with matters such as occupational health and safety, and defending the legal structure of collective bargaining against a determined effort to destroy it. The union movement does understand its task to be the extension of social reform, but its leadership has been skeptical of the possibility (and, indeed, the desirability) of advocating structural alterations in market relationships. We are on the familiar terrain of the exceptional nature of American social development, the absence of American socialism.

The first thing to be said is that socialism has not been absent. There was at the turn of the century a mass socialist movement that gave some promise, at least, of attaining the dimensions and importance of its European counterparts. Populism in essential aspects was hostile to the newer forms of financial capitalism, however incapable the movement and its leaders were of alliance with the industrial working class. There were even American groups attached to what in Europe would be termed anarchosyndicalism, where a broad interpretation would place the Industrial Workers of the World, recruited from loggers and miners, among others. The question of the absence, or more precisely, the failure of American socialism has provoked a large recrudescence of historical scholarship. The culture of the working class and that of middle-class reform have been studied; the political and organizational problems of the unions and the socialist movement (divided as it was into competing factions) have been examined. What we now possess is not only a new range of findings, a historical image of depth and detail of aspects of our recent past insufficiently studied previously. These have been connected to larger interpretations of American society to give us a new version or new versions of the view that the United States is (or was) exceptional.

One major theme may be termed the history of consumption. It is a commonplace that a generally rising standard of living, the early development of a large domestic market for consumer goods, gave the American working class a view of its fate that did not allow the unequivocal application of ideas of exploitation. That an aristocracy of labor of this sort also developed its own militancy in workplace struggles is a complexity but not a contradiction. Consumption had an individualizing function, the more so as it was promulgated by new uses of the press. In the place of the moral and religious instruction inseparable from political discourse in nineteenth-century America, a new pedagogy portrayed consumption as an aspect of personal development. Combining an appeal to status aspirations with the manipulation of the anxieties induced by secularization, the cult (or religion) of consumption reversed the productive ethos of the early Protestant nation. Lears's work on consumption, the most original contribution of its kind, does focus on the educated middle class. It was a society, however, in which the new consumption ethos was not confined to one class. The cultural boundaries between the classes were hardly closed. Middle-class white Protestant control of the education of the ethnic masses was far from total: there were parochial schools. Insofar as control was exercised, it imposed what was, increasingly, a model of consumption on the rest of society. (The migration to the cities from the farms, meanwhile, was Protestant and northern European.) In any case, mass media peculiarly adapted to a stratified cultural market spread the gospel (or gospels) of consumption.

It is significant that Lears's analysis of the earlier cultural significance of consumption, on the way in which it was embedded in advertising and widely read magazines and newspapers, complements Lasch's analysis of the present consumption of self. Lasch deals with a cult of personality distributed throughout a society in which neither class nor community nor ethnic group nor family nor religion (nor any coherent set of beliefs) provides either meaning or support. He attributes much of it to the incessant rationalization of capitalism in its American form, a process extending into the minds and lives of every member of the society. Lears's argument is that the process began earlier, that it is connected to what he calls modern cultural weightlessness, and that its relationship to the religious components in American history is not one of simple succession but of interpenetration and transformation. The argument connects with other kinds of historical work on American working-class communities, which emphasize the extraordinary weight attached by American workers and their families from early in the industrialization process onward to church, family, leisure, neighborhood. Obviously, there is a large difference between a view of American culture as failing to generate radical alternatives because of its fragmenting and isolating qualities, and a view that argues that precisely the satisfactions derived from institutions other than economic made market experiences tolerable.

Which, then, is it—alienation or traditionalism, weightlessness or provincial satisfaction? No doubt much depends upon the particular class (and ethnic, occupational, regional, and religious contexts). Much depends upon time as well as place: a large break in historical continuity is now generally situated between the end of the Civil War and the beginning of the century. It is clear that these newer cultural analyses give the rather general term *embourgeoisement* rather specific meaning, or meanings. These connect with an earlier tradition of studies of color and ethnicity to suggest that a historical topography of the American class structure remains to be completed, that questions about the formation of class consciousness cannot be answered until that is done. A primary objection to pursuing this inquiry is that it blurs the distinctions between occupational groups, positions in the system of exchange and production, and the differential ownership of property. Quite so: those differences in the United States have been historically indistinct, or unclear, just at moments of historical change, or in those areas of the class structure most directly affected by market alterations. We can even challenge some commonly held notions of the past decades. It was believed that the United States has advanced from relatively clear class differentiations (and antagonisms) to the present situation of corporatism, fragmentation, and regionalism. Suppose, however, that we have been undergoing a continuous if jagged process of homogenization—of which, after the compromise of the welfare state, the counterattack by capital of the Reagan period is but the first expression?

The reinterpretation of the nineteenth-century conflict over slavery not only tells us much about the antecedents of modern America; it provides a model of analysis that can be extrapolated to the present. Foner, in a series of studies, has shown that slavery became a popular political issue when it was seen as a threat to free labor. Abolitionism was transformed from the moral crusade of a determined moral minority to a program when the antislavery forces coalesced against the extension of slavery to the territories. The defense of free labor (often, in fact, fused with antiblack ideology and sentiment) provided an ideology upon which northern capital and labor could and did unite. The eventual elimination of slavery, the reduction of the agrarian South to dependency (before the emergence of the New South), as well as the economic impulsion of the Civil War itself, accelerated the transformation of a nation of freeholders and mechanics and entrepreneurs to one of large concentrations of capital dominating farmers and workers. The early Republican motto "Free Soil, Free Men" led to very different consequences than those envisaged by the founders of the party.

The history of the American welfare state is rather more complicated, but is no less a case of the supersession of the original ends of the social movements that struggled for it. Hofstadter and the historians of the postwar period insisted on the moralizing and antipopular character of reform. The work of proponents of the word (Protestant clergy and lawyers and university teachers), the reform movement of the century's initial years abjured anarchy and socialism from below and reviled corruption and egoism at the top of the new corporate America. The Populists themselves were crabbed opponents of the new urban America, the socialists relatively insignificant advocates of ideas that could not really take root in American soil. This analysis, which gravely underestimated the weight of protest and interpreted class conflict to a surprising extent in psychocultural terms, has now been replaced by another. Reform, from the beginning of the century through the Great Society, has been depicted as a compromise, half forced upon, half conceded by, corporate elites fearful at times of actual revolution, at others of systematic and deep limitations of their sovereignty over property. The analysis of the New Deal as the work of social movements from below (where most radical), and of technocratic elites and corporatist bureaucrats (where most acceptable to capital) has at least the virtue of treating politics as the conflict of classes as well as the emanation of ideas. A retroactive analysis (the same, no doubt, can be said for the summary interpretation of the slavery conflict some paragraphs above), however, does knit together what actual history rent asunder. American capitalism was in a severe crisis, and it was the crisis that permitted the mobilization and utilization by Franklin Roosevelt of the accumulated intellectual and political resources of three previous decades of reform. The New Deal did encompass in a historical bloc popular movements, a radical intelligentsia, the more prescient sectors of corporate and financial capital, and a technocratic elite that (whatever the outcome of the social conflicts it mediated) emerged from the period greatly strengthened.

Full employment came to the United States, however, only as the result of war and the initial period of postwar imperial advance. The Great Society program was, no doubt, the result of a response to social turbulence and racial conflict, to the black movement led for a while by Martin Luther King, Jr. It was also an explicit program to supplement (not oppose or nullify) the working of the market by state intervention in education and employment. The program was initiated after industrial unionism had reached its high point, and if it was supported by the industrial unions, was sponsored most resolutely by public-sector unions (in some of which blacks and Hispanics were numerous). The Great Society, in other words, was a technocratic refraction of a social movement—a technocratic effort to render the movement disciplined and malleable.

The present situation with respect to the American welfare state is not quite obscured by the quite astonishingly vulgar level of public discussion about it. There are, in fact, multiple welfare states in the United States, rather as in the other industrial democracies. One important conclusion of recent inquiry is that the salaried middle class (and everyone else in the intermediate income categories) profits enormously from the governmental distribution of national income. Federal retirement pensions (Social Security) and medical-assistance programs have the indirect but important consequence, by increasing the standard of living of the elderly, of relieving families of the burdens of supporting aged parents. Projects that intend the privatization of these programs are unlikely to succeed. Indeed, the entire counterattack on the welfare state seems likely to have the consequences of restricting its growth. To this, there is one large exception: programs for the impoverished, the unemployable, and the undereducated have been drastically cut. Some of this is due to racism (many in these categories are black or Hispanic), some to class cruelty motivated by the residues of the Protestant ethic— far easier to apply when it comes to others. The fusion of racism and what I have termed class cruelty (the anxious pursuit of advantage at the expense of less privileged groups) is surely not new in the United States. In parts of the union movement, it has been averted by strict adherence to racial equality in the allocation of the contractual rights of workers. In others it has been stimulated or reinforced by the affirmative-action programs that seek to redress the imbalance in racial access to skilled jobs created by generations of prejudice. That these programs have set white workers against blacks attests to the ways in which racism has become a component of every part of the institutional structure. It also shows how weak is the egalitarian component in actual American ideology as opposed to the individualistic one: white workers have been especially receptive to the view that they owe their employment to their merits. In their rejection of any personal incidence of responsibility for the nation's racist past, they also demonstrate that curious disengagement from history that marks American national consciousness—or its most widely diffused versions. The gap, indeed abyss, between the finely detailed and historically grounded work on racism in the economy in the universities and public awareness of that racism is immense—evidence, if evidence were needed, of the isolation of the academy from the public arena.

The same isolation is as evident in the larger areas of economic policy. There is a certain amount of diffuse perception of a decline of manufacturing as opposed to service industries, a good deal of anxiety about the loss of "competitiveness" on the world market, some worry about the fragility of the banks and the emphasis on the financial manipulation of productive property, as well as doubts about American managerial skill, worker competence, and "productivity." The matter is not one of the usual discrepancy between serious knowledge and superficial commentary. The ideological counteroffensive of capital intends the diminution of the political capacity of the recent centers of American resistance to an entirely free hand for corporate enterprise (the unions, the environmental movement, consumerism, and public-interest jurisprudence). That counteroffensive can count a large triumph: it has confined critical economic thought to the universities and the margins of the political process. In this, of course, its chief allies have been the academic economists themselves—policing their disciplines lest "questions of value" or "politicization" or *(horribile dictu)* "softness" intrude. (One of the pecularities of discussion in American social science that lends itself only to psychoanalytic parody is the use of the vocabulary of "hardness" and "softness" to distinguish between methods. "Hard" are matters of fact, quantitative findings, models with rigorously specified and limited variables. "Soft" are interpretations, not least historical ones, and those expressions of value preference that do not call for the sacrifice of compassion, fraternity, and sympathy to the iron workings of society. In one approach, we deal with the vocabulary of tumescence. In another, since for otherwise inexplicable reasons the phrase "hard-nosed" is often used to describe a methodological attitude, we touch not merely olfactory processes but, through them, poorly disguised defenses against anality. "Hard-nosed" are those who can ignore the odors rising from humanity.)

The new generation of political economists of the left have replaced, in their critique of prevailing belief, the older liberal Keynesians. One of their beginning points is institutional: they insist that it is not the economists' function to caricature the managerial quest for short-term profits by confining analysis to the immediate workings of the economy, sector by sector. They are prepared to attempt, at least, an integration of the economy with the world economy. Indeed, one of their major points is the extent to which the United States has become both a *rentier* nation, living off investments (and cheap labor) abroad, and an international debtor. Another point is the predominant function of financial capital in the entire economy—for which a synonym they do not shrink from using is "speculative capital." Inquiries both historical and contemporary have demonstrated that there is no automatic mechanism to technological innovation. Indeed, the demonstration of distortion and misallocation in the utilization of science and technology (largely but not exclusively for arms production) is one of their central themes. It connects with questions of the possibilities of enlarging public access to control of technology, the education (and autonomy) of the labor force, with issues of the nature of work. Working parallel to the natural scientists, they have frequently arrived at some of the same conclusions: the American version of a scientific-technological society is in important respects nonrational, even irrational. A book that culminates the past decades of more reflective work in economics bears the title *Beyond the Waste Land:* it makes waste a central category of analysis.

The most obvious effect of economic change upon the society, of course, is upon class structure—if we conceive of class as location in a hierarchy of access to the means of production. Nothing new has been written about class in the United States recently; older themes have been reworked. The discussion about a "new class" has given rise to political polemics: a sector of the right sees the new professional stratum as dangerously receptive to socially critical ideas, as profiting from its own position in the public sector. It is difficult, however, to see what distinguishes a conservative thinker on the payroll of a center of research financed by capital from an intellectual working for a union, if not a political and social choice of alliances. The discussion of a putative new class is utterly confused, mixing class position, educational attainment, occupation, and political preference. The confusion extends to the left—as in a desperate effort to identify an agency of change in our society, Gouldner reposed his hopes on the bearers of what he termed critical discourse. A variant of this debate came from the students of "postmaterialist" values. Why, however, a penchant for short hours, long vacations, and the delights of life should be thought historically new is entirely unclear. What is interesting is the decomposition of Protestantism in sectors of the middle class. The argument that recruits from the working class will hasten to take the place of the lapsed Protestants or Puritans is a way to repeat the obvious, that society will shape the motives it requires for certain functions. What will become of the working-class or lower-middle-class recruits to the managerial elite when they discover that they are neither as managerial or as elite as they initially imagined is another question. The spread of a taste for leisure throughout industrial society is, of course, a consequence of the shortening of the working day, and an inner disengagement from the values of production may be a consequence of the fact that these values pushed to their limits have served their historical purpose. We appear to have come far from structural questions, but this cultural digression is interesting in that we learn that large changes in value seem consonant with the maintenance of considerable differences in power and property. Finally, "postmaterialist" values do not appear to include excessive amounts of sympathy for those without the resources or social position of the "postmaterialists." There is a question whether this is a variant of a phenomenon described by David Riesman over thirty years ago as "other direction"—or depicted, not without irony, by Daniel Bell as the necessary hedonism of a capitalism dependent upon a large market for consumer goods. For all of the disquisitions, pro and con, about a new politics in the United States, "postmaterialism" does not appear to have resulted in a movement like the German Green Party, committed to a rigorous alteration of the values of industrialism.

It is difficult, for the moment, to see how it could do so, the experiences of the decade 1960–70 notwithstanding. The interconnection of public and private sectors is different in the United States than in other nations, beginning with universities. (Some time ago, a former president of Yale said perhaps more than he intended when he appealed to corporate capital to support universities, describing both as instances of private ownership. The usual American rhetoric is to speak of a "nonprofit" sector. The president was quite honest: culture and power in America, despite the technocratic form these take, flow from the sphere of capital. The great exception proves the rule: the large bureaucracies that direct the empire constitute a system in perpetual exchange with the private sector.) It is possible for serious analysis of certain sorts of social movements in, for instance, the German Federal Republic to point to the fact that these are constituted by public employees, teachers, and journalists. From this to explaining their propensity to support the Greens or the Social Democrats or Citizens' Initiatives or a range of alternative solutions to social problems—even within the parties now governing Germany—is but a short step. To suppose that a government one of whose central functions is world domination could generate similar attitudes is implausible: one might as well have expected an anticipatory Green movement from Bismarck's bureaucrats. It is true that schoolteachers (as opposed to university professors), postal and health-service workers and some local and state government employees in the United States behave somewhat like their European counterparts—but their weight in the society is far less. It is still a society that struggles with a large amount of false consciousness: the public sector serves as a critical control and relay station, but its indispensability and social value are continually denied or denigrated. The likening of the federal budget to that of a firm or a household bespeak a widespread economic illiteracy that is functional. The market may work imperfectly, but in one respect it functions: it sets many of the terms of American discourse.

In brief, then, the new class system is not quite so new. The large increase in the number of service workers, the decline in the number of industrial workers, simply continues a tendency long since evident. The dependent condition of the worker continues, accentuated by the fact that unionization was never firmly implanted in the sectors of the labor market that are growing the fastest. An increase in the number of managerial, professional, and technical workers has not entailed an increase in the stability of their employment or in their own autonomy vis-à-vis their employers. In terms of income, the recent wave of inflation (combined with unemployment and poorer wage bargains negotiated in the shrinking sector of unionized labor) has meant a net decline in the real wages of a majority of the employed, a decline masked by multiple employment in families. Moreover, the impoverished parts of the society have become more impoverished, the wealthy ones wealthier. Whatever slight tendency toward narrowing the income gap may have been evident in the years of prosperity and Great Society social programs (difficult to disentangle in their effects, at times) has been reversed. Within the nation, regional differences have become salient, different industries and different parts of the service sector have had extremely unequal fortunes. A general process of homogenization has assumed, in other words, diverse local forms. In the circumstances, public awareness of the entire process has been limited—and open to manipulation. Historically, no doubt, economic processes affect politics through changes in class structure, but politics, as the realm of consciousness and organization, has a large amount of autonomy. It is to that autonomy—much exaggerated by some, seriously underestimated by others—that I now turn.

V

The Decline of
Liberal Democracy

Postwar affirmations of the strength and vitality of American democracy insisted upon its success in harmonizing the separate demands of the groups making up an extremely diverse polity, in mobilizing the nation for tasks as diverse as the expansion of the economy domestically and the establishment of empire abroad, in giving some sense of membership and participation to tens of millions of citizens. The maintenance of fundamental liberties was mentioned as a pious afterthought: after all, these were not in danger after the period of McCarthyism had passed. The Supreme Court's injunction to proceed with school desegregation "with all deliberate speed" meant that the judicial process was contributing its weight to the normal functioning of the system. Indeed, the Court (despite its conspicuous reluctance to venture into the terrain of foreign policy) was praised as a guarantor of civil liberties and democratic values generally.

This highly schematic optimism had assumptions, stated and unstated. They came from two intellectual sources: Hartz's view of the United States as a society whose central agreement was that it was a democracy of property owners, and Hofstadter's pervasive skepticism about the extent to which democracy could dominate property (to which was added an even more pronounced skepticism about the *bona fides* and efficacy of many of the tribunes of democracy). They were also produced by the euphoria of empire, tempered somewhat by the nagging realization that the blacks and the poor somehow participated little in the democratic process—and benefited less.

The critique of the decade 1960–70 altered much. The relatively low (and declining) levels of voter participation in the United States may have suggested to some that the nonvoters were often satisfied with their lot. To others, they suggested that either the nonvoters did not think voting made a difference or that they were so privatized that they did not pose the question to themselves. In either case, a large part of the populace did not assume the minimal burdens of citizenship. The parties were not mass organizations, however much they may have approached that in parts of the nineteenth and earlier twentieth centuries. They were, instead, loose coalitions of local elites, lobbies, and specific-interest groups. There were ideological differences between the parties, determined by the different constituencies to which they appealed. There were significant groups within each party (and its congressional and senatorial representatives) willing and at times eager to coalesce on important issues with the party to which they were nominally-opposed. Much was changed in party organization and function by the replacement of newspapers (not least, local newspapers) by television as a source of news and opinion. Meanwhile, the rising cost of political campaigns and the looseness of organization combined to turn candidates for office into entrepreneurs, trading off past and present favors to donors— usually, one or another interest group. (Organized ethnic lobbies were no less important in foreign-policy areas, and the unvarying backing of Israel by the Democrats owes much to Jewish influence in the Democratic Party. Greeks and Poles and Cubans play similar roles. What is interesting in the literature that depicts this as a triumph of American ethnicity is what it overlooks. The ethnic lobbies can influence foreign policy when their aims and that of the imperial apparatus more or less coincide: America's Afro-Americans and poorer Hispanics have had far less success in arguing the case for assistance to the globally impoverished, despite the fact that they are more numerous than the other lobbies.)

The argument about ethnicity is a variant of the argument about what has been termed single-issue politics. Abortion, or gun control (more contra than pro), or school prayer have served as foci of concentrated pressure, mobilizing determined if minority constituencies to reward political friends and punish foes. The work of the consumer movement, environmentalists, the peace movement, and women's-rights groups has been likened to single-issue groups, wrongly. These entail complex approaches to complex questions, not symbolic reduction of complexity. If *The Authoritarian Personality* were being rewritten, its authors might well place the single-issue-politics groups rather prominently on their F scale: they certainly show the philistine credulity, large rage, and paranoiac determination remarked upon a generation ago. An inverted populism, which is aimed less at praising popular sense and virtue than at denigrating the educated, precludes that sort of analysis. In rather general form—Kohlberg's treatment of moral development—the academy is prepared to admit that there are lower and higher forms of the moral life. What is surprising is, some enclaves apart, that the degradation of public discourse, the cretinization of the public, is so little studied.

More attention, to be sure, has gone to one of its major structural preconditions. The proliferation and fragmentation of issues has produced a literature on the difficulties, if not the demise, of democracy— by which these critics mean the recalcitrance of modern populations to treat elites with deference and to take their orders. Suppose, however, that modern elites in the United States act rather more subtly to frame and direct the course of public debate. The ideological hegemony of a limited number of ideas is a product of something other than their intellectual persuasiveness. It has to do with the interpenetration of elites, their symbiosis with (or parasitism upon) the major structures of power in the nation—the large corporations and the foreign-policy apparatus. It is not a paradox that the ideological elites working in or for these two concentrations of power spend much of their time denouncing "elitism," by which they mean the suggestion by some reflective citizens that our institutions could be improved, or that present elites are acting irresponsibly, selfishly, or stupidly. They do so in the name, of course, of the supposed good sense, convictions, and values of the American people or a majority of them, but define convictions, good sense, and values in terms which exclude any systematic challenge to the existing distribution of opinion or power. Earlier, I referred to the left's desperate search for a group or groups that could serve as a political vanguard, a search moved by the hope that somehow new vanguard and old main body could be joined. The right's exercise in self-legitimation is more refined, if appreciably more dishonest. Insisting to the public that there are no alternatives, it then interprets the public's apparent acquiesence as a directive. Its policies, of course, reinforce the society's immobility—

except where it can safely extend the privileges of the groups that constitute the right itself.

What has emerged, then, from an uneven combination of ideological and structural analysis by the critical party in American thought is a severe portrayal of our politics as a form of pseudopluralism. The agitation and interplay of groups, the diversity of economic, ethnic, regional, and religious interests, and the conflict of cultures provide entertainment for the public, work for journalists, and subject matter for professors. In fact, it is almost a tale of sound and fury, told by idiots if not an idiot, and signifying if not nothing then not as much as its tellers think. Behind the diversity lie unifying, or rather centralizing, forces—now manipulating the montage, now using it, able to maintain sovereignty because the one principle that unites the whole is the relatively untouchable status of capital and the imperial apparatus. Every analysis we have of the separate American cultures, of the economic and regional groups, of tradition and revolt, depicts these groups and movements in their relations to these concentrations of wealth and power. I am anticipating the cultural section of the essay somewhat, but that is inevitable: American culture is most deeply politicized precisely where it is ostensibly most remote from the questions that concern the political elites. That is no less true, as Bellah and his colleagues have shown, of the psyche. A quite extraordinary testimony to this proposition has come from avowed and intelligent opponents of the American left, Berger and Neuhaus. They believe that the tawdriness of modern America is due to the destruction, or encapsulation, of what they term mediating institutions: local church, local community, family. Their argument is somewhat vitiated by the fact that local churches are far more numerous and vital, membership and participation in them far higher, than in other industrial nations. As for local communities and families, these bear the weight of larger social processes. Decisions made outside communities determine their fate. Economic and cultural developments quite beyond the scope of families to control alter their structure, the very texture of relationships within them. It is disconcerting when we remind ourselves that a European originally close to the Frankfurt School, Paul Lazarsfeld, in his inquiries four decades ago into opinion formation in the United

States attached much importance to local and primary groups, where ideas from the larger society were distilled, somehow made consonant with the experience of the group, and circulated. Now, for large areas of society, it is entirely unclear that primary groups have this assimilating or transforming function: opinions come ready-made from the mass media, especially television. Sometimes, of course, the immediacy of experience speaks almost for itself: the war in Vietnam was difficult to sanitize in words when pictures of it were so disturbing.

A good deal of energy has been expended, of course, on the question of why the United States did not or does not have a large socialist movement. Walter Burnham's answer is perhaps the most elegant, because most simple: the groups which in Europe vote for the socialist or social democratic parties do not participate very much in the American political process. Another answer is that large groups who could support a socialist movement remain unorganized. Suppose, however, that there is a different set of answers. Some historians have pointed out that the association between Enlightenment and socialism, positivism and reform, was attenuated in the United States by the religiosity of the working class—and of an influential group of middle-class social reformers. The Christian component in the early union movement, in social reform, in populism and socialism, too, legitimated these movements but also generated inhibitions on the formation of ideologies of a countersociety or an alternative one. The churches absorbed energies which in Europe went into the mass socialist parties. Theological notions of personal goodness, however crudified, worked against the construction of popular notions of social causation like those the Europeans derived from Marxism. It is true that with the development of welfare states in Europe the eschatological energy also left the most secularized of socialist movements. That energy, in the United States, alternately infused and left the public sphere—but the sphere itself hardly gained in autonomy or dignity. That the same difficulties were encountered by American liberalism is true, but since liberalism had won many of its struggles, it was not seriously limited by the encounter. Moreover, since liberalism had a large individualistic component, it was quite consonant with much Protestant thought. What for most reflective American historians is a commonplace, that the churches as communities and religious beliefs as ideologies had and have primary roles in American social history, remains a matter of some bewilderment—where it has not somehow escaped their attention—to a number of otherwise critical spirits.

What is even more striking is that the distinctiveness of social movements in American history has escaped sustained attention, despite the fact that a number of social scientists participated in some recent ones. From the religious movements of the eighteenth century to the antiimperial protest of the Vietnam period, the most varied movements have risen in the United States, often dominated culture and politics for a period, and then have either been absorbed in routine politics (somewhat transformed) or have disappeared. We know that the politics of the period before and during the Civil War are inexplicable without attention to abolitionism, that nativism, agrarian populism, early unionism, and middle-class social reform uneasily coexisted (and convulsively influenced one another) from the end of the Civil War to the First World War. The New Deal period was not just a matter of the Congress voting reform programs proposed by the president: a great deal of activity in the society provided political incentives for the elites.

These movements included American unionism in many of its phases, the early socialist movement, and projects as diverse as women's rights and anti-imperial protest. The difficulty with all of them is that they remained sectional or partial. Even when they proposed programs that would have entailed major changes in the society as a whole, they addressed specific issues and constituencies. The common denominator that would have connected their interests to those of others was lacking. Is this simply a way of repeating what we already know, that the multiple fragmentations and segmentations in American society make it very difficult to develop a coherent project for reform of the whole? We are led back to the (increasingly mechanical and obsessive) promulgation of a shallow unifying ideology, an unstable mixture of corroded beliefs in individualism and property, beliefs that define the actual American idea (and even more the practice) of freedom. It is in this setting that the actual clash of interests, often disavowed or depicted as its own opposite, proceeds, making of our politics a singular combination of brutal selfishness and hypocritical falsity, not unmixed with ignorance and stupidity. Is that, however, all?

VI

American Culture, American Promise: What de Tocqueville Did Not Know

The crudity, mediocrity, and monotony of our politics, Leo Marx once observed, is in startling contrast with the energy, the originality, the vitality of our culture. Others have remarked on the almost instinctive democratization of impulse and judgment in the American people, a phenomenon often enough difficult to distinguish from *Ressentiment*— or from the spurious consensus (the sociologist Robert Merton once termed it pseudo-*Gemeinschaft*) induced by the cultural industry.

De Tocqueville wrote about a preindustrial society: the recurrence of his thought may suggest something else than a commendable desire to go to the historical roots of our political culture. The nation has changed immensely since de Tocqueville's visit. The French thinker, a recalcitrant liberal (in the European sense) with deep doubts about democracy, has served to legitimate the ambivalence of Americans about their own nation. He, or his ideas, have also served to avert our gaze from problems presented by industrialization, by immigration, by the end of slavery, and by empire. The place to begin is with new interpretations of our culture, deliberately destructive of received notions. It is precisely in this area that American social thought has shown, recently, the most critical energy. Can we move beyond the legacy of Weber? Weber, it will be recalled, visited the United States before the First World War. In addition to his impressions of the pervasive effect of Protestantism, he took others, more complex, back with him. The Protestantism he saw in the United States was not merely a spiritual press that stamped out capitalist personalities in a uniform series. It was communitarian and congregationalist in its effects. Weber suggested that Americans, in their repugnance for hierarchy, would rather live with corrupt civil servants whom they could censure than take orders from zealous bureaucrats with impeccable moral credentials.

The newer work on Protestantism, and on religion in America in general, has emphasized a communal dimension, a sense of social responsibility, overlooked in mechanical applications of Weber. Indeed, some of it may not be so new, since it recalls Perry Miller's studies of the Covenant, and H. Richard Niebuhr's analysis of the achieved millennium in America. The newer studies are so many blows to the view that American culture is ineradicably individualistic, or—its caricature in a crude reading of de Tocqueville—conformist, nay, servile before utterly standardized norms. Indeed, the two are organically related, since an iron individualism expresses an internalization of norms so rigid that they become inaccessible to criticism: Sinclair Lewis's pathetic heroes believed they were actually thinking for themselves.

The countercultural upsurge of the period 1960–70 was a wholly ambiguous revolt against Protestantism. It was a revolt against a caricature of the Protestant ethic, institutionalized in the routines of a bureaucratized society. The impulses of the revolt led, indeed, to a new appreciation of the Protestant dimension in American culture. Conscience was opposed to convention: Thoreau's protest at the Mexican War was discovered by those who rejected the intervention in Vietnam. Inwardness was opposed to submission to a harsh superego. Limits were set against grandiosity. Well before the notion of an imperial presidency, after all, the idea of an imperial self had made its appearance.

We can identify three periods in American studies. The work of F. O. Matthiessen and Perry Miller (continued in different, less restrained, accents by Alfred Kazin) established a complex tradition—quite distinct from the genteel pieties of some, the unidimensional Jacksonianism of others. The postwar reevaluation of Melville and Henry James legitimated a turning inward of the spirit, a rueful retreat from engagement— not at all what Matthiessen and Miller intended or practiced. American studies between 1945 and 1960 became to some extent a cultural pendant to the anticonflictual politics of Hartz and Hofstadter. In an America where no social conflict could be resolved because, fundamentally, none could mobilize the entire nation, moral energies were to be cultivated elsewhere, in selfhood or in family, in neighborhood or in region. Inwardness was the privilege of some, just as the obsessive preoccupation with inheritance gave meaning to others. The third period dispensed with historical condensations, insisted on discontinuity, on change in the substance of American society and the American spirit.

These alterations were also reflected in depictions of Protestantism—by Protestants themselves. A very positive view of social Protestantism paralleled the discovery of American literature in the first period, the period of the New Deal. The period of empire, however, brought with it a melancholy rather than a triumphalist vision of Protestantism—a view of Protestantism as appreciative of, if not insistent upon, ambiguity. Reinhold Niebuhr's *Moral Man and Immoral Society* was the characteristic work of this period, an argument that God's work in the world required acceptance of the world's imperfections—including power and wealth. The third period brought with it a historical appreciation of Protestantism's own ambiguity or polyvalence. An earlier liberal Protestantism had attempted to assimilate Darwinism, fragments of Marxism, modern science and scholarship, in an intellectually tenuous but affectively strong fusion with American optimism and progressivism. The critical Protestantism of the third period was self-consciously hermeneutic, depicting itself as engaged in a perpetual process of self-explication. Fragments of linguistic philosophy, parts of the Marxist theory of alienation, notions of ideology, and ideas of a constructed historical identity gave Protestant theology a new lingua franca. The awareness of the historical rootedness of the varieties of American Protestantism legitimated the new cultural pluralism. If it allowed any Protestant to say anything and claim that it was canonical, or at least permitted, it also broke the cultural power of the belief that there was a single line of descent from Jonathan Edwards to Reinhold Niebuhr. Here the intellectual patron of the movement was a Weimar émigré, Paul Tillich, who dealt with God as ultimate being. Tillich had been a religious socialist, but preferred in the United States to substitute for that a historicized metaphysics of being. Curiously, this encouraged his American students to proceed to endorse far more social experimentation, and radicalism, than much Protestant social teaching allowed. This was inextricably connected with the idea of the United States as a chosen nation, of our society as actually or potentially sanctified. Once that belief was critically examined, an infinity of other possibilities could develop. Finally, Robert Bellah in two works drew up provisional accounts with the Protestant tradition. In *The Broken Covenant*, he argued that the attenuation of the idea of national sanctification had led to the ideological vacuum into which poor substitutes flowed. In *Habits of the Heart*, he (and his collaborators) argued that individualism driven to its limits had engendered a social vacuum: Americans had no sense of the common life.

Yet one of four Americans is a Roman Catholic. The history of Catholicism in America has also been reinterpreted, and the most recent work is significantly entitled *American Catholics*. That is, it deals not with the Church but with its people. The period in which Catholics could be flattered as honorable Protestants is behind us. True, in many ways Catholics and Protestants behave alike: birth rates and the practice of divorce show no large differences between them. A Catholic vanguard, at least, has reclaimed an aspect of its tradition in America not much discussed a generation ago—a tradition of social Catholicism. Looking back, we are now able to appreciate how much of the early labor movement, of the defense of ethnic distinctiveness against the demands of a Protestant culture, of the cultivation of an idea of community and the practice of solidarity, were the work of Catholics. The history of a mechanical process of cultural integration has been rejected in favor of the idea of a distinctive Catholic presence in American society. That presence, moreover, was and is not just a matter of the hierarchy of the Church, of Catholic institutions, of an enclave. It entailed drawing a line around values deemed impervious to the corrosion of the market. It is quite true that an often narrow defensiveness marked much of the Catholic response to American society, a defensiveness encouraged by often hateful and violent prejudice. Perhaps this accounted for the extreme chauvinism and mechanical anticommunism with which many Catholics (and their bishops) supported American foreign policy in the years 1945–65. The newer forms of integration in American society allow a far more critical and generous view, and this has culminated in the bishops' pastoral letters on nuclear weapons and the economy, each of them strikingly insistent on universal values and utterly remote from the new American tribalism. A process of integration has had its grotesque sides: the bishops have been criticized by wealthy Catholics (and their ideological spokesmen) for failing to see that Americanism and unrestricted capitalism are identical, and by apologists for American arms policy for neglecting the positive moral aspects of nuclear missiles.

A number of causes occasioned the change in our view of Catholicism. One was the American response to the Second Vatican Council. A new generation of Catholic theologians and a very self-conscious laity drew from the council legitimation for what they would have sought in any case: a new modus vivendi with a pluralistic society, with a Protestantism that seemed much more alive than the antimodernism incorporated in the ossified legacy of Pope John's predecessors. The new generation, of course, made contact with a tradition of open Catholicism, and with another of left Catholicism, both possessing the inestimable advantage of a unique purchase on the American experience. If these views entailed a conflict, subsequently, with the restored conservatism of Pope John Paul II's Vatican—and of course with important elements in the American Catholic community—they also constitute a major element in that reevaluation of our history that is the most substantial part of the critical thought of recent years.

While the political scientists in the universities, further, were trying to extricate themselves from the historical lugubriousness of "modernization" doctrines—or supplying apologetics for the imperial apparatus—the Catholic theologians were making us aware of liberation theology in Latin America. The cosmopolitanism and historical sense of the Catholics, often enough, provided an antidote to the Calvinist arrogance and historical narrowness of much American thought. The Catholics, too, thought and think our experience unique, but they do not believe this is a warrant for claiming that it is spiritually superior.

No such restraint, alas, governed a vocal but not dominant segment of the Jewish intelligentsia. The openness and pluralism of American society, its self-depiction as a nation made up of groups who were originally strangers, renders it especially congenial to Jews—in contrast with the harshness and hatred so evident in modern Europe. The Calvinist component in American Protestantism was and is no less important: a welcome to the people of the book was theologically required. The postwar ascent of the East European Jewish migration, the elimination or large attenuation of cultural and social prejudice in institutions

and occupations practically barred to Jews until 1945, also had its consequences. Jews figure prominently, moreover, in the imperial apparatus.
Withal, something else is at work beside the comprehensible loyalty of
a group that has every reason to view the United States as home.

Earlier generations of Jewish intellectuals, particularly from the East
European migration, allied themselves with the progressive strand in the
American tradition. It was (and is) possible to think affirmatively of the
United States while criticizing its institutions. The conservative, or
neoconservative, Jewish thinkers have denied that: they have invested
the United States as it is with tribal loyalty. It is quite true that many
of them are epigones, others vulgar publicists. They have, however,
systematized ideas taken from more serious figures like Isaiah Berlin and
Karl Popper—a rigidified liberalism—and turned these not only against
American progressivism, but against the idea of progress as a whole. The
question about the fate of poetry after Auschwitz has taken on a rather
different focus in America: what Jew can really believe in a benign
human future? Beneath the ostensibly optimistic reading of the American experience, there lies a rather desperate pessimism. By a singular
paradox, then, American Jews are nowhere and never so Jewish as when
they proclaim their routinized Americanism and Americanization. Un-
derneath lies terror, a profound disbelief in the Enlightenment, and a
curious reification of what may prove to be a passing moment in American history.

Much of this was anticipated, however stiltedly and even obscurely,
by Lionel Trilling in his cultural criticism in the decade 1950–60. (His
Sincerity and Authenticity, per contra, returns to a more universalist
idiom and theme, as if Trilling found the vulgarization of his earlier work
distasteful but did not quite wish to say so.) The only profound treatment of it I know is to be found in the work of another, younger,
Columbia University teacher (New York as a vantage point still
counts)—Yosef Yerushalmi. His reconsideration of the entire modern
Jewish experience goes well beyond a concentration on America, but it
may tell us more about American Jews than many of them are prepared
to admit. For the moment, treatments of the situation in terms of the
social mobility (or integration) of the Jewish community are predominant, but they make one point and miss the major one.

(Are not Berlin and Popper proponents of Enlightenment? They are certainly not obscurantists. However, they are thinkers so frightened by the coupled experiences of Nazism and Stalinism, so reassured by Great Britain—and to a lesser extent, perhaps, by American democracy—that their reading of Western tradition is a defensive one. Progress is behind us, and has culminated in the structures of liberty and politics we now possess. The rest is detail, piecemeal social engineering, in Popper's phrase. Reinforcement for their view came from Raymond Aron, promoted to the status of an honorable Anglo-Saxon. Western liberties were the fruit of careful cultivation in an oasis surrounded by sands of brutality and tyranny. The Jewish component of the neoconservative movement has only rather banal intellectual roots in America, and it has drawn uncritically upon a rigidified liberalism formulated in Europe.)

A peculiarity of American culture is the tension between universal rhetoric and very specific interest. Rights in America may be defined in an unlimited extension of universal claims. The institutions of the market have constituted a barrier to the extension or elaboration of economic rights, and that extension has come indirectly when it has come at all. The courts, for instance, have hedged the assertion that rights to social assistance (welfare) are universal—and have derived these from notions of due process and federalism rather than from an articulated theory of citizenship. Equally, rights are demanded by virtue of the opposite of universal claims, by virtue of their indispensability to the coexistence of communities and groups in a divided and segmented society. The recent rise in ethnic and racial consciousness, the reawakening of a women's movement after a long period of mid-century somnolence, the assorted values of American versions of what in Europe are termed alternative cultures ("counterculture" is an American misnomer, since it is frequently unclear what specifically they are supposed to counter), have brought this contradiction to a permanent condition of exquisite tension. Its philosophic refraction (in the work of Dworkin and Rawls) we considered earlier. What is of interest now is the way it has heightened our appreciation of the historical diversity of American cultures.

The thesis of the assimilation of ethnic and racial minorities into a dominant white, Protestant, northern European model of culture is no longer tenable. An antithetical thesis, that our culture is the changing sum of its parts, that we exist as a segmented, tribalized society, is more plausible but, in the last analysis, not entirely convincing. How, in that case, deal with the homogenizing effects of the industrial fabrication of culture, with the phenomenon of American nationalism, with the one sort of integration that is beyond doubt—economic integration? Perhaps these questions cannot be answered until the work of historical reconstruction of the diversity of the past is complete. That reconstruction has been most pronounced with the group hitherto least visible—or, at any rate, least looked into—the blacks. Differences between northern freedmen (and southern ones, too) and slaves, the familial structures of the blacks, their economic and occupational histories, have been depicted. We possess an increasingly complex and detailed description of black culture, with important derivatives for our general understanding of cultures of oppression. In fact, however, many of the scholars working on these materials have been skeptical of the legacy of the work of Oscar Lewis. There is no generalized culture of oppression or poverty, they argue, since historical situations are not easily subsumable under abstract categories. The black experience in America has been a singular compound of African legacy, cultural interaction with white society, and the economic and social (and more recently, political) vicissitudes of the black population. Some of the analysis of black American society (if it can be so sharply distinguished) is part of a reconsideration of the entire history of the slavery question—ideological and institutional, and political. Part of it is an aspect of the history of the American working class. More recently, work on twentieth-century black cultural and social movements has provided a larger context for the reconsideration of the black movement of recent decades.

No unequivocal political conclusions result: the debate continues. Present divisions within the black community, between an employed and skilled segment (depicted as socially integrated on that account) and an unemployed and unemployable segment (in a condition of proletarianization and, worse, social disintegration) are the bases of considerable polemics. The question of a distinctive black culture, or rather the necessity of maintaining one, has receded somewhat into the background as economic and social issues have become salient. What is interesting is that the receding wave of black militancy has left as an intellectual residue an extraordinarily heightened awareness (among blacks and some whites) of the complexity and depth of black history in America. A somewhat heightened activity on behalf of, for instance, the struggle against apartheid in South Africa does not amount to the full engagement on behalf of the Third World expected a while ago. An educated elite (increased in numbers by the social programs of the Great Society but with access to it now being restricted by reductions in those programs) is the bearer of the new consciousness. Its solidarity with the black underclass, however, is far from total.

An analogous situation prevails with respect to women. The new women's movement is in fact (like the black movement of recent decades) a revival of an earlier one. Like the black movement, it has engendered countermovements by those threatened by it. Like the black movement, its most immediate and visible beneficiaries have been an educated elite. Both movements can be interpreted, also, as consequences of long-term economic and ideological processes: the absorption of blacks and women into the new labor force, and the increasingly obvious contradiction between doctrines of equality and institutions of domination. There the analogy ends. The crisis of patriarchal attitudes and practices leaves hardly any area of society, any group, untouched. The problem of blacks can be ignored temporarily, even fled; the problem of the alteration in the relationship of the sexes cannot. Women are not a minority in the United States (indeed, statistically they are a majority). Despite profound ambivalence about the women's movement among segments of the female population, ideological and institutional change has occurred.

The intellectual derivatives, however, have if anything been more confused than in the case of the problem of blacks. Arguments about the consequences of slavery, the immutability or otherwise of racism, the nature of black culture, the past and future consequences of economic change, are relatively specific. Arguments about the feminine character, about the mutability of gender, about the dimensions and possibilities of change, seem to call into question received knowledge about human nature and institutional function. Not surprisingly, we have again expanded our historical knowledge of the role of women in America. Stereotypes have been discarded, and controversy is so intense that new ones have hardly been fixed. We do have sharper delineation of the place of women in the labor force, of the history of the family, of the fabrication of a woman's role in the early phases of the development of mass consumption. The earlier phases of the women's movement—and anticipations of it in the nineteenth century—have been sketched. What remain open are questions to which no definitive answer is likely. Are there biopsychic limits to mutability in women's role, and what are they? What consequences for character formation follow from the fact that a majority of mothers work outside the home while raising children? Some of the most challenging issues are raised by thinkers like Barbara Ehrenreich and Jean Baker Miller, who argue that the assumption by women of men's roles would betray the human promise of feminism. Competitiveness, exaggerated individualism, and careerist relentlessness, they declare, are already men's diseases: why should women eagerly seek these maladies? Cooperativeness, solidarity, and empathy are what they instinctively (a word in itself debatable) bring to what was a man's world—and no one needs these traits more than men. Ehrenreich, indeed, holds that the revival of feminism is a consequence of a male revolt against the rigidities of bureaucratic capitalism. If these thinkers are right, however, the trouble lies not with men but with a society which cultivates in its elites characters unattractive at best, destructive at worst. Carol Gilligan, in a discussion of moral psychology which insisted that women brought to moral questions a larger degree of empathy, termed her work *In a Different Voice.* If these feminists are to be believed, we will all have to speak with a different voice.

We come, finally, to the question of alternatives to the dominant bureaucratic and capitalist culture of America. Ethnic multiplicity, the presence of large enclaves and islands of startling diversity to the contrary, a standardized sensibility, one sort of moral discourse, counts as normative. This is embedded in the culture of large organizations, in market-consonant behavior. That culture, that behavior, seem to generate their own antitheses. Inglehart has argued that "postmaterialist values" originate at the very apex of the system, among those who find the career sequence, the psychic burdens, of the large American organizations aesthetically and philosophically unacceptable. Bell, borrowing from John Wesley and Max Weber, has argued that the capitalist market requires constant consumption—which in turn requires values that undermine an older Protestant-like ethos of labor discipline and productivity. Whatever the case, clearly the normative structures of American capitalism must be in doubt—or how else explain their utter trivialization and compulsive reiteration in neoconservative ideology, whether in its polysyllabic or technocratic form, or in the dreadful vulgarization of the media and conversation? No doubt a desperate (and often defensive) acquisitiveness motivates many Americans, but it hardly provides meaningful answers to questions about community, family, psyche, and society. It is in these realms, beneath and increasingly alongside the standardization of market-consonant behavior, that a plethora of American cultural worlds constitute an errant historical galaxy.

In this setting, the American opposition has been singularly unable to formulate a convincing project. Initially, its own analysis of the historically specific character of American nationhood was determined by its own variant of the American millennial or missionary idea, a derivative of both social Protestantism and the Judaic component in modern America social reform. More recently, the opposition has moved to a stringent defense of cultural and ethnic pluralism, without providing a canon (or even an idea) of beliefs that might unite rather than divide the various American groups. Some in the opposition insist that the central problem is the supersession of the domination of the economy and public life by giant corporate structures. Others assert that the central problem is the destruction or relativization of a standardized ethos, the general affirmation of cultural multiplicity. The antithesis caricatures the ideology of the right, as if in a funhouse mirror. The right, after all, insists that if exchange, production, and property are left as they are (or surrendered even more completely to the market), control can be exercised in the communal and private spheres of aesthetics and morality. The right, moreover, has the honesty to recognize (and declare) that mobilization for empire has positive ideological consequences. The opposition's vision of a postimperial America veers between a systematic program for the reconstruction of urban sewers and transit, and a gigantic expansion of the Peace Corps. Despite that cultural vitality which forever astonishes Europeans, the United States has no oppositional cultural model. Multiplicity, and pluralism, are not matters for programs, they are already matters of fact. Whether these phenomena themselves—combined with the confusion and discontent of the modern epoch—will produce an authoritarian cultural-political reaction is not a new question. It was raised not only by the authors of

The Authoritarian Personality but by a set of authors with very different political ideas, thirty years ago. It has lost none of its force. The integration of a reactive cultural politics with mobilization for imperial tasks (Reaganism, in short) suggests that much of the work of the Enlightenment, for much of American society, remains to be accomplished.

At the end of the decade 1930–40, Matthiessen and Miller sought in the American past for cultural (and religious) sources of a modern civic view. They thought that they had found them. Suppose, however, that dwelling upon the New England and Puritan tradition is rather like those interminable exercises in which de Tocqueville appears as anticipating twentieth-century industrial America. Suppose, in other words, that we experience a radical, almost total discontinuity in national cultural experience. Lasch and Lears have seen that much; so has Bellah (and his colleague in comparative studies, Geertz). The situation provides a beginning point for reflection still to be undertaken.

VII

Psyche and Society

The intellectual migration engendered by fascism and war in Europe also brought to the United States a number of psychoanalysts, many of them quite original and significant thinkers. The United States had already been quite receptive to Freud's work, despite a certain skepticism on Freud's part as to the depth of the reception. Jacoby has recently insisted (following an internal critique of psychoanalysis by Kovel) on the fact of a retreat from social concerns by European psychoanalysts who found themselves in an American milieu. Mentioning Fenichel and Simmel, among others, Jacoby suggests that these Europeans found their previous engagement in the socialist movement an encumberment if not an obstacle to integration in American medicine and American society. Perhaps: if our Federal Bureau of Investigation regarded Einstein as dangerous (well before his widely publicized doubts about nuclear politics), these relatively unknown and unprotected émigrés had reason to be cautious. However, the period of their arrival was marked in America by the work of Harold Lasswell, Margaret Mead, Edward Sapir, and others who were attempting a synthesis of psychoanalysis and social science (Jerome Frank had done as much in jurisprudence). To be sure, it was not a synthesis of Marxism or socialism and psychoanalysis, but progressive notions (in the American sense) were clearly present. Indeed, the American attempt at synthesis followed Dewey in proposing, in effect, a social pedagogy that would incorporate psychoanalysis as a means of cultivating the cooperative and rational aspects of human nature. Wilhelm Reich, when he arrived, took a tragically idiosyncratic course.

The Americanization of psychoanalysis, then, was not a single process or an ideologically one-dimensional project. It is true that character analysis and its derivative, ego psychology, were treated by Hartmann, Kris, and Loewenstein in relative autonomy from social analysis. It is also true that a connection with social analysis was always possible: witness the use Erikson made of these psychoanalytic concepts. Why reproach the Europeans for their alleged betrayal of a project—the radical transformation of human nature—that was no longer an article of faith in the United States or the Europe from which they fled?

The period 1940–60, however, brought the most contradictory psychoanalytic discussion of human nature. Quite apart from *The Authoritarian Personality,* Fromm in his much-read *Escape from Freedom* gave a simplified view of the Frankfurt School's work. His own later efforts to develop a theory of an autonomous personality were connected with his stubborn adherence to a socialist vision, which also led him to participate in the revival of Marxist humanism toward the end of the period. American social science accepted a psychoanalysis it could reduce to empirical dimensions in its rhetoric—that is, it emptied Freud's own work of historical and philosophical meaning. In a radical farewell to thoughts of emancipation, Norman O. Brown in *Life Against Death* transmuted psychoanalysis into a new form of pantheism and did not merely relativize social conflict: he dismissed it as unimportant, or as an epiphenomenon in the play of fundamental psychic forces. Marcuse, per contra, took Freud's historical approach to human nature seriously. By developing the notion of "surplus repression," he enabled us to think of a situation in which emancipation would be made possible by the historical development of the psyche. He was also able to take the conventional view, that the temporary affluence and productivity of postwar capitalism had deadened revolutionary impulse, and reverse it. The development of the productive forces could be reinterpreted as a new *via regis* to the kingdom of freedom. What was most striking was Marcuse's rejection of those revisions of Freud which held that psychoanalysis was insufficiently historical or social in its theoretic structure. Marcuse argued that Freud had seized upon a historical structure (extending over centuries and indeed millennia) and that he was entirely correct to suppose that psychic structures could not be changed in relatively short periods of time.

Marx once said of Balzac that it did not matter that his art was devoid of explicit criticism of capitalism. The master's realism was criticism enough. We can turn this method on psychoanalysis. Some of its most critical aspects, precisely those that enable us to see an entire society's conflicts mirrored in the psyche's wounds, have nothing to do with explicit sociological intent. Three recent clusters of work in psychoanalysis (with roots in the past of the movement, of course) belong in any account of recent social thought.

One theme has been set by Kohut's work on narcissism. That self-love and self-preoccupation are primordial themes of Western culture (and not only ours) will not surprise readers of *The Sorrows of Young Werther*. Kohut's own work was the product of a lifetime, and it can hardly be deemed an anticipation of later themes of social thought. It was, however, incorporated by Lasch in his *Culture of Narcissism*. We can say that modern narcissism is encouraged by two quite incompatible tendencies. The first is the social Darwinism that seems inextricably bound to the functioning of the market as a central economic principle. The second is the therapeutic definition of the personality (derided by Lasch in his other works), which conceives of persons as perpetual objects of cure. Clearly, psychoanalytic treatments of narcissism connect with the traditional analysis of alienation and rootlessness in modern social thought. That connection, however, appears very different when we ask if narcissism is the result of an overevaluation of the individual rather than a systematic if implicit underevaluation, even obliteration. Once again, the use we make of psychoanalytic concepts and data depends upon the larger framework that we select. It is impossible to declare that social structure encourages phenomena we group as narcissism without specifying the structural processes at work. Moreover, it is difficult to answer the question of an irreducible extent of narcissism in human nature. The value of psychoanalytic work is, not despite but because of these perplexities, great: it obliges us to consider a more complex system of causation, to avoid simple derivatives of human nature from immediate and limited historical situations.

At first glance, Kohut's work on the self is a contribution, if an elegant one, to that pervasive search for authentic subjectivity that marks so much of the recent cultural situation. Does not Kohut argue that the self, to become healthy, must learn to love itself? Appearances deceive. His work is more subtle, and it is intricately connected to the ego psychology that preceded it. It offers, indeed, another perspective on those questions of historical self-location (termed identity) that so concerned Erikson. Kohut's self is most definitely not an entity that can be maintained in enforced or willed social isolation. It requires (above all for that healthy narcissism that Kohut insists is human maturity) a great deal of solidarity—and love.

Ego psychology arose from reflection on the vicissitudes of drives. The healthy ego could reconcile drive and the demands of the world. The examination of the ego's defenses led directly to inquiry into character: a pattern of defenses was, in the last analysis, character. Kohut's idea of self rests on a rather more specific set of experiences. Self arises not from the entire set of human tasks but from relationships to archaic objects. Kohut uses the term "archaic" in three senses. It refers to the earliest experiences, but also to the most enduring and, equally, the deepest ones. We encounter the irresistible attraction and angry disappointment inseparable from the internalization of parental models. The term "models," certainly, is inaccurate: we deal instead with archetypes. The child unable to integrate early love and early rejection (or what is imagined as rejection) into a growing and constant core of affect and insight will develop pathological narcissism. The child cannot regard his or her self with love while it struggles with overwhelming ambivalence toward its archetypes. No doubt, the description reminds us of the ego psychologist's description of humans devoid of autonomy and self-respect, suffering from the diffuse malaise of the modern psyche. Here, however, diffuse pain is given a name, and a source.

Kohut originally held that ego psychology and self psychology move on parallel tracks, complementing one another. I am reminded of the late Aldo Moro's witty formula for the rapprochement of Italy's Catholics and Communists: parallel convergences. The ego psychologists, close to Freud in thought and time, depicted the resolution of the oedipal conflict as the critical early event. They then spent their therapeutic energies and theoretic acumen on matters that could hardly be ascribed in any linear fashion to that event: to the diffuse incapacities and vulnerabilities of the ego in its life course. Kohut takes the oedipal crisis seriously enough. He argues that the insufficiently developed self will be unable to bear the strain of resolving the oedipal conflict. In fact, with the argument, he terminates parallelism. What we get, instead, is a new map of the soul, a new history of its metapsychological course.

Kohut's archaicism is no doubt the premise of his work. When the time comes for the child to develop, however jaggedly or painfully, a fixed and strong character, many fail. They do so because they do not love themselves. Fixated on others, not as models but as sources of their being, they cannot aspire to the autonomy further development requires. What Kohut terms a healthy narcissism is found in the self that has achieved differentiation from its parents. Fatally bound in its earliest passion, the incomplete self cannot love itself.

Another dimension marks Kohut's work. He likens psychoanalytic method to hermeneutics. Transference in the therapeutic relationship alters the patient's self—but also the analyst's. We deal not with an isolable structure seen from outside, as in a classical description of ego function. We deal with a human process that we attempt to recreate from within. The experience of self is a result of an inner struggle with the feelings attached to primary relationships. A large degree of inward awareness and selfhood are synonymous.

The connection with the discussion of inner objects in the British school of psychoanalysis is clear enough. What makes Kohut's use of notions of inner objects so distinctive is his contextual awareness, especially in his later writings. Our historical situation affords little continuity. Only those with a healthy minimum of narcissism can function outside of the near total environments once constituted by communities and families. Kohut's later thought reminds us by implication of Lifton's reflections on the protean character of the modern psyche. Kohut states the inner conditions for the maintenance of a sense of cohesion under the shock of existence in a world resembling a film projected at insanely high speed.

Kohut began with a rigorously metapsychological language, and was at pains to mark his distances from those who, like Mahler, studied interaction directly. In the end, he saw the value of his work in its historical fit. Tragic man, he claims, has now replaced guilty man. The tragedy is our inability to experience ourselves as whole. The difference from the ego psychologists' formulation is, however, not impossibly great. Kohut's ultimate conclusion, that healthy narcissism is impossible outside of the immediate experience of love, endows his metapsychology with a sustaining body. Inner process and outer support, self-love and the love of others, appear inextricably connected.

The second set of psychoanalytic materials concerns the theory of separation, more precisely, of early-childhood separation from the mother. Empirical findings based in some measure upon observation (rather than solely upon clinical reconstruction) suggest that internal self-conceptions, emotively highly charged and perduring, begin to form very early in infancy. The importance of the matrix, then, is its bearing upon questions that the enlarged participation of women in the labor force, and the great increase in the number of single-parent households, makes salient. What are the consequences for total personal development of early separation from continuous contact with a mother? What qualitative (as opposed to quantitative) alterations in maternal attitude follow from work outside the home—or, for that matter, from confinement to the home? We may also regard the importance attached to mother-child relationships in infancy, following the earlier work of Melanie Klein, as an anticipation of feminist themes in psychology, if one that not all feminists would greet with unqualified enthusiasm. Just as with the question of the irreducible nature of narcissism, it is impossible to depict mother-child relationships solely or primarily as refractions of larger social processes. Rather, these fuse with those processes, giving them concrete psychic content.

Finally, psychoanalysis has given much attention to the processes of internalization. The earlier domination of American psychoanalytic thought by ego psychology, in a rather straight line of descent from Freud's own work, has been replaced by a multiplication of perspectives. Among these, the earlier writings of Melanie Klein and the later ones of Winnicott have been very influential. A depiction of superego development as due to the internalization of paternal authority has been superseded by a far more complex idea, in which mother-child relationships, sequences of inner splitting, and narcissistic fixations play their varied parts. All of this, of course, is much removed from analyses of the supposed tyranny of the family (common enough twenty years ago under the influence of Cooper and Laing) in inflicting psychic deformation. The concept of deformation, however, implies that we know psychic health or wholeness when we see it—a difficult vision to generate when our very ideas of pathology alter with new ideas of psychic structure. Again, we face a situation in which the uses of psychoanalysis are many, and depend upon the content and intentions of social (and political) analysis.

Feminist ideas fall under the rubric of alternative conceptions of culture. It is a sign of the diffuseness (and the pervasiveness) of the issues raised by feminism that these may also be treated under the psyche. Gilligan's insistence that women think in a different moral voice, Jean Baker Miller's depiction of the unhappiness of career women who seek to behave like men, are very contemporary versions of a view of women as empathic and nurturant. Ehrenreich's reversal of the argument, in her assertion that men have suffered more than women from the repression of these traits in their psyches and society, is original in accent and content. In implication, it joins a long tradition of analysis which holds that our society is antithetical to the expression of primary (and valuable) human needs.

The psychoanalytic movement can hardly claim that the theory of femininity is one of its titles of honor. Freud himself intimated that he was not clear about the answer to his question "What does woman want?" It is striking that much of the recent discussion of femininity uses Freud's earliest work on hysteria as an occasion for rethinking. In particular, the case of Dora has been revived. The questions being asked again—or, more precisely, being asked differently—are several.

Within the boundaries of psychoanalysis, the structure of oedipal processes in women has been described anew. Freud thought that girls

became women by half accepting, half denying, their own lack of pe-
nises. The search for the surrogate penis led to the male, who could alone
give a penis temporarily, a child (a symbolic replacement) permanently.
A later argument retains Freud's notion of hopeless competition with
the mother, but interprets it as the source of the acceptance of standard
feminine roles. Girls identify with men as victors in the struggle for
power: penis envy concerns the phallus as a symbol of domination.

The discussion has been enlarged by the linguistic transformation of
psychoanalysis wrought by Lacan. Not surprisingly, students of cultural
theory and literature have become enthusiastic appropriators of Lacan's
work. The psychoanalytic guild has been decidedly more reserved.
Lacan, of course, has moved psychoanalysis away from the description
of drive to the realm of symbolism. The feminist critique of the eternali-
zation of culturally derived roles in the biosocial theory of classical
psychoanalysis found in Lacan an armature of concepts apparently
ready-made for their requirements. In fact, the clinical inquiries of those
discussing inner objects may be—in the long run—more telling. It is
true that work like that of Kernberg is exceedingly abstract—a metapsychology to end other metapsychologies. In its clinical aspects, however,
the analysis of the inner life of the early years does not assume that the
patriarchal social relationships of the beginning of our century were
replicated in the psyche. Patriarchy in any event was rather like the
military occupation of a passively resistant country. In large sectors of
late Victorian or early modern society, women had ways of holding their
own. Clinical work which insists that in the early years of life mothers
are at least as important as fathers may be laboring the obvious. It does
make possible new views of femininity and feminine roles—and not
least, of the feminine components in the male psyche.

Here, where once anthropologists called our attention to cultural
variability, the historians of our own society are now heard. Smith-
Rosenberg has shown how the very categories of masculinity and femininity, biological predisposition and human possibility, express a struggle
for power between men and women. Her analysis of the world of
women, and of relations between men and women in nineteenth-
century America, describes spheres of existence narrowed or extirpated
later. In particular, middle-class women inhabited a region rich in feeling, from which men were excluded. Smith-Rosenberg also deals with

what was termed the New Woman of the early twentieth century, of the resistance she incurred, of her failure to establish a female presence in the arts and professions. That presence was opposed by another kind of female presence, enunciating doctrines not of personal autonomy but of sexual liberation. The liberation in question, from a repressive definition of permitted sexuality, accepted the masculine-feminine boundaries the New Woman sought to transcend. In the long run, by claiming sexual freedom for women, it may have done much to undermine the patriarchy the New Women opposed. Had not Freud declared that it would take years from the invention of certain contraceptive methods, but that these would bring a profound alteration in our sexual lives?

We are returned to the question of the biological basis, and the permanence, of our ideas and practice of gender. Consider Sulloway's inquiry into Freud's debt to the Darwinian biology of his formative years. His exploration of sexuality within an evolutionary framework was uncompromising: it laid bare the hidden assumptions of prevalent ideas. Freud's very attachment to the biological dimensions of thought codified these in a way that rendered them vulnerable. Mitchell has said that by depicting the psychic consequences of patriarchy, Freud made it possible to treat patriarchy historically. Marcuse has employed the same sort of argument: Freud's depiction of the limits of liberation was truer to the historical moment than facile accounts of the possibility of freedom. The biological determination of cultural categories, in Freud, ended where it did not serve his theoretic purposes. There, he began to develop his metapsychology—and was led, ineluctably, to enter upon cultural and social terrain. We cannot stand Freud on his head and replace biological determinism by cultural analysis. Freud's own biologicism was already culturally tempered—preconsciously if not half-consciously so. We now confront the task of analyzing a complex system of interdependent relationships in the genesis of femininity. Perhaps, we may have to admit, there is no one structure of femininity but many, created by the interaction of culture and biology in the psyche. Freud insisted that psychological events were overdetermined. We are now able to reinterpret the injunction as a generalized methodological precept.

The revival of social Darwinism, wars and rumors of wars, and preparation for the nuclear extirpation of the entire human race (absurdly described as "defense") raise anew the question of intrinsic aggressivity. Surprisingly, aggressivity (the death instinct of Freud) has not been much discussed. Perhaps, after the trivialization of the behavioristic connection between frustration and aggression in the academic psychology of the previous generation, the problem seemed too difficult. Perhaps the debate around Norman Brown and Marcuse exhausted our resources for a while. The more likely explanation is this: Aggression is so pervasive in daily life, in our experience of history, that its reduction to a single source seems to require huge simplifications. Put in another way, every analysis we make of the psyche confronts us with the omnipresence of aggression, and an apparent multiplicity of causes.

Perhaps an indirect confrontation with the aggressivity of the human psyche is a more promising approach. American social thought has been struggling with the Holocaust, with anticipations of nuclear destruction, with questions of collective and individual responsibility. The revival of interest in the content and the causes of the Holocaust (in which the role of the victims and of ordinary, or tacit, accomplices has had as much attention as the psyche of the murderers) has been no less striking in the United States than in Europe and Israel. The historian David Wyman has demonstrated that a variety of reasons (bureaucratic inertia, routine anti-Semitism, and the failure of the imagination) accounted for American official indifference—at best—to the fate of European Jewry. Robert Lifton's work has proceeded in a straight line from his study of survivors of Hiroshima to his analysis of the Nazi practice of medicine in the death camps. He is interested in the fusion of precipitating circumstance, ideological legitimation, and destructive impulse that leads scientific and technical elites to moral crime. In other work, best described in the title of a major book, *The Broken Connection*, he has depicted the contemporary Western psyche as deprived of the certainty of continuity that sustained what Freud termed Eros in previous generations. Put schematically, if Lifton is right, it is not so much aggressivity that generates the modern possibility of total extirpation, but that possibility that generates aggressivity.

Lifton's work portrays all of us in extreme situations—either victims or executioners, actual or potential. He began by studying the survivors of the Hiroshima bombing, who sought to give meaning to their survival by constant interpretation and reinterpretation of it. He proceeded to treat the rest of humanity as anticipatory survivors, potential victims of the final catastrophe. On the way, he has written of the protean capacities (or, more precisely, aspirations) of the modern psyche, our effort to inhabit several selves or construct several identities. A fundamental fact about our identity as biological beings that is most difficult for humanity to acknowledge is the certainty of our own death. Lifton, to be sure, thinks that preoccupation with death is a major theme of the unconscious—not second to sexuality. Symbolic defenses against the anxiety of death, effective simulacra of immortality, can be found in communal and familial continuity, in the affirmation of a human identity across generations. History now threatens that continuity: our connections with past and future are broken. The pervasive despair of contemporary psyches comes, then, not alone from rising (or falling) expectations, role conflicts, or moral argument, but from a fundamental transformation in the compact between generations.

Why cannot humanity respond to this central threat with a spiritual (and political) mobilization, an angry refusal of ideological and technical soporifics? Lifton adduces the idea of numbing, a defense by a self paralyzed by anxiety and emotion, (and overwhelmed, intellectually, by complexity, too). This can hardly be termed a reaction to excessive concern. It is more accurate to describe it as an inappropriate response to excessive but real threat—inappropriate because it denies selves and society the opportunity to develop rational measures against it.

Lifton has now carried, in a study of Nazi physicians who worked in the death camps, his inquiries into contemporary extremity to the limit. The difficulty is that in our history, extremity and normalcy merge. Does not Lifton cite a remark to the effect that the terrible Mengele, under other circumstances, might have been just an ordinarily sadistic German physician? Lifton also cites a survivor of these horrors describing the response of other prisoners in her concentration camp: those who experienced them found it impossible to believe what was occurring in their midst—genocide organized with bureaucratic pedantry and industrial efficiency. Freud once remarked that before the mysteries of art, even psychoanalysis had to lay down its arms. Before evil, must the analytical and historical imagination resign itself to (relative) banality?

Lifton thinks not, and under the rubric of "doubling" has developed a theory of inhuman behavior by humans. Those who have studied genocide (or talked at length with former Nazis in Germany) will recognize the extraordinary pain Lifton had to overcome to conduct his inquiry.

It must be said that the depth and realism of his clinical insights into his Nazi interlocutors often renders his theoretic categories pale. That is inevitable. What is striking about his theoretic conclusions is their transcendence of the one case. Lifton employs the notion of doubling to describe the ways in which selves manage extreme contradictions. Devoted heads of family command death camps, not so much by splitting parts of themselves but by finding acceptable legitimations for the connection between their roles. The human demand for something like spiritual wholeness here exacts a terrible price: can irrationality and murder be integrated in the psyche as well as anything else? Lifton's description of the ideological context (the social-biological obsessions of the Nazis, instrumental neutrality in the practice of medicine, and the supposed threat to German national existence) does remind us of other, nearer settings. Lifton does not hesitate to discuss the similarities between the ideologists and executioners of genocide and the apologists and planners for future nuclear wars.

Their psyches, too, are doubled—protected by a contemporary version of moral casuistry from repugnance for what they are doing. To be sure, Lifton's data includes the ambivalence of many of the Nazi physicians, the residual guilt of those who after the war resumed the practice of medicine. Guilt, clearly, is not enough to deter evil. In any event, after nuclear war, there will be nothing to resume.

Reading Lifton, we are reminded that at the very beginning of psychoanalysis Freud sublimated his critical and liberal politics in his work. With consummate delicacy and mastery, Schorske has analyzed the dream of revolution in *The Interpretation of Dreams.* So far from politics expressing the oedipal conflict, argues Schorske, the theory of oedipal conflict was a sublimation of Freud's own bitter enmity to the irrationality of arrogant authority and power. The burden of Lifton's work is that the understanding of the psyche cannot turn us away from these conflicts in reality. Psychological insight teaches us that there is no alternative to the attempt to master them. So far from diluting Freud, then, Lifton has returned us to the great political end of the healing project, enlightenment.

We are, clearly, at some distance from classical psychoanalysis. The unconscious, in its benign as well as its dreadful aspects, is present even in those American studies that deal with cognitive functioning or the direct play of social influence upon the psyche. Milgram's horrifying study of the compliance of experimental subjects (in the event, students at an elite university, Yale) in inflicting pain on others is by now a minor classic. The study suggests that the implicit authority of modern science (if in the form of a university psychologist) can and does outweigh individual empathy and responsibility. Kohlberg, per contra, depicts the moral development of the psyche in rather more reassuring terms. His is not, to be sure, a mindless optimism. Rather, his work entails an implicit demand upon society—for institutions that will sustain the moral sense and structure that are basic components of psychic development.

There is, of course, no one American character: how could there be in a society so mixed, so fragmented, whose history has proceeded by discontinuous accretion? Yet the United States, precisely because of its variety of contexts and multicultural mixing, may also be understood as a historical laboratory for the psyche. In the absence of a single national character (or even of a limited spectrum of characters), industrial America must show us the psyche in its immediacy, with character like litmus paper registering immediate alterations in the socioeconomic environment. Alas, the situation is not so simple. We can understand specific American cultures (ethnically or religiously constructed) as constituting nodal points of resistance to socioeconomic change. Alternatively, we can understand certain cultures as cultivating characters most responsive to those changes. The distance between character and culture in general remains impossible of precise measurement, the causal connection between the two obscure.

Just as every religion or fragment of one, and a large number of secularized derivatives of religion or imitations of it, claims residence in the United States, every sort of character is naturalized, or domesticated, in some part of our society. Monolithic notions of the society as producing the psychic symptoms of alienation are true, but they miss another essential point: the United States is not a nation or a society in any received sense of the term. The idea of certain Europeans, that Americans are free to make or remake themselves, is absurd. Some Americans are free (by virtue of economic and cultural circumstance) to attempt that, but most are not. The attempts, meanwhile, have not materially advanced our understanding of either human nature in general or of the ultimate limits of the American experiment.

In sum, then, the specific nature of American society sets limits on the universal applicability of recent American attempts to depict the psyche. Those Americans who have had the most to say have quite explicitly attempted to make contact with larger contexts of experience, to relativize the American one. Alternatively, they have drawn upon intellectual traditions specifically European. (An American tradition in psychology, from William James to Edward Tolman, appears to have exhausted itself.) Whether this is a statement about our entire intellectual condition is a matter to which I now turn.

VIII

The Fate of Theory

If there is one positive and promising aspect of the decades just behind us, it is the secularization of social theory. A quite religious positivism, or unreflective empiricism, has marked much American social thought for a good part of the century. This took on, alternately, conservative or reformist political functions, but its basic intellectual structure was unchanged. There was a substratum of social reality, and empirical procedures combined with an abstract analysis on the model of the natural sciences could apprehend it directly. There were, indeed, laws of social and psychological function (a term borrowed from biology and medicine); it remained only to state and verify these.

What I have termed secularization is the result of a number of influences. The critical party (or *a* critical party, as there were several) in social science pointed to the striking similarity between the laws ostensibly inherent in social structure and the notions of social order congenial to dominant ideologies. Historians, a converted minority excepted, remained skeptical of the reductionist emphases of much social science. The social reality they knew was too complex, had too many levels, and developed over too long a stretch of time to lend itself to laboratorylike inquiry. Critical thinkers influenced by Marxism and historians skeptical of it both conveyed, at times, the view that social science generalized excessively from the present. Kuhn's work on scientific revolutions had ambiguous effects. It opened contemporary models of society and social process to scrutiny on the grounds that these were historically relative. It also, however, seemed to bring social science and natural science closer: if all were paradigm, our social-scientific paradigms were (almost) as good as their natural-science paradigms.

Some of what happened was the result of an intellectual long wave movement. The historicization of thought typified by the work of Troeltsch, and even Weber, the legacy of Mannheim's personal synthesis of German historicism with some elements of Marxism, the sort of perspective employed by Durkheim, found their way into the assumptions of American social science. There these coexisted uneasily with the tradition of pragmatism. What is striking, when we look back, is that— acute, lively, and at times spirited methodological debate to the contrary—most social scientists, without much intellectual effort, subscribed generally to one or another methodological position, and did their work unconcerned about finer points of epistemology. Discussions of the political dimensions of social thought, of value neutrality and value relevance, were more common. These, of course, were often inextricably connected to philosophical issues—although not every participant in political discussion was philosophically literate.

Let us say that American social science is now pervaded by the idea that perspective is important, indeed decisive. Some align themselves with Weber's formal position, that philosophical and political perspective determines the choice of problem, but that scientific canons of empirical rigor have to determine its precise formulation and solution. Others go further and see social-science discourse as a dialogue between or among alternative or competing moral universes. The recent offensive by conservative thought has done much, curiously, to second the work of those in the Marxist tradition. If the liberal (in the American sense— that is, hesitantly reformist) party in the universities, and of course, the radical one, were biased at best, prejudiced and even persecutory of truth at worst, the conservatives were in a poor position to claim exclusive possession of scientific truths. To the credit of many, they did not, and instead argued for the superiority of their value systems. A few declared that the universities should be policed, intellectually, to eliminate an alleged Marxist threat. Only the naïve, in these circumstances, argue that they do so to maintain the objectivity of the social sciences: their aim is, quite avowedly, the ideological domination of society.

The result, interestingly, is a condition of methodological pluralism in fact. Every political and philosophical doctrine, if in very uneven measure, is found in our social-science departments. The disintegration of the consensual social science of the period 1945–60, and of its impoverished philosophical justification, has generated a vacuum into which a number of competing forces have rushed. Methodological pluralism, however, is perhaps another way to fix or situate an equivalent substantive condition. Perhaps the term "equivalent" is not quite right. What appears as pluralism is pluralism *malgré soi-même*—the absence of much conviction and all certainty.

The loss of public space, the decline of public existence, the inauthenticity of the substitutes we have for it, has been a theme of much of our more telling social criticism. A singular conflation of liberal demands for an elevated practice of citizenship and radical ones for participation, the idea of the decline of public life entails assertions about what we are not, not about what we are. It parallels, and at times mixes with, depictions of all the social world as a stage. The steady ascent of Erving Goffman's work in esteem—well beyond the narrow confines of sociology as a discipline—is evidence for the omnipresence of the belief that appearances are all. The otherwise inexplicable fashion by which in ostensibly serious discussions of international politics, a shallow, even silly, theory of the constitution of international relations by systems of perception has become nearly dominant is further evidence. (So, too, is the election to the presidency of a rather mediocre screen actor.) What these things attest to is the absence of an idea of society. Even the critical party has no realized version of society in mind, no counterproject, and must content itself with a frantic effort to confront the jagged contours of a reality which, especially in its contemporary form, escapes us.

Another parallel is provided by the theory of the psyche. In each epoch in which an enormous amount of institutional legitimation for the unleashing of aggression is available, discussions of the limits, the plasticity, of human nature seem beside the point. (Popular American television dramas now feature soulfully neurotic policemen, their health endangered by the struggle to uphold order.) The idea of development, of characterological maturity, seems as nothing when contrasted with the systematic diminution of the spirit pursued by the culture industry.

Critical social thought in the United States, then, suffers from the absence of a counterproject, an alternative view of historical possibility. The recapture of substantial fragments of the past by historians, hope for the future engendered by those with radical views of the possibility of alteration in our institutions and our selves, seem not to have mobilized conviction, energy, or ideas for a profoundly different politics. These function negatively—if importantly—as a reservoir for moral criticism of a present that seems immutable. The destruction of the conviction of the immutability of our society (the explicit and implicit message of both unreflective belief and most systematic thought) is for the moment the most that critical thought can hope for. Even that would be a great deal.

2

THE POLITICS
OF SOCIAL
KNOWLEDGE

I

Between Ideology
and Enlightenment

When, in the midst of the turbulence of a defeated Germany, Max Weber addressed the students of the University of Munich, he warned them against revolutionary enthusiasm—or even hope. He ended his talk, "Politics As a Vocation," with a quotation from Shakespeare's Sonnet 102.

> Our love was new, and then but in the spring,
> When I was wont to greet it with my lays;
> As Philomel in summer's front doth sing,
> And stops her pipe in growth of riper days.

"Such," Weber concluded, "is not the case. Not summer's bloom lies ahead of us, but rather a polar night of icy darkness and hardness, no matter which group may triumph externally now."

The meaning is unequivocal: politics is not a matter for youthful enthusiasm and its more permanent residue, utopian hopes. It is, instead, a matter of stoic confrontation of harsh, often punitive, realities. We can at the moment hardly accuse most of our colleagues in the American social sciences of either excessive passion or utopianism. The question is whether behind their arid prose, beneath their intellectual sobriety, there lies a huge disappointment, a sense of irretrievable loss. There is, indeed, something depressive about the very language of normal social science, something that is not relentless discipline but is more like a compulsive repression of spontaneity. One explanation is obvious: heirs to a tradition that depicted social science as a linear continuation of the natural sciences, as capable of those decisive alterations of our entire way of thinking and seeing personified in the lives of Galileo and Newton and Einstein, or more prosaically represented by Nobel laure-

97

ates, the social scientists experience a double burden. One is the weight of the past, of extreme anticipations of intellectual, nay moral, progress. Another is the realization that their position is like that of the Christians described by Ernest Renan: they looked forward to the Kingdom of Heaven, but got the Roman Catholic Church. Our colleagues know that in the beginning the social sciences promised a new social world. What they got was (a small part of) the National Science Foundation.

Perhaps they have taken too literally Freud's bitter conclusion to his *Civilization and its Discontents.* He knew, he said, that he would be reproached for offering no consolation to humanity—for consolation in his view was what they all wanted, "the most ferocious revolutionary no less than the most obedient believer." A vision without consolation, however, presupposes precisely what most social scientists implicitly refuse: a tortured spiritual analysis of the human condition. Some social scientists reserve that sort of inquiry for after hours— many tell themselves that a sphere of values may be connected to their work in the sphere of fact, but that it most definitely does not intrude upon it.

The most religious (or, at least, ecclesiastically organized) of the industrial societies, we are also the most secularized: our elites and the institutions they command, the ordinary functioning of patterned social relationships, seem utterly bereft of religious (or even moral) drives. Perhaps there is a more accurate way to phrase the paradox: the very absence of reference to (or recourse to) transcendent standards in our daily lives has the quality of a reaction formation, a defense against saturation by belief. No defense is perfect and all bear the mark of the forces against which they are erected. Secularization in America is still half guilty, still religious.

In the not so distant past, the social sciences were in the vanguard of American intellectual creativity and social reflection. They are in their present nearly homogenized condition still witnesses to that past, and to the major role of religion in it. Secularization in the social sciences separates them from moral analysis, from questions about the historical equivalents of first and last things, but leaves just that affective vacuum into which a joyless and unavowed belief flows. It is the most vulgar of beliefs, the conviction that things being the way they appear, they cannot be otherwise. Once, American thought was a battlefield of contention between Calvinism and the Enlightenment. Is it possible that the pervasive rupture of historical consciousness, of intellectual continuity, which is so prominent in our intellectual life, remains incomplete, unachieved? Memories, however dim or distorted, falsely systematized or in the form of unconnected if truthful fragments, fitfully stimulate conscience, and so render less perfect the homogenization of which I complain. The social sciences may flatter themselves that they are instruments of domination (poorly disguised as ancillary techniques of administration). It is entirely unclear, however, that the agencies of power need them for anything more than apologetics—an apologetics not nullified but at least challenged by the slightest hint of authentic pluralism. We shall return to the theme of broken ideological circuits, if that is the term, shortly. For the moment, these lines raises a question. If the social sciences are so jaggedly devoid of moral coherence, so unmoved by the impulse to shape history, must we simply discard them—if necessary, in the cruelest of ways, by ignoring them? Many do, and turn instead to novel and film, or the plastic arts, for instruction about society and for the rudiments of moral coherence.

In fact, what is true of normal or routine social science is not invariably true of the most spirited thinkers in the field. Consider the American universities in the decade 1920–30, in which the proponents of a new history, pragmatism, psychoanalysis, and legal realism struggled against other schools (and the institutional economists, in an anticipation of the later arguments over Keynesianism argued with the neoclassicists). Certainly, the conflict had much about it that was political. The advocates of reform, those who took a critical view of the normalcy espoused and apotheosized by Harding, Coolidge, and Hoover, were generally to be found among the innovators.

Political perspective as such was not at issue. What mattered was the way in which politics provided moral and intellectual energy for a different scrutiny of human nature and society, of thought and the psyche. The passions that animated William James and Holmes, Dewey and Beard and Veblen, were not political in any narrow sense. They involved questions of human autonomy and purposiveness, of history, tradition, and responsibility, of constraint and freedom. They were clearly political in a larger sense, if we understand politics as the assumptions and conditions, as well as the organized forms, of our common life. The domestication of the social sciences had proceeded apace for a generation: the new thinkers threatened to introduce again questions of compassion and hatred, love and fear—in short, to reverse the kind of secularization of thought reduced to the ascetic rationality of a supposedly neutral social science. Those described by Morton White in his study of the group as revolting against formalism were indeed in the vanguard of that larger movement in American thought and life that was to eventuate in the New Deal. Roosevelt's programs of social reform were not only responses to crisis by a new generation of technocrats seizing their chance. Technical and institutional innovation in administration, government, and law presupposed, or was inseparable from, new analyses and new values in the social sciences—a new conception, indeed, of the relationship of thought to its setting.

Does the history of the New Deal provide us with a model, or serious indications, for the present? Let us suppose that a president of considerable capacity takes office as, about him and everyone else, the institutional framework begins to disintegrate. We can envisage another economic crisis, compounded perhaps by serious social disturbances and losses in our imperial system (let us say, the withdrawal from NATO military obligations of the German Federal Republic). Upon what intellectual resources, reserves of political ideas, could a new administration draw? No doubt 1993 or 2001 will not resemble 1933. The economy has changed; our world position is much different; our population and our politics are organized (or fragmented, as the case may be) on other bases. Still, the question is worth asking—its heuristic implications are large.

An initial objection is entirely just: the modes of connection between the academy, the other institutions that house and communicate the work of the mind, and the polity have changed. Our politics are already ideologicized, our technocrats in place. Entire ranges of organizations (the research centers and foundations, the schools of public policy and law) specialize in supplying government, the Congress, the parties (and the private sector) with educated experts and systematic expertise. Government itself (and significant parts of the private sector) are full of academically educated specialists, often engaged in inquiry as well as administration. Indeed, so politicized is the process that much inquiry is quite specifically directed to political ends. It aims to convince, or to justify, or to reassure: it is not matter for academic reflection alone. Indeed, much of the academy would be discountenanced were it restricted to academic tasks in a conventional sense. It is not as if the universities—above all, the large centers of research and education—did their work *sine ira et studio* and then asked: what may we offer to the agencies of power? The work is directly conceived, and executed, for those agencies.

The dean of the Kennedy School of Government at Harvard, announcing in 1985 that he was a consultant to the secretary of defense, also pronounced the latter a man of profound philosophical qualities— these unjustly, in the dean's view, ignored by the public. At first sight, it would appear that the dean, a political scientist, was at pains to show that, with the naked eye, the triumphs of his colleagues in microbiology can be repeated; no one else, at any rate, had claimed to have caught a glimpse of the side of Caspar Weinberger that situates him in a line of descent from Aristotle. Perhaps the explanation for this encomium is to be found in competitiveness among Harvard's social scientists. Surely, the university prize for calling a thing by anything but its name has hitherto been in the uncontested possession of Samuel Huntington for his unforgettable description of free-fire zones, defoliation, and enforced relocation in concentration camps in Vietnam as a particularly rapid process of urbanization. The dean's avowal of reflectiveness in a secretary of defense whose public pronouncements suggest that he thinks, as well as speaks, in words of one syllable is more than evidence for the persistence in our academy of a universal human trait, sycophancy; it illuminates the technocratic bondage of our institutions. What matters is not the education of the public; what counts is the legitimation sought by the university through its connection to power. Speaking truth to power is, no doubt, possible in many circumstances (court jesters had this function once). Altering the conditions in which power is exercised by addressing a public directly is very different from concentrating on rendering advice to the powerful.

The intellectual conflicts that preceded the New Deal, the long travail of the American spirit from populism, through progressivism (and social-ism), the engagement in this argument of the theologians, took as an unvarying substratum of debate the existence of a public. Views might differ on the extent to which the public needed new capacities; what was not (or not much, at any rate) doubted was the public's ability to develop those capacities. For all of the brutality and corruption of American politics, the unashamed pursuit of interests at the cost of solidarity, those who were revulsed by these national traits thought that there was more substance to the nation. There was a citizenry, a court of historical last resort. Consider, by contrast, the very language of most contemporary political consultants. (And reflect for a moment on the fact that the AFL-CIO, mobilizing for election, relies not on volunteers from union ranks but on specially employed staff.) Not only does that language use the rhetoric of marketing; it manipulates segmented markets as if no common discourse were possible. The election of an ignorant and un-comprehending actor as president, the reduction of politics to media events—events that testify to the acuity of Bishop Berkeley's vision, since their existence, and even more their significance, depends entirely upon their having been contrived in the eyes of a political promoter—is but one piece of evidence for the decline, nay near destruction, of political discourse in America.

It is this, no doubt, that has reduced a large segment of the critical party in our universities to self-pitying impotence. If none will listen, why not speak and write only for the initiated few? Alternatively, we witness a desperate search on the critics' part for new agents of historical change. An American tradition—that social movements and not parties are the architects (and artisans) of major political transformations—here seems most compelling to those who consider, with reason, that current notions of the mainstream in our national life are cynically distorted or absurdly beside the point, or both. That tradition lives still, and those who make such frequent use of the term "mainstream" to denigrate these movements usually testify to nothing so much as their irreducible vulgarity or to a near totalitarian conception of politics in which those not in the fictive mainstream are depicted as irrelevant, or pathologically eccentric, or subversive if not traitorous. Neither the media, nor the academy, then, need take the arguments of these outsiders seriously.

The media—and, to some extent, also the centers of intellectual production that claim more depth—are fixated on the surface of events. They now underestimate the movements that emerged in the decade 1960–70 (a new black consciousness, feminism, ethnic groupings of all kinds, the general demand for more participation), which themselves flowed alongside currents that had already disturbed the sleep of the decade 1950–60: consumerism and environmentalism, and the persistent demand for human survival voiced by the peace movement in its several stages. Anything resembling a new New Deal will mobilize, or rather canalize, their energies: the Great Society program did so in instructive fashion. What could be learned from that experience was that another aspect of the traditional function of American social movements persists: insofar as they are successful, they lend themselves to incorporation in the standard political process, no doubt altering it, but often losing their own specificity at the same time.

The belief that these social movements will constitute the elements of a new reformist coalition, that the search for new agents of historical change has ended successfully where it began (in the aftermath of the turbulence of the decade 1960–70), ignores or underestimates two other aspects of the American political tradition. One is that new social movements can coalesce with other political groupings much more easily when a new ideological common denominator is found. By that I mean a social project, a notion of a new ordering of the polity and the community that calls into play ideas of order and equity, of historical opportunity and cultural consensus. The discrete addition of separate demands will not serve. The other usual condition for the success of new social movements is rather opposite: their readiness to contract alliances with very different or even hostile groups for the sake of agreed immediate ends. The abolitionists, in the Republican Party, found themselves aligned with northern racists who were opposed to slavery since they did not wish to see blacks in the new states. The segments of the New Deal coalition bitterly critical of American business worked under Roosevelt with the more farsighted financiers and industrialists, who believed (rightly) that the concessions they had to make in the form of a rudimentary American welfare state (with an expansionary economic policy) were a necessary price to pay for the survival of capitalism. In the struggle over Vietnam, the anti-imperial movement eventually found itself allied with the more rational of the imperialists (first McNamara and then Kissinger), who knew that their losses had to be cut. The name of McNamara reminds us, finally, that the contemporary peace movement can now cite figures like McNamara and Kennan on the suicidal absurdity of nuclear weaponry. It remains true that nothing of an enduring kind can be won by a merely additive politics (the French have a phrase, *cartel des nons*).

It is equally true that those seeking major changes in the United States (for which the idea of another New Deal serves as a shorthand expression) may be excessively drawn to models of political mobilization and ideological development from a past that lies behind us in two senses. The large historical generalizations advanced above notwithstanding, it is entirely possible that the politics of the industrial democracies have entered a new phase. The ideological disorientation of the reformist parties (from the Italian Communists through the left wing of our own Democrats), the fragmentation and attenuation of their electorates, and the failure of an (internationalized) economy to respond to national corrective policies are so much evidence for the exhaustion of the ideas and alliances of the postwar period. The rise of social Darwinism, again, as a (temporarily) plausible politics constitutes additional evidence. We face a rather new historical setting, but we do so, to a large extent, without the conceptual resources to explain our situation to ourselves. It follows that we cannot generate the rhetorical conviction that would be necessary to persuade the public that in the midst of that singular synthesis of cacophony and monotony that characterizes the contemporary intellectual market, those of us who call for purposive and radical alterations should be listened to.

II

New Thought
or Old Despair

I am aware that I presuppose what a good deal of the analysis in these initial pages so strenuously denies, that there is a public, still. That is also a matter for inquiry. We come, if somewhat abruptly, to the set of questions to be asked in this book. Can we scrutinize the social sciences in the United States, despite the technocratic bondage of our institutions of learning, and find new ideas that would serve as the elements of a reformist politics? By new, I mean more adequate to our changed historical situation—and that, too, is an object of analysis. I also intend, by new, an application to social sciences of what Harold Rosenberg once termed the tradition of the new, a continuous process of intellectual development through relentless criticism of fixed assumptions. For the social sciences, this clearly entails breaking with the notion of a cumulative progression of knowledge on the model of the self-correction of the natural sciences. It means a continuous hermeneutic process, but one applied to the knowledge or knowers as well as to the human objects of inquiry. It involves continuous attention to the historicity of social science. The static examination and reexamination of assumptions and methods is (often among those who proclaim their attachment to historical method) a new form of scholasticism—a scholasticism, to be sure, without a church. An authentic historicity implies constant movement between the objects of social inquiry and the ideas by which they are construed.

It does not follow that a self-consciously critical or radical social science is the only or most probable repository of new ideas. American university radicalism, alas, too often lends itself to the kind of caricature recently advanced (and woefully overdone) by Frederick Crews. Marx, I have recalled, once remarked about art that not explicit political purpose but a certain aesthetic honesty was the essential thing. Balzac was not a critic of capitalism, but his portrait of nineteenth-century French society (in which *"Enrichissez-vous"* was a prominent motto) omitted none of its ugliness. Saul Bellow has joined those who argue that systematic criticism of American culture and society is, objectively and essentially, service to the Soviet Union and a betrayal of our responsibilities to defend freedom. Nevertheless, his description of our society in *Mr. Sammler's Planet* or *The Dean's December* leaves little to the critical imagination: if his friends at the Committee for the Free World see these as affirmations, we may sympathize with their fear of negations—these would be truly terrible. Suffice it to say that critical intent is not the equivalent of intellectual accomplishment. Indeed, a new view of society may come as the by-product of a thorough examination of character formation (think of the use Lasch and others have made of studies of narcissism), or of aspects of the past seemingly unconnected to the present. (Slotkin's assertion of a connection between the extirpation of the Indians and a fear of working-class savagery tells us more about the psychic dimensions of American class conflict than a stereotyped treatment of the cultural hegemony of an American bourgeoisie.)

Newness, then, is not merely a matter of rearrangement, or of a different perspective. It is the use of the imagination to recall from oblivion (since things new may be matters rediscovered) or raise from obscurity connections hitherto hidden. Perhaps the idea of progress in knowledge has this much to it: newness must also entail a deepening of what is already known. Under the influence of Kuhn and the newer critical philosophy of sciences, we have become used to constant reference to the term "paradigm," to making distinctions between normal or routine science and intellectual innovations or breakthroughs in revolutionary science. Kuhn himself has voiced reservations, indeed skepticism, about the application of his account of the history of science to the social sciences. It has indeed been abused.

In one version, it has justified the promulgation of an indiscriminating plurality of epistemological universes—existing not in society but in the very small segment of it constituted by academic schools or sects. It is rather like the absurd use of the term "perception" to avoid intellectual (and political) choices among and between competing explanations. (The American farmers who became Populists, for instance, have been depicted as "perceiving" the eastern financial elite as their enemies.) In a world constituted by "perceptions," no one version of reality is better or more true than another. In a scholarly language organized by "paradigms," those who speak in this way can feign reflective detachment from events—while having none, or very little. If one paradigm is as good as another, or if social science is simply a succession of paradigms without systematic relationship to the purposive construction of human society by humans, no test of social thought by its capacity to shape reality is possible.

Another version of the abuse of Kuhn's thought takes what we may term a scientistic form. In this variant, the social scientists combine a self-flattering identification with natural science with a simulacrum of critical distance. The succession of models in the social sciences, even shifts in emphasis from one discipline to another, are explained as results of the confrontation of paradigms with reality, and the idea of scientific cumulation is retained, appropriately adorned by a knowing reference to a historical context that remains very largely unexamined. Normal science, in Kuhn's sense, is what interests these social scientists, but they hardly ever ask themselves if social science is capable of normal science at all. The historical world isn't made up of unvarying relationships, and the question of the essential elements of social process is one that does not allow the construction of a periodic table.

The questions I shall ask of social science are, then, not the ones posed in recent assessments, positive in the case of Karl Deutsch, negative from Daniel Bell, of progress in the social sciences. I ask not if social science can correspond to some schematic notion of cumulation in knowledge, but if it has something about it of *sagesse,* of the kind of reflectiveness that is inseparable from purposive moral action. The idea of a social science, or the social sciences, as a purely technical resource for politics removes them from political discussion and so contributes to the reification of a world, to the exclusion of a citizenry from consideration of its own fate.

I ask if there is in the American social sciences systematic insight into character, culture, and society that would help us see ourselves, visualize our historical situation, more clearly. Perhaps I should eschew the term "social science" on grounds of its conventionality, its suggestion of a method borrowed from the natural sciences. It is more accurate to describe this work as concerned with social thought—with ethical and moral questions about politics and society and with historical inquiry into the course of our experience. The question of character, too, must have its due: we expect humans to act on their own behalf, and we are obliged to consider the wellsprings of action. More than the question of rationality is at issue. If we seek a society with heightened solidarity, and one capable of controlling the enormous destructive potential of what is (absurdly) termed the mastery of nature, we have to confront again the questions raised by Freud with his ideas of Eros and Thanatos. And it would be astonishing if the women's movement were to affect us everywhere but in our conceptions of human psychic possibility.

Whenever I read a new idea, said Justice Holmes, I go back to Aristotle and Plato to see which of the two said it first. Perhaps some subsequent generation of intellectual historians will flatter us (when we have long since gone) by deciding that we are not all epigones. For the moment, the least that can be said is that in social thought there are few new discernible master ideas, no compelling syntheses, and even remarkably little evidence for the existence of contested terrain: intellectual passes under attack from ideological armies striving to advance onto plains of public acceptance. Indeed, much of what is written is discussed only in smaller circles, within the confines of separate disciplines. The British social theorist Ernst Gellner, reviewing a work on ethics that did not exhaust his reserves of enthusiasm, once declared that great advances in substantive ethics are always made in the next chapter. For the public, significant ideas in the social sciences are found only in marginal advertisements in the *New York Times Book Review* or the *New York Review of Books.* Substantively, the public reads a good many reviews calling to its attention a plethora of findings and issues, but no convincing argument as to why any one text or set of texts is worth more attention than another. And Washington's quintessential house journal of public affairs, the *National Journal,* recently listed fourteen academics as having influence on current policy debates. With the possible exception of one, none on the list seems excessively burdened by an effort to find a place in the tradition that runs from the Greeks through Machiavelli and Locke to the founders of the American Republic and the thinkers of our own Progressive epoch; indeed, one suspects that most would be hard put to swear that they had read widely in that tradition. They concern themselves with the technical discussion of very immediate and specific public issues.

Nevertheless, there are at least hints of a set of new ideas in the recent literature of social science and social thought. These are often most conspicuous where they may be least expected: not in efforts at explicit development of a conceptual structure, but in attempts to understand a contradictory or an ambiguous social phenomenon. The historians, for their part, in working on aspects of the past may well be more contemporary than the technocrats serving some client or other: they teach us new ideas of agency, cause, sequence. I do not underestimate the influence of disinterested curiosity, but disinterested curiosity in scholarship usually turns out to be the carefully regulated (indeed, policed) code of a highly organized group, a discipline. Most of the new ideas at issue have emerged in the setting of a very interested or politically charged effort to discern precisely the possibilities of a different politics. In no small number of instances—conservative, liberal, or radical—the thinkers in question are responding to the inadequacy of a model of politics strenuously advocated by themselves but no less strenuously resisted by society. It is clear that the boundaries between political and social project and model of society or conception of human nature are by no means obvious or fixed; projects tend to call into existence their own conceptions of psychological and social fact. I indicate some of the ideas, and leave to later the question of how—in the light of other things we know—we may evaluate them.

Was it but thirty years ago that Louis Hartz and Richard Hofstadter still dominated the discussion of the basic political philosophy of the American Republic? The one advanced a view that liberalism was uncontested and pervasive, the other the idea that contestation was likely to be inauthentic or feigned and in any event short-lived. The domination of our politics by the market was not in their view unequivocally good, but it was a fact; and generations of Americans had obviously preferred the protection of their material stake in society (however small) to the risks of experiments in collective action. The liberalism they described had a far deeper structure, and a more complex one, than that of a political system guaranteeing individual rights and representative institutions. It entailed the notion of a permanent social contract, or an ever renewable one, between autonomous individuals. It entailed, no less, the assertion of an organic connection between that autonomy and the very definition and existence of political liberty and the sovereignty of the market. Briefly, market was more important than nation—not a substitute polity but its highest form. Hartz and Hofstadter were neither fools nor ideologues and they were deeply ambivalent about this ideology, but they saw no practicable, much less tolerable, substitute or successor for it. It was this conviction on the part of small men and women, further, which allowed those with much larger stakes to take common action to consolidate and extend their own advantages. The only kind of class warfare congenial to the American ideology was one from above, which did not dare to avow its name. Its presupposition, far from tacit and quite openly articulated in reform movements from progressivism to the Great Society, was that the privileged and propertied were not to push their luck too far. By implication with Hartz and quite outspokenly in Hofstadter, there was a corollary. Americans were interested in their income, and property, their families, communities, churches; a public sphere as such interested them only occasionally or not at all. Privatization was built into the dominant liberalism—except for those who had effective reason to consider themselves guardians of it.

Those who now seem most skeptical of the effectiveness of two (or three) centuries of indoctrination in liberal ideology are not radicals but the conservatives. Peter Steinfels has declared that if one reads the neoconservatives, one has the impression of an America (even Reagan's America) seized by an egalitarian convulsion. Set aside theologians of the free market like Milton Friedman, or the philistine votaries of a reductionist economic theory of behavior like Gary Becker or Richard Posner. In the curious and contradictory mixture of doctrine, presupposition, and gnawing anxiety (in which fantasies of annihilation and incorporation seem to play a major role) that constitutes Reaganism, two recent criticisms of liberalism have evoked obsessive attention.

One is an ostensibly familiar one: pluralism. After all, a version of pluralism was a response to the obvious difficulties for liberalism posed by corporate America, with its heavy structures of economic domination. Organized group interests would counter each other and by a process of bargaining analogous to a market—a political market, in fact—would make good the increasingly evident defects of formal representation. As new groups entered the system, or as new bases for organization emerged, indirect representation became more complex—but, somehow, more representative. Churches, ethnic groups, economic organizations, ideological communities, and regions could all be accomodated. What bewilders and enrages the Reaganites—and not only they—is that the new pluralists have taken the logic of pluralism to its conclusion. They see no reason why some groups should be more powerful than others, and insist that both economy and polity respond to the demands of groups not prepared to tolerate exclusion or deprivation. The newer social movements, with their systematic emendation and extension of ideas of rights, have seized upon what was a halfhearted or hesitant modification of original liberalism and converted it into its opposite. They do so not in the name of abstract principles of autonomy and individualism but for the sake of specific groups in the conditions of American society—in the language of specificity.

If this were all there were to the new critique of liberalism, it might be contained. It is joined, however, if in no very convincing synthesis as yet, by a demand that legitimates itself by recurring to a liberal notion of citizenship—the demand for participation. It is interesting that Benjamin Barber has chosen to call his own plea for participation *Strong Democracy*, borrowing "strong" from philosophical usage in which it means "rigorous." The demand for participation does not as yet unite, but draws upon, themes taken from what was once the literature of alienation, from the current of radical democracy in America that begins not with Jackson but with the Anti-Federalists, and from the analysis of bureaucratization. Its very undifferentiation and indistinctness are, for the moment, advantages: it can decompose into a generalized antinomianism, make pious obedience to Thoreau, and relapse into insignificance. But the idea of participation can also serve to legitimate a newer and deeper idea of citizenship. It can do so by functioning, further, as a common language for old liberals—embittered by the distortions of liberalism and the disappearance of liberal institutions and their replacement by bureaucratic corporatism—and both old and new radicals.

III

Citizens
or Subjects

I mentioned the Anti-Federalists, which suggests that nothing is quite so contemporary as an old tradition. As the federal government was used by both Progressives and New Dealers to oppose the concentrated power of capital, as "states' rights" served to justify refusal to accept the welfare state or federally mandated extensions of citizens' rights, the tradition was forgotten. The decade 1960–70 gave us a revival of the critique of bigness or centralization, a rediscovery of Thoreau. (More recently, Bourne has come under renewed and positive scrutiny.) Exercises in political and social philosophy in the United States, however, must remain just that—exercises—unless they connect not only with the legislative process but also with constitutional jurisprudence. We have our own version of philosopher-kings, who are not legislators but judges in the federal appellate courts and, above all, the Supreme Court. After the New Deal court disposed of "substantive due process" as an obstacle to the economic intervention of the state, the Warren Court extended the content of citizens' rights in areas as diverse as education; relations between parents and children, between the sexes, and among the races; as well as in confrontation with organized power in consumer exploitation and environmental degradation. A common complaint of the right is that law schools are responsible: professors out of touch with ordinary American opinion (the "mainstream," it appears, when it does not flow can be pumped into ideological ditches) have managed to subvert the common sense of otherwise sound judges, often recruited from the harder schools of corporate law or politics. They do so by writing articles in law reviews, read by their recent students, Supreme Court clerks, who, it appears, are the nation's hidden rulers. Let us take these critics at their word: are there new ideas of rights in the law reviews, in constitutional discussion? One point is clear: we have come a long distance from simple notions of adversary relationships, and class actions can and do allow not single plaintiffs but the public to reenter constitutional conflict as an actor with full rights. The Reagan administration has been able to recruit its own legal theorists into the judiciary and the executive, but the extent to which this is a reactive movement suggests that the effort to rethink the philosophical and social fundaments of the Constitution is too important to be left to lawyers. An elegantly ambiguous and discreet forerunner of a good deal of conservative jurisprudence, Alexander Bickel, has written of the pedagogic functions of the courts. In the often convoluted, and frequently dishonest, debate over judicial usurpation it remains to examine its philosophical content. In another epoch, we could have declared that past and future contend for the interpretation of the balance of contending rights. (A spurious sort of populism is for the moment advanced by the right, which insists on legislative sovereignty where it thinks it can win.) We are wiser now, and have learned that the past is a matter of interpretation and the future open: historically, we do not put our trust in progressive sequences of a philosophically or politically irresistible kind. We have experienced, in other terms, too many reversals.

In one respect, as we shall see, the courts have left the citizenry to its fate. Questions of foreign affairs have been deemed "political" and not subject to court intervention or judgment. Successive presidents could conduct wars, expend blood and treasure, without fear of judicial censure. Here the pedagogy of the court has been distinctly restrained: it has refused to make common cause with those in the nation (by no means bereft of legal argument) who see in the new imperial state a threat to democracy, morality, and the substance as well as the existence of the nation. The analysis of our imperial present is in part a consequence of a reconsideration of our supposedly nonimperial, indeed antiimperial past, which now, under the critical gloss of newer historians, seems to have been imperial by other names. The question is whether distinctions between analyses of domestic and foreign politics, between description of the structure of our national society and consideration of our global role, are any longer tenable. It is not the difficulty of completing a plausible chain of causal analysis that has challenged some colleagues to join these inquiries. It is an evaluative or political concern.

The very notion of citizenship, of representation, of democracy, seem to dissolve in these areas: who can believe for one moment that the Congress will be asked to vote on the next (which may be the last) employment of nuclear weapons—or our entry into a war? Studies of the imperial state entail issues of the centralization of power, of elite command not simply of decision but of the processes of opinion-making (in every sense, fabrication).

Meanwhile, economists, political scientists, and sociologists split asunder what history has joined together. An international division of labor has altered our class system, changing the very categories of social differentiation. The imperial state may have preempted the decision-making processes of representative democracy. Those who command the imperial state have in turn been preempted by the internationalization of economic decision. American society is no longer contained within its boundaries. A movement that terms itself the new populism proposes a new onslaught on remote centers of economic decision in the name of popular sovereignty. Suppose, however, these are in Frankfurt, London, Tokyo (that is, suppose that the international bankers are in fact international). We have few concepts to connect these processes with received notions of center and periphery, top, middle, and bottom, metropolis and province, in our society.

Consider the (not unreasonable) conservative demand for a renewal of what is termed mediating structures: family, church, neighborhood, local community. These are supposed to serve as links to larger social and political processes, and to defend the values of the members of the society against the otherwise homogenizing force of centralized cultural production. Suppose, however, that family, church, local community are irrelevant to the centers of decision, that these proceed on criteria of power enhancement and profit accumulation that may well entail the extirpation of precisely those qualities prized by the advocates of mediating structures. We face, again, a situation for which no rhetoric prepares us—and which few concepts can seize.

Not the least of the paradoxes of the present intellectual situation is this. For the longest time, a certain kind of social science denied that social classes were important in the United States. The denial took the form of an insistence on the saliency of other modes of organization— ethnic, regional, religious. Of course, the notion of a society so attached to market values that its own members did not (perhaps could not) think in terms of classes was compelling. The Great Society program intended to reduce (even eliminate) the severe disadvantages suffered by the underclass, who were to be integrated into a nation of (relatively) happy workers and (enthusiastic) consumers. The critical movements of the 1960s had themes other than the direct alteration of the class system. Since then, a certain vocabulary (if only at a fairly vulgar level of description) has acknowledged the existence of classes. We hear of an underclass and of the virtues of an established working class, or of the necessity of winning back for reformist or redistributionist or a new productivist politics the middle class. As these matters have been admitted to limited spheres of consciousness, or public discourse, a larger phenomenon has gone not unnoticed but not much discussed. The standard of living of important groups of wage earners is falling, although the decline in many instances has been softened in its impact by multiple employment in the same family, and by previous possession of what are now rather low-interest-rate mortgages on residential property, itself increased in value. Moreover, with the numerical decline of the skilled industrial working class, and the automation of clerical labor, we are entitled to refer to an increasing homogenization of the labor force. The restriction of some kinds of political discussion to culture and values has the function (if not the intention) of distracting attention from this process. Our society may be culturally fragmented to an extraordinary degree, but the material bases for a new class politics lie at hand. Few thinkers have caught the significance of this (those who refer to the interest of unions with large proportions of ethnic and racial minority members, or women, generally underpaid, in social reform programs are honorable exceptions). It is true, it was fifty years ago that Roosevelt in the election of 1936 (and even more in 1940) used a vocabulary of class, and class conflict, of a kind many Americans think of as reserved for ideologically narrow Europeans. Very likely, the quantitative and qualitative decline of our unions has something to do with this: a traditional working class seems an increasingly improbable agent of large-scale change. Does the new form of American capitalism (extreme financial speculation on the one hand, productive innovation or innovation in supplying services initially concentrated in smaller enterprises on the other hand) mean that no one can any longer easily discern an exploiting or opposing social class? The plausibility of Reagan's ideological appeal (attacks on the underclass and appeals to national harmony) rest on this sort of social alignment.

New ideas of the possibility of the renewal of democratic citizenship, then, will have to deal with the utter transformation in the (largely unspoken) terms of the debate. It is here that America's historians may come to our aid: they are, after all, witnesses to the permanence of change.

IV

The Past Present

In her book on the teaching of American history in our schools, Frances FitzGerald used the title *America Revised.* She might have used *America Forgotten:* class and racial conflict, exploitation and injustice, the particularity of the immigrant experience or experiences, the fate of the Indian, are not allowed to mar these texts. Cultural conservatives have demanded that our schools teach more history: it is an interesting question as to what they would think of a serious treatment of the resistance to the war against the Philippine independence movement. Our nation lives not in its history but (for large parts of the populace) by systematically denying it—not, to be sure, by international standards an unusual situation. The gap between the serious work done in the universities on our past and public awareness of that past is, however, very great. What has been termed the search for a usable past has been instrumentalized or thoroughly politicized: whose past, and for what uses, are the important questions.

What we now have (the sense in which we have it is also worth thinking about) is an idea of the United States in which complexity precludes easy generalization. To the Federalists we may oppose the Anti-Federalists, suspicious of central power, determinedly local in espousing ideas of direct democracy. To the constitutionalists' distrust of human political nature, we can contrast the severe demands in their own ranks (and in subsequent generations) for a republic of virtue. To the Calvinists and fundamentalists insisting on the permanent presence of the darkest forces in the soul, we may cite the tradition of the Enlightenment and the belief in the nation as the bearer of progress. The deep and at times frenetic racism of multitudes was countered by the moral egalitarianism of the abolitionists. The atomizing individualism of an attachment to the market that had idolatrous qualities (and has these, still) evoked expressions of solidarity with deep roots in the structures of daily life. The arrogance of a drive to domination (poorly disguised as a humble effort to improve the world) has conflicted with the realization that, sooner rather than later, imperialism abroad would corrupt democracy at home. Above all, in the face of the contemporary effort to redefine citizenship as a lower synthesis of ideological cretinism and privatized conformism, Americans have drawn in our history upon enormous reserves of antiauthoritarianism.

All of these conflicts have been concretized in the work of historians who initially set aside the study of politics and the state. Blacks, artisans, women, immigrants, workers, farmers, cultural and religious dissenters and eccentrics have been studied, as have social movements, from the Shays' Rebellion to the student revolt of the past decades (the very juxtaposition gives us an idea of one use of history). The development of the industrial social structure, the emergence of an industrial culture, the invention of a cultural market, and the rise of an obsessively policed educational system have been depicted. The brutal underside of conquest, expansion, and war have been described, and the accretion of influence and the consolidation of power, by cultural and religious elites as well as by economic and political ones, have been chronicled. The emergence of new class formations has been sketched, and the interplay of centralization and localism has been treated and treated again.

The work of the historians is not a record of triumph, particularly the triumph of democratic values. It is often enough a record of limited success, of disappointed hopes, of a millennialism become secular as its horizons sank (where they remain) into perpetual recession. In recovering a past more real than its idealized distortion, truer than the progressivism that is our version of Whig history, the work of the historians demonstrates that behind seemingly descriptive or neutral phrases like "fragmentation" or a putative "search for order" there lie sequences of deep conflict. Other nations live, however poorly or gracelessly or reluctantly, with their conflicts. The United States, in a fabricated and politically instrumentalized ideology, in almost official ways seeks to deny these. Between the parents scandalized by textbooks that do not treat figures like Washington with sufficient respect and a secretary of education who suggests that history will ready students, if properly taught, to serve in the next Vietnam conflict (the secretary was busy with a very successful career at home during the last one), there is an almost instinctual bond. Our historians may be likened to psychotherapists, and it is little cause for wonder that so few citizens present themselves for treatment: too many certainties have to be discarded, too much that is solid threatens, if not to melt into air, to begin to shake.

It is easy enough to ironize on the vacuity of the view of our past held or espoused at the approximate level of philosophical cultivation, moral sensitivity, and mastery of fact we associate with anchormen and -women on early-morning national television. What, however, about the incidence of recent historiography on an American left that forever proclaims its readiness to confront reality? Our historians of the left are, after all, chroniclers of defeat. The democratic upsurge of the Revolution was followed by a Constitution that quite purposely initiated a conservative republic. The Jacksonian revolution was the work of artisans and smallholders, but opened the way for something far different from a republic of virtue. Abolitionism, that singular fusion of Calvinist morality and a theory of free labor, triumphed over slavery, but segregation in the South and the new corporate capitalism elsewhere followed. The enormous ideological and political energies of populism and socialism served in the end to justify the reforms of the Progressives, who modernized American capitalism partly against the will of the capitalists. The New Deal repeated the experience: it was not the social movements of 1936 but the new imperial consensus of 1946 that brought full employment. Meanwhile, a combination of the American sense of mission and a new nationalism was turned outward, to justify from the end of the last century onward our own version of what it was sworn we abjured, imperialism. Racism, prejudice, and social Darwinism precluded the consolidation of a multiethnic republic proud of its diversity. The melting pot, to be sure, seemed to have been made of metal not resistant to the heat of subsequent experience. The serious claims of white Anglo-Saxon Protestantism to moral leadership have been reduced to Reagan's grinning intimations of hatred and self-satisfaction. It is quite untrue that of the excitement and exaltation of the sixties not a trace remains: there are more residues than contained in *The Big Chill*, more serious effects than evident in reunions of veterans of what was once termed the movement. Enough has been put back in place of the former structures of belief and control to suggest that these are far more durable than we thought. Is a cyclical theory given some substance by ideas of generational alternation all that can be drawn from three and a half centuries of national history? Here the melancholy of the left calls for deeper consolation.

The newer work in history is, no doubt, a continuation of beginnings quite further back than the politics of the generation that came to awareness in the turbulence of 1960 onward. John Higham's *Reconstruction of American History* (1962) may be compared with Kammen's *Past Before Us* (1980): there is as much continuity as not. The theoretic implications are striking. When we look back, the much-praised American consensus consists of the nation's achievement in avoiding all but one civil war. Was it the very size and scale of the society (increasing for most of our history and increasing, too, through an imperial reach that may now have attained its limits) that permitted the encapsulation of very intense social conflicts that took predominantly local forms?

The recent domestic critics of American democracy, who suggest that we suffer from an excess rather than a deficit of it, take as a model of stable institutional functioning a nation of passive political consumers. To what extent is there an odd core of truth in their demands for an end to demands upon the society (voiced for instance, with insistence by Huntington)? The activation of large numbers of citizens, challenges to established modes of conducting politics, entail at least temporary cessation of that privatization which is one side of the domination of American society by the market. The spokesmen for a Reaganite version of populism (entirely self-styled, to be sure) meanwhile provide another hint for those who need one. They are untiring in their denunciation of the supposed domination of our culture and politics (their attacks on economic elites appear to be far more muted) by what they describe as eastern and liberal elites. Harvard (whether because of its association with the Kennedys, or because of Mr. Justice Frankfurter and Franklin Roosevelt) serves as a convenient target of their antagonism. They have, apparently, not given much attention to Dean Allison's praise for Caspar Weinberger (but he, too, went to Harvard, as did Donald Regan). In a somewhat different idiom, Irving Kristol has advanced the view that the welfare state has engendered a near-parasitic class of elite and subelite beneficiaries (academics and bureaucrats) who propagate its virtues in the interest of employment, influence, and power for themselves. All of these animadversions from the right do seem to confirm views advanced by historians like James Weinstein on the nature and structure of a "corporate liberalism" by which American capitalism defended itself against the more strenuous demands for reform by incorporating or co-opting the reformers. There are other historical references—quite unknown to the Reaganites, one trusts—to work by Bledstein and Haskell and Veysey and others on the emergence of a new professionalism and on the technocratic functions of universities. The Reaganites seem also to be parodying, however unintendedly, Hofstadter's analysis of populism as negative and reactive. Busy occupying positions in the governmental and private bureaucracies, anxious to serve those with large concentrations of economic power, the new populists speak the language of simple citizens uttering simple verities. Compared with William Jennings Bryan and Tom Watson, the likes of William Bennett, Edwin Meese, and Richard Viguerie are convincingly inauthentic. The theoretic question for those who retain a minimum honesty, and a minimal regard for their fellow citizens, is not whether we can find traces of virtue in the citizenry but how a citizenry may be realized.

Much recent historical work, as acute and critical as it is, sets the question aside. It is concerned with the long waves of American history, with the accretion of practices and the consolidation of institutions, with the conflict of interests (and occasionally classes), with the rise (and subsequent fall) of social movements. The historian of labor David Montgomery recently remarked that many historians of labor tend to think of the American working class in abstract and indeed passive terms. The fact that the early labor movements studied with such care by Montgomery himself were the work of purposive human actors has been, in his view, too little stressed. Lawrence Goodwyn, by contrast, has written the history of populism (the authentic movement of the last century) from within, so that its protagonists appear heroes frustrated by impossible or implacable fate.

V

Character and History

There is no single answer to these problems, and our more complex, more differentiated idea of American history, appropriately informed by deference to the capacities (moral and political) of generations long since gone, still has to ask questions (and answer them) that burden the proponents of democracy everywhere. When all the institutional accounts are calculated, on what human and psychic forces may we rely? That institutions form or deform the psyche we know; and that there are no individuals, only human organisms acting within a cultural and social context, we know too. A striking reflection of the capacity of some of our thinkers not to be overly dominated by ideologies may be found in an American tradition of psychology. Nowhere else has psychology (and psychiatry) been so resolutely cultural and social in its emphases—a practical denial of the legacy (political) of Locke by those who may well have lacked heart or taste for, let us say, Marxist political economy.

Perhaps this is a tribute to de Tocqueville's interpretation of the modal American character as so fully integrated in local group or primary group and larger society that autonomy or self-expression becomes the problem. The recent disquisition on a theme from de Tocqueville by Bellah and his associates showed that a good deal of integration is compatible with fundamental political isolation: the Americans in *Habits of the Heart* were integrated with everyone and everything except our polity. Lifton's analysis of what he calls *The Broken Connection* (a sense of the possibility of making contact or attaining wholeness) takes human survival as a primordial psychic theme, but survival presupposes a community and an engagement across generations. An engaged struggle for survival in a symbolic sense entails politics. At any rate, we have come a long way from the embarrassing simplicity of notions of a direct and manipulable connection between frustration and aggression.

William James, who founded pragmatism, was also an early American sponsor of Freud. He had good reason, given not only his own exquisite awareness of the unconscious but his own symptomatology: he converted a good deal of psychic distress into bodily pain and was quite responsive to the notion that the relationship was reversible. Writing about the period, Jackson Lears has attributed the new American preoccupation with neuropsychic disorder (neurasthenia) to the feeling of weightlessness, of being cut off from connections and of floating in some space unanchored by traditions upon which to draw, of being unrelated to or unembedded in enduring institutions. Briefly, Lears was describing a sublimated politics of the unconscious through which the American middle class converted into psychosomatic terms its crisis of political and social autonomy. Did not Schorske, dealing with Freud, suggest that the theory of the Oedipus complex was a metaphor for his own political liberalism, frustrated in the authoritarian (and anti-Semitic) politics of the late Austro-Hungarian Empire?

The origins of a distinctively American psychology, then, are closely connected with politics. It is by now utterly conventional for radicals to decry the excessive psychological emphasis of much American social criticism, or its turn to a therapeutic language. Better the indirect expression of social criticism than none at all. Is the indirection, however, so very great? It does not, at any rate, seem to impress those critics from the right who still think of a therapeutic approach to human beings as likely to undermine morality and social order. Marcuse held that Freud was a more radical critic of capitalism than many who sought to revise his views in an ostensibly radical or socially critical fashion—in his insistence with uncompromising rigor on the alterations in the psyche and its relatively permanent structures wrought by experience and history.

In examining the legacy of studies of the spirit, then, we do well to assume that not all is as it seems. The promise of relief may be more honest (and socially more critical) than a (vacuous) anticipation of liberation. The movements of personal growth or the various cults of experience, if flights from the disappointments of politics for many of their votaries, may still express a desire for change that can flow into politics or energize politics in the future.

The idea of the possibility of human transformation is not the only conceivable basis for a politics of change. Even a mordantly pessimistic Calvinism may provide one. Reinhold Niebuhr, in his *Moral Man and Immoral Society*, argued that politics was a very limited affair and not one that demanded of us absolute moral superiority. We had only to be relatively moral, or discernibly superior to those we were struggling against. Since he thought of Joseph Stalin as our antagonist (and before him, Hitler) it was easy enough for Niebuhr to attribute moral superiority to the United States. The argument has a more general implication. If the only morality humans may attain is a relatively benign one, if dreams of total social transformation are precisely that—dreams—the argument for the search for possibilities of amelioration becomes not less but more compelling. Freud referred to psychoanalysis as a movement and thought its cultural and pedagogic implications were at least as important as its medical, therapeutic ones. Even a politics of small psychological steps is to be preferred to one in which an irredeemable human nature is taken as an excuse for resignation, or for that particular variant of the savagery of the imagination in which those who think they know better look down upon the struggles of those they think know less or nothing at all.

It was not so long ago that, in the shadow of fascism and the European Holocaust, studies of *The Authoritarian Personality* sought to analyze an authoritarian political potential in the United States. Forty years later, the authoritarians are for the time being in office, and the country is divided over cultural and sexual issues that carry enormous affect. The liberal view, that these should be left to a private sphere, suffers from two defects. One is that a large number of Americans (and especially, vocal and skillful leaders well able to mobilize their anxieties) do not think of these matters as private. Another is that

even if there is obviously some connection between the characterological capacity to experience—for instance, empathy for others—and political values such as solidarity and a willingness to tolerate cultural
pluralism, we are at a loss to convert these very complex and imperfectly systematized insights into a political program. The work of Wilhelm Reich, Erich Fromm, and Erik Erikson lies well behind us in
time, but, if anything, we seem to have retreated from the implications of their politics. Our retreat has been discreet and not devoid of
a large if superficial plausibility. Construct a better society and—somehow—these matters will work themselves out. Perhaps the Calvinist
moralists of the early Republic (or their secular descendants like Emerson and, of course, Dewey) were in their directness, their sense of the
immediacy of character, more realistic and even more modern. Put
briefly, the most effective defense against authoritarianism may be a
population raised differently. Are our psychological resources such that
we could even envisage a program of this sort, a series of educational
reforms or a different politics of the family?

It is possible that a curious fusion of old and new may assist us. Lasch
has repeatedly warned that it would be a mistake to dismiss popular
dismay or revulsion at drugs, at familial disintegration, and at the generalized moral vacuity of the mass media. It is exceedingly difficult to
begin with a large social project, but we could begin in an ostensibly
unlikely place—in the more reflective parts of the feminist movement.
Carol Gilligan's *In A Different Voice* argued that women do speak
differently, morally, that their capacities for empathy and for transcend-
ing the brutality of interest conflict are larger than those of men. Barbara
Ehrenreich has held that much of what we think of as a feminist revolt
(the demand for new qualities in public life, a criticism of institutionalized social Darwinism) may have begun with men. The discussion of
postmaterialist values, meanwhile, could be far more important than the
conclusion that a growing segment of the labor force seeks to work less
and enjoy more. If these values have a structure other than a systematiza-
tion of inducements to more consumption, they must entail different
psychological demands upon the society, demands that cannot be met
by a rigid antithesis of work and leisure, public and private activity.
Perhaps the gradual reorganization of production to adapt to familial
imperatives could be a beginning point.

On a very different plane, work on character formation and child development has provided us with an empirical differentiation and grounding of psychoanalytic theory. Our problem is to identify a human capacity for both autonomy and solidarity; it may be that Mahler's studies of individuation and separation in infancy enable us to state what kinds of contexts are likely to be most productive of humans with a fuller range of capacities. At any rate, following Lasch, we will have to turn away from the belief that the reaches of the human soul are beyond politics.

Psychoanalysis apart, are there elements of cognitive and developmental psychology that promise help—or at least relief—in an epoch in which a politics of systematic cretinization (intended or not) flows from the combined defects of our cultural industry (including its public sector, education). Kohlberg's adaptation of Piaget is in an honorable American tradition, that of a natural history of morals. Bruner's work on education (in a large sense) is no less generous and open in its perspectives. Both, to be sure, insist on the existence of human capacities in principle and in practice susceptible of education. They do not, however, respond to the question Marx put to Helvétius: who educates the educator? Under what conditions can schools function as moral rather than custodial institutions?

The question is, I trust, more than the iteration of a banality. Of course, everything is connected to everything else—and no more so than in a society like our own, in which moral fragmentation and cultural homogenization alternate mechanically, the one seeming to evoke the other until a new cycle begins with old elements. Still, it is a matter of more than curiosity. We seek ideas that could give us a programmatic sketch of the future (or at least allow us to avoid the grosser errors of the past). We do need to know at what point institutional opportunity and human potential can be best joined.

VI

Varieties
of Belief

We come to the penultimate theme in this survey of the possible intellectual origins of a (limited) American revolution—religious ideas. Of course, much attention has been given of late to the Protestant fundamentalists. The Catholic bishops' active intervention in public debate on the economy, foreign policy, and nuclear weaponry has hardly gone unnoticed. The turn to conservatism of some Jewish intellectuals has had undue attention, a tribute less to the depth of their ideas than to their skills at marketing; the supposed conservative drift of the Jewish community as a whole is a far more equivocal matter. American religious pluralism, of course, is such in fact that no single religious tradition can any longer dominate a new political coalition: its ideas will have to possess general attractiveness. At the least, reflection within the group must have the consequence of increasing its capacity to enter a coalition and to do so creatively—that is, not only on the basis of strictly defined and negotiated interests but by making its own tradition available to others. If Lincoln's Republicanism had a strong Calvinist component, Roosevelt's New Deal combined the varieties of social Protestantism, Catholic social doctrine, and a measure of Jewish moralism.

It is absurd, then, to demand a strict separation of religion and politics: ideas of community, person, and power in the secular epoch are saturated with religious meanings. What we can ask is that the religions accept that their public role is pedagogic (this is the self-understanding of the American Catholic bishops and makes of their recent letters invitations to this sort of dialogue). This in turn presupposes that we seek to go beyond a narrow pluralism in our conception of an American public sphere. That sphere has not been neglected: it has, indeed, been continually fought over. Separate groups, with their real and ideological interests, have attempted to occupy space in it—excluding, or preempting, similar moves by others. At times (think of abolitionism or its desiccated heir, Prohibition, or the Catholic engagement in the New Deal and in the wave of unionization of the 1930s), the churches have energized the public sphere, only to withdraw to a more particular and protected space, the battle done. (Recall as well the Jewish moral energies in recent American public life, not all of them contributed by organized Judaism but much coming from individual, even secularized, Jews still beholden to their own tradition.) Put briefly, we require a conception of a public sphere that can reconcile the antithetical exigencies of American politics—our omnipresent pluralism, and our desperate need for a minimum of common understanding. Only a conception of politics as a process of self-education by a citizenry will meet this task, and (it has to be acknowledged) imperfectly. Suppose the groups, not least religious ones, to which the citizens separately belong hold irreconcilable values, pose exceedingly conflicting demands? Not all religions, historically, have been conspicuous for their capacity to induce in believers empathy with others. However, we are in an ecumenical age—in fact and in the consciousness of the churches. The idea of America as a pluralistic society has possibilities other than our usual recourse to a political market. It can also involve a certain interpenetration of values as a precondition for the reconciliation of conflict.

A static idea of the perpetual coexistence of the American religions, then, is unlikely to do justice to the probable future course of events. There are, to be sure, serious problems entailed by the educational (and ideological) gap between many theologians and ordinary believers—which is part of the general cultural division between a professionally educated group and the rest of society. The theologians' difficulty in bringing ideas to Americans immersed in routine is quite analogous to the troubles of our intellectuals in general when they seek to speak to economic and political elites, or try, through the resistant media, to reach their fellow citizens with complex ideas.

Finally, we ought to consider political philosophy itself. More precisely, we ought to consider it directly as a source of new ideas. Every other sort of analysis of culture, psyche, or society has, at the least, political implications. In most cases, these are hardly buried; they are not merely open for inspection but ready for use. What about the thinkers who draw upon other inquiries but who make no detours or use no circumlocutions, that is, theorists of the polity? Do any offer us a way out of our interest-bound existence (an existence complicated by the fact that it is extremely difficult for most citizens to determine what, in the longer run, their interests are)?

The work of John Rawls has so thoroughly dominated discussion that it is perfectly plausible to concentrate on it and its critics. Rawls attempted several things at once. He sought a political philosophy that was compatible with theoretic advance in welfare economics and that would not contradict what we know, in a very general way, of human nature. He also sought one that was consonant with an American mode of political rhetoric, and that therefore could be transmuted into policy. Indeed, the publication of his *Theory of Justice* in 1971 can be understood (despite the fact he indeed had been working on the problem for decades) as a reflection or refraction of the Great Society program.

Rawls asked what choices human beings would make about a social order if they could not anticipate their own fate? That is, if they did not know whether they would be rich or poor, healthy or ill, beautiful or not, talented or not, what precautionary measures would they take to ensure that the social order would not or could not deal too harshly with them. It is striking that he began with a view of humans as self-interested, with a notion of individuals as separate from institutions, with a version in other words of the familiar social contract. Sociability (or Eros), excluded from his initial design, makes its entry very quickly thereafter. Among the human qualities he takes as the source of interests is a desire to be approved, or integrated. What, then, of a society in which approval was obtainable only by some sort of contribution to, or expression of, solidarity? Rawls's strongly implied answer is that our model of a just polity ought to possess a maximum of realism.

Rawls, in so many words, excludes what conventional opinion would describe as utopian thinking. The question is, however, to what extent has he presented us with a schematic utopia in the guise of a systematic model of the interplay of interest and choice. Humans, after all, do not choose their institutions: one does not need to be Edmund Burke to suggest that we are born into particular historical contexts. The contexts also shape (if they do not largely determine) our capacity to conceive of ranges or structures of moral choice.

Rawls's humans shrewdly design or accept social arrangements that would produce advantages for some only if others were compensated equally. The problem, however, is less the abstract design of a principle of justice than the development of conditions under which moral reasoning (and effective moral reasoning at that) is possible. Our own communal and social structures are so pervasive because they are so incorporated in ourselves. Perhaps the term "pervasive" is too vague—and I should use "immovable" or "rigid"—to describe their responsiveness to moral force.

At any rate, the two central challenges to Rawls (if respectful ones) come from opposite poles of the spectrum of philosophic options. Walzer argues that justice begins in concrete social circumstances that engender primary loyalties; since these are always with us, balances always have to be struck with more general or universal attachments. Dworkin also suggests the utility of a natural history of morals, but thinks that the implicit philosophical content of practical jurisprudence is evidence for a recognition of a natural set of rights, an innate moral grammar. Rawls had indeed acknowledged something like an innate drive to moral recognition, without dwelling on the problem Socrates raised with Thrasymachus, of the difference between appearing and being moral. The burden of Rawls's argument does fall upon the construction by individuals of self-serving conventions that take living in society and social constraints into account: as much solidarity as necessary, as much selfishness as possible. That fusion of self and society which, if modern psychology and sociology have anything to teach us, renders classical notions of individualism dubious has had little impact on Rawls. If the veil of ignorance is removed, would not his humans—negotiating terms to establish a society—find themselves to be liberal and skeptical Americans from our own mid-century?

VII

Radical Ideas and Conservative Contexts

Our intellectual universe is as fragmented as the rest of our culture. Flashes of insight contend with lugubrious adumbrations not of the obvious alone but also of propositions that are obviously untrue. Economists propound absurd, even illiterate, notions of social structure. Sociologists ignore those changes in the economy that (if acknowledged) would nullify their historical assumptions about relative constants in our society. Philosophers promulgate notions of human moral possibility utterly remote from, if not antithetical to, what psychologists know. Political scientists isolate political processes and, insofar as they apprehend these, may well overestimate their importance. There are, no doubt, redeeming aspects of our situation. The historians, or many of them, use distance from the past to treat it as a context: those working on specific problems frequently keep the larger epoch and the society in which it is situated in view. It is not surprising that Geertz's work on culture, or rather his practice (as well as his theory) of cultural analysis have had such effect on historians. Geertz himself is in a line of anthropoligical inquiry that invariably began with cultural wholes, or which saw in a detail the possibility of expanding vision to the whole.

Lawyers in the common-law tradition are not supposed to indulge a passion for general social ideas but to concentrate on an adversarial reading of matters immediately at hand. Matters immediately at hand, however, tend rather rapidly to get out of hand when we seek to demarcate their boundaries. Lawyers, as American society's supreme social technologists, may be vulgar fixers or cynical manipulators; some of them, however, just because they eschew the caution incumbent upon disciplinary specialists may be able to seize our society in movement. And if social philosophers often lose themselves in or confine themselves to esoterica, by raising (from time to time) questions of ultimate value, they function rather like theologians, dealing with first and last things, or important ones in between.

Two large questions remain unanswered at the end of this jagged survey of the field. Does a self-consciously reformist or radical party in the social sciences have something different, and valuable, to say? The differences between this grouping and more conventional social scientists (those who adhere to ideas of neutrality or objectivity) are several. The notion of a social science closer to actual human purposes, in this case political ones, may bring it closer to reality (a justification used by the technocrats, of course, to abjure the work of colleagues who serve no clients). If we use the term "radical," we imply as a precondition of an attempt to tear things up by their roots the capacity to locate those roots. Radical social scientists are not necessarily revolutionaries, least of all in a situation that offers so little promise of revolutionary success. They, however, are sufficiently in possession of critical vision to think in terms other than the dominant common sense or the conventional rhetoric of a discipline.

We now have a radical party, at least in this last sense, in our academy. Do they have things to tell us more worthwhile than the views of their colleagues? If so, how can their ideas gain a hearing? Before a more detailed examination of these matters, I propose that we reflect a bit on the social fate of American thought—on the ways in which ideas, and their bearers, become institutionalized, and the paths by which their proponents and producers seek (and occasionally obtain) access to the larger society.

Ideas are not direct derivatives, much less mechanical ones, of social contexts. Ideas represent responses to the problems of action, morality, and reflection posed by both the unvarying and the new elements of social existence. Ideas, then, do have a certain autonomy—exactly how much is hardly a matter for generalization, since some historical situations are more open than others. Meanwhile, no doubt, both the relationship of the groups that circulate, cultivate, and originate ideas to society as a whole and the politics of the organized guardians of ideas are important. I could have titled this book *The Politics of Social*

Knowledge because social knowledge is in fact eminently political: it entails conceptions of our common life whose genesis and propagation concerns both the powerful and those subject to them—as well as everyone struggling between these groups. I have also insisted that our own production of social knowledge is impeded by the fact that so much of it goes not to a critical and democratic public, the educated citizenry, but to those who seek knowledge to enhance their power.

It never pays to idealize the past. Whether the United States was ever an educated republic may be doubted. At several points, however, it did appear that we might become one. A look back, historically, may help us to discern what is new (and troubling) about our present situation.

We may doubt that we were ever, despite the literacy of the Founding Fathers and the high level of public debate immediately before and after the Revolution, an educated republic. For a long time, however, we were not a philistine one. The diffusion of biblical literacy made a difference. Men of the book and the word were the lawyers, physicians, pastors, editors, and teachers who formed opinion. Emerson wrote for a reasonably educated general public; Douglas and Lincoln debated before one. The recent literature on women (Ann Douglas on the feminization of American culture, for instance) suggests that there may have been a transfer of cultural influence to women, but it also suggests that this influence was neither confined to the family nor otherwise insulated from the larger currents of American life. To the recent recovery of the past belongs a positive reassessment of the role of women. It is in any case curious that a republic founded by the cultivated gentry of the eighteenth century should within half a century have come to regard reflection and reflectiveness as feminine, or more precisely, as womanly in a man's world. Perhaps this was an unconscious tribute by the men of the word to the more empathic and sympathetic sides of their own natures. Readers of *The Public Interest* will note that, if so, contemporary men—less of the word than of the word processor—have cast off this as well as many other American traditions. A technocrat fears nothing so much as the accusation that he is overly tender, too sympathetic to immediate evidence of pain. Much of the standard literature in economic and social policy is a compulsive attempt by its authors (and their sponsoring institutions) to deny (anticipated) charges that, in the inimitably vulgar language so current, their hearts bleed.

These, however, in the nineteenth century were not matters salient in public debate. The men of the word were often enough repelled by the crudity, real or imagined, of the frontier, just as their direct heirs in the second half of the century were repulsed by the greed and vulgarity of the new capitalists. Well before that, however, the problems of urbanization and immigration had given rise to an effort at devising ideas of social control and reform that were developed outside the university system, that is, quite independent of that professionalization of social science that was still to come. The American Social Science Association was an association of concerned citizens, public officials, some academics, physicians, lawyers, and churchmen. Founded in 1865 in New England, it disbanded in 1909. It had yielded the terrain to the new disciplinary organizations in social science, whose leadership and membership were constituted largely of professional specialists in the research universities—themselves, of course, new institutions. We can say that the professionalization of social science was a far more complex process than the simple exclusion of citizens with amateur status. It was an effort both to address a new public and to offer technical service to the agencies of power. Indeed, in the constitution of the new agencies of power in the regulatory state of the Progressive epoch, the professionals had much to say.

The dates are interesting. All in some connection with the Social Science Association, the American Bar Association was founded in 1878, the American Historical Association in 1884, the American Economic Association in 1885, the American Political Science Association in 1903, and the American Sociological Association in 1905. More interesting than the dates, of course, are the institutional and ideological conflicts that marked professionalization. A decisive impetus for the entire process came from Daniel Gilman, the president of the newly founded Johns Hopkins, a university explicitly designed on the German model of a research university rather than on the English model of an institution providing for the general education of a cultivated citizenry, or at least the education in this fashion of an elite segment of the citizenry. Gilman was responding, of course, to the same imperatives that accounted for the reorganization of the universities. No doubt much of this had been anticipated in 1862 with the founding of the land-grant colleges and universities, which was legislated by a Congress that specifically wished to encourage the "useful arts and sciences." It is striking how many of the founders of these associations sought for something other than the organization of new disciplines in consensual communities of knowers. They strove for more effective ways to bring knowledge into the public realm. Their conception of the public realm, however, reflected the changes in American society which in fact rendered obsolete the idea that educated citizens alone could effect reform. The secretary, for many years, of the American Social Science Association was a figure who had known and worked with Emerson. The founders of the new associations included the historian and political scientist Woodrow Wilson.

The Progressive movement, and later Wilson's New Freedom (as well as the mobilization of America's thinkers and experts for wartime service), were vehicles for mind's reentry into American politics. The intellectual leadenness of the period between Lincoln and the first Roosevelt seemed a thing of the past. The structural conditions under which this was possible, however, were results of social changes destructive of the cultural supremacy of the older men of the word, whether moralizing secularists, Protestant pastors, or educated lawyers and merchants.

I have remarked on the end of amateurism, the rise of professionalism. The public, once prepared to accept the intellectual leadership of the amateurs or educated gentry, had now changed, too. In the place of an America of local communities, states, and regions there was now a national and, indeed, a mass public. Decades before radio and television, the mass media in printed form had begun to supersede those primary or local modes of cultural transmission we identify in community, church, family, and school. The increasing class division of society— joined in uneven and jagged ways to ethnic and religious divisions— entailed an increasing stratification of culture. Parts of the public were receptive to ideas: Edward Bellamy and Henry George wrote best-sellers, and later, Lincoln Steffens and the other muckrakers were widely read. The new professionals were prepared to accept that very general, if simple, ideas should circulate in this way; they were also prepared to accept as allies in a general project of social reform investigative journalists and social theologians. What disturbed many of them, however, were new social movements and unfamiliar and even alien ideas like socialism or the new social emphases of American Catholicism.

The Progressive political triumph, it will be recalled, followed the election of 1896 in which populism, having captured the Democratic Party, seemed to threaten upheaval. The Republicans won, but the Progressives were able to exploit the fright they evoked—as well as widespread fears of nascent unionism and socialism. A minimally reflective segment of the financial and industrial elite realized that they had pushed their luck too far. Reformism now seemed credible—and useful.

The depiction of progressivism as the work of a displaced and literate middle class in a world it never made may be true. The Progressive intellectuals were indeed in the middle, between a potentially militant working class, a discontented rural population, and the new American plutocracy. They solved their problem, however, by escaping it—by transforming themselves from intellectuals into an American intelligentsia, technocrats with useful and serviceable knowledge to vend. Of course, there were tensions within the group, and a bipolar reorganization of the American intellect. Not two decades later, Charles Beard lost his chair at Columbia for opposing the war, and many of his erstwhile admirers were in Washington prosecuting it. The peculiar twentieth-century American combination (not unknown in either Great Britain or Germany) of a reformist technocracy integrated into an imperial project does not date from 1942 or 1948: much of what we have experienced was not simply anticipated but rehearsed in 1917. Indeed, the inner tensions and palpable contradictions we also experience are not quite new either, but they may have been heightened, recently, by the quite insupportable moral burdens of late twentieth-century empire. However, we are getting ahead of ourselves.

A new mode of integration for some thinkers with conventional politics (the politics of progressivism having rapidly become conventional) and the state contrasted with new forms of distance for others. The academic disciplines consolidated themselves in the universities. Others with academic backgrounds took posts in government. Within the universities, those with applied or practical interests in social matters worked in a different idiom from those with more theoretic interests. These differences did not always coincide with political ones: there were academics who attached themselves to groups like the unions or to political formations like the Socialists or (later) the Farmer-Labor Party and the Communist Party. Still, the largest and most accessible market of academic services was provided by the newly technicized spheres of the economy and the state. Political philosophers, no doubt, still worked alone in their studies; constitutional lawyers, mobilizing (if not always self-consciously) philosophical resources, now worked increasingly in large legal firms.

The universities, and the several disciplines, had to deal with the conflicting political perspectives of the newly expanded and newly important social sciences. The formation of the American Economic Association was accompanied by severe conflicts: a charter statement, later modified, required of members that they abjure ideas of a free market in favor of a socially regulated economy. These internal conflicts were exacerbated by pressures from regents, trustees, and the other custodians of orthodoxy (however transitory their conceptions of what was orthodox). The organization of the American Association of University Professors in this period (1914) was the work of academics who had good reason to think of ideas as at least potentially disturbing: Charles Beard, John Dewey, Thorstein Veblen. It also followed years in which scholars (by no means all of them younger or unknown figures) were often dismissed from one year to the next for quite explicit political reasons. Soon enough, to be sure, the internal processes of intellectual discipline in the university brought, if not consensus, a somewhat domesticated academy. That there was a genuine (if limited) pluralism cannot be doubted. Upon examination, much of it was due to the political protection given to critical or querulous academics by influential sponsors or vocal segments of the public.

Was there, however, a public worthy of the name? The question is hardly secondary: it brings us to the center of the search for agencies and structures capable of activating or reactivating our democratic tradition. If there was a public at the end of the first two decades of the century, what has become of it? We may begin with the new journalism, a counterpart to the new academy. The new journalists worked for a segmented public, and some of them crudified, others blunted, others denied or denigrated the ideas circulating, however uncertainly, in the academy. It is unclear, however, that the most important impulses and

motivating ideas, and the sensibilities that responded to them, originated in the academy. I have referred to the political protection given
to groups and schools in the academy by sponsors (or supporters or
patrons).

One of the advantages of the new American situation was that once
the political and social weight or utility of academic work was recognized, it was not left to the academics. They had to live, with conspicu-
ously varying degrees of enthusiasm, with public scrutiny. Some of it
came from a higher journalism. Often conventional, if not laughably
pompous or tediously stuffy, occasionally tiresomely vacuous, it did serve
to relay (often in concrete and immediate form) the organized or stylized
preoccupations of the educated elites. There was also a radical journalism, sometimes reportorial, sometimes a continuous social commentary.
Unconfined by the newly and rather rapidly rigidifying rules of academic
discourse, it too communicated experiences, perspectives, and ideas that
could be reflected upon, or elaborated, by those who could take their
dissonant character without undue psychological shock. Finally, there
were actually thinkers not employed in universities who had serious
ideas: Randolph Bourne and Walter Lippmann were extraordinary early-
twentieth-century examples, if with very different views (and careers).

I asked about the public and turned, at once, to the new academi-
cian's journalistic or independent contemporaries and competitors.
With the decline of amateurism, it appeared, there also declined a series
of local and regional clubs, forums for the circulation of ideas. Culture
was also nationalized: the new journalism represented a national public,
however segmented.

Thinkers in the academy responded in two very different ways. Some,
cultivating the newer disciplinary groupings, cultivated esoteric truths,
available only within the disciplines, and occasionally made known to
colleagues in other fields. Others turned to segments of the public, in
many cases to organized elite groups that could use their ideas. The
Council on Foreign Relations, in the initial years of its work between
the two wars, recruited a number of academics who with Nicholas
Murray Butler collaborated with bankers, businessmen, lawyers in making plans for a future American world role.

Others chose very different allies, working in and with municipal and
state governments of a reforming kind. Still others of a reformist and

even more radical persuasion retreated into the academy *faute de mieux:* there were in their immediate vicinity no elite or governmental groups with which they could ally themselves. Not all of these reformers and radicals, however, withdrew to academic quiescence. As segmented as the public might be, they persisted in an effort to raise large questions, to evoke a social conscience, to deal with the foundations of our public life. A good deal of the work of Charles and Mary Beard, and of John Dewey, was addressed to a general public. In a sense, we may say that their writings constituted or created a public where there might only have been fragments of amateurism or disoriented curiosity, or a blind will to social improvement helpless before a capitulation to routine disguised as realism.

No doubt the universities of the lengthened decade between the end of World War I and the New Deal were dominated by a conservative ethos. The speculative frenzy of the twenties, the new cultural developments epitomized by the automobile and jazz, were not of the sort likely to make the patrician Protestants who dominated American higher education feel entirely at home in their own country. Theodor Adorno once said of Europe that as formal and even priggish much of the humanistic tradition had become, it was still a barrier against the total rationalization of culture, still retained a breath of a general human discourse. We may say the same about the guardians of the genteel tradition of the twenties. Far from enamored of the newer social criticism, certainly not in a hurry to think of Hemingway as a master in literature (they had not made any reckoning with Melville and hardly knew what to make of Eliot), their very insulation or stiffness rendered them resistant to the total organization of existence by the market.

In the next decade, the field known as American studies (even if not yet institutionalized) acquired in the writing of Miller and Matthiessen its early masterpieces. Outside the universities, the cultural modernists and social realists attacked the genteel tradition, if from very different beginning points. Perhaps we now see what they all had in common. They were all distressed by the transformation of consciousness and sensibility, or their homogenization, in the new industrial fabrication of culture.

Where the universities did touch the market, they did so in the field of law—insulated in its own way. The gulf between the practice of law and the legal acdemy was not invariably great, and many teachers of law were quite conventional. The conventions of the academic study of law, however, were changing: legal realism was making its way in the faculties. The newer legal academics were generalists, or could use the study of the law to purvey general ideas that in more open form or language might have been too disturbing. The economics departments might have been in the hands of classical economists, arguing here and there with the institutionalists. The law schools were full, in the guise of professors of contract and torts and commercial law, with analysts of the actual processes of the economy (the late William O. Douglas's autobiography is instructive in this respect). The constitutionalists, meanwhile (or enough of them), were preparing the arguments that would later legitimate New Deal legislation.

I have written of a general public, and suggested that it was no passive or static group but composed of those who stuck to the notion of a self-cultivated citizenry. The idea of a public is, without further qualification, vague. Was it the educated elite of the cities, the business and professional leadership of local and regional society joined to national elites? The press of the period (over 90 percent of which subsequently did not support Roosevelt) was hardly receptive to large ideas or to a vision of the United States very much different than the prevailing Republicanism. The Democratic Party as a national entity was simply a union of state and local parties and, despite the urbanization of its electorate, not self-consciously programmatic. The public's venue may well have been at the intersection of the academy and journalism, in the weeklies and monthlies that dealt in culture, ideas, literature.

In fact, we can say that the general public was dispersed if not fragmented. Only the implicit appeal to it in the writings of thinkers like the Beards and pressing events called it into life. The idea itself, even then, was half real, half project.

Before we consider the New Deal and its complex embeddedness in and encouragement of thought, what about American radicalism? It was, of course, divided into segments, some with a more positive view of the Soviet Union, some already skeptical (at least) that it could have model functions for the United States. The radical groups had their own journals and clubs, which often compensated in intensity for their difficulty in making connections with much of the rest of society.

What did keep a general public alive may have been literature. Those who read Hemingway or Lewis were unlikely to accept that reality was exhausted by what they saw. They were, at least, open to other possibilities in existence. The decade 1920–30 was also the decade of a cultural anthropology, joined to psychoanalysis, that took its distance from vulgar American assumptions about human nature. Read by those who were not anthropologists or social scientists, these studies had a novelistic or perhaps touristic quality: they were literally trips to another land. The anthropologists' intentions—to show that matters could be arranged differently—were thoroughly political.

Radical movements may be understood as schools—from which the students graduate not quite the same as when they entered. They also, of course, affect and influence far more persons than their members. That not all graduates of these schools cherish positive feelings for alma mater is not new: some turn into postgraduate rebels, their whole lives (rather like the antiheroes of those British novels about the consequences of attendance at boarding school) dominated by their ambivalence toward the experience. At any rate, in the first four decades of the century millions of Americans did pass through radical movements and rejoin what we may term ordinary life. (Millions more did so in the decade that began in 1960, and the inner result—in terms of a political predisposition to accept radical solutions under unexpected conditions—may not have been entirely described by films and novels of disillusionment or by the shrill self-accusations of a handful of political exhibitionists.)

I have said that perhaps thinkers like the Beards and Dewey did not address the public or a public, but created one. We may look at the intellectual experimentation (a word that Dewey surely would have found congenial) of the first three decades of the century as a form of social accumulation, in which ideas were banked in the minds of an intelligentsia (and a receptive segment of the public, if we wish to distinguish between more and less active members of the intelligentsia) for future use. Occasionally, in the states (New York under Smith and Roosevelt) actual social experimentation both drew upon this stock of ideas and altered and enriched it. At the least, without necessarily committing the experience to paper or explicitly reflecting upon it, the experimenters learned something of the limits of the conceptions they drew upon. It was the Depression, and the readiness to experiment Roosevelt brought to the presidency (or developed so rapidly as the crisis deepened) that drew a set of ideas, far from coherent or consonant with one another, into use. The common conception is that a partly radical, partly reformist intelligentsia (the lines were not always clear) left the statehouses, universities, law firms, and the press to occupy the federal government. Perhaps it would be more accurate to say that the New Deal called this intelligentsia into life. It did so not only in government, but outside it, by creating an instant interest in and market for comment, criticism, and reflection on the New Deal experience, by enlarging the public space for thought.

VIII

Intellectuals— of Several Kinds

I have described the New Deal as an uneasy amalgam of progressivism, Catholic social reform, Keynesianism (despite Franklin Roosevelt's own almost instinctive dislike of deficit spending). It altered the ethnic and religious composition of government, as well as of politics, bringing many Catholics and Jews into important office. It was a bridge, at least—particularly in the turbulent years of triumph and labor organization of the mid-thirties—to the radicalism of the American socialist movement and the Communist Party. It also—in the South and the West—not only evoked memories of populism but (if in different circumstances) mobilized those who had been active in the movement.

Despite its obvious characteristics as a coalition, it also reinforced a dualism evident since at least the New Freedom and the wartime government of Woodrow Wilson. By and large, economists and lawyers concentrated on drafting legislation, frequently assuming political as well as administrative tasks in bringing these new laws through Congress and institutionalizing them. Indeed, administrative and political tasks were often enough inseparable. Others one step removed from daily politics were left to think. The New Deal, however, also stimulated no small amount of interpenetration of thought and politics. Those performing political tasks asked academics for help, and so set the limits and aims of thought in the universities. Anticipated practical difficulties led to the avoidance of ideas that might have enlarged our conception of politics. The division between practice and thought, then, narrowed—not always to the advantage of thought. The law schools, and a bit later the newly Keynesian departments of economics, became recruiting grounds for a new officialdom. Many scholars moved back and forth to and from government (never, of course, wholly leaving it behind). What thirty years later was to be attacked as "corporate liberalism" (a phrase not much heard these days, but which has entered the academy in the somewhat depoliticized form of work on the new corporativism) institutionalized itself. Its ideology of "pragmatic" government (a use of the term Dewey most emphatically did not invent and which deformed his thought) served to rationalize a relatively narrow set of options.

Much of the creativity and excitement of the New Deal, however, had to do with other and opposite currents. The Roosevelt administration was diverse and often wracked by conflicts of policies as well as persons. If an ideological right wing departed early (Dean Acheson and Raymond Moley), the very controversies among those who remained had as a by-product the widening of perspective. The Communist Party presented itself as the New Deal's left wing, but its potential for creativity was diminished by its intellectual woodenness and its concentration on tactical gains. The union movement, and particularly the new industrial unions, seemed to stimulate thought, and so did the revivified consumer and environmental movements. A certain distance from the commanding center of politics may have enabled some to see the New Deal more whole.

Something else was at work. The New Deal enlarged our conception of politics. It did so not only by creating new agencies like the Social Security Administration or by its excursion, through the Works Progess Administration (WPA), into the arts, literature, and the universities. It did so by demanding different conceptions of politics, of the relationship between self and society, of the ordering of community and income and property. The deep antipathy, even hatred, of Roosevelt and the New Deal felt by the wealthy and a segment of the middle class has been derided by historians as it was laughed at by perspicacious contemporaries. These imbeciles did not see that Roosevelt was saving capitalism from itself, although such solid figures as the wealthy Texan, Jesse Jones, and the elder Kennedy joined him in the effort. Perhaps, however, those figures in evening dress pictured in the famous *New Yorker* cartoon ("Come along, we're going to the Trans Lux to hiss Roosevelt . . .") were right. As hesitant as it was, as incomplete and finally defeated its socioeconomic program, the New Deal at the very least encouraged another American public ethos. I have referred to the beginnings of what was later to be the discipline or area, more precisely, of American studies in the work of Matthiessen and Miller. This new grasp of the American past was perhaps made possible by the release of energies, the widening of national possibility, Matthiessen and Miller experienced as young scholars. While they, to be sure, worked on Emerson and Jonathan Edwards, a much different segment of the intelligentsia argued about Trotsky.

They also argued about everything else. The New York intellectuals, now that they have disappeared as a group, have assumed legendary status—with the qualification that no two survivors of the group, or memorialists of it, can agree on quite what the legend is about or what its enduring value may be. America had of course seen groups concentrated in one place before (Concord antedated Greenwich Village). Rarely, however, have the members of a group by so assiduously talking only to each other convinced others that they had something to say. From a relatively small set of editors, contributors, and readers of one avant-garde magazine *(Partisan Review),* their influence gradually extended to the universities, to the more literate segments of the general media. That influence was, perhaps, largest just as the group lost its originality and merged with the larger currents of American thought after the war.

In the New Deal period, however, it concerned itself with aesthetic matters quite remote from the concerns of most WPA cultural projects, and with historical discussion not at all connected to the arguments of New Deal lawyers in Washington. As a unionization campaign transformed the industrial belt of America (and so affected the balance of American politics for a generation), the *Partisan Review* group speculated about world revolution. Looking back, we can say that the group had an indispensable function on the eve of our postwar imperial expansion. It served as a channel for the introduction of a more cosmopolitan culture, a more refined and theoretic politics (its very abstractness was useful). The original *Partisan Review* group was convinced that it was alienated from American culture but in the end it turned out, in its most self-consciously (and self pityingly) oppositional moments to have been doing the nation's work.

I take as a focal group the initial and early editors of and contributors to *Partisan Review*. The journal had plenty of readers outside of New York, no doubt, but it spoke to (and for) an urban milieu constituted by this group. New York had been a cultural and literary center, of course, well before. Recall the New York of Henry James's visits from England, of John Reed, the city to which the young Edmund Wilson came. The new New York intellectuals brought to the city's cultural life (or to their initially encapsulated sector of it) an infusion of vitality, even crudity, a conviction of newness—due in large measure to their recent American origins, their roots in the East European Jewish immigration of the end of the last century and the beginning of this one. They were often precocious, had gone to City College, expected to live by their wits, and had to construct or fashion their own relationships to America—and to everything and everyone else. They were different from the German Jews represented by Lippmann (with his own dreadful ambivalence about his Jewishness), from the cultivated European exiles who came to the city in the thirties.

The group was not, to be sure, entirely Jewish. There were Dwight Macdonald, and Mary McCarthy, Frederick Dupee, James Burnham, James Farrell. Edmund Wilson kept a half-benign, half-derisive distance, but he was there. The cultural newness, responsiveness, of the Jews, however, seemed to allow them to move with extreme rapidity to exploit the discontinuities in ideology and sensibility caused by the Depression and by the long-term effects of secularization.

An intellectual group is characterized, of course, by its ideas. Three central ideas preoccupied the group. These were the idea of secular transcendence, the idea of a modernist aesthetics, and the idea of a

revolutionary politics. The idea of transcendence, a secularized derivative of Judaic messianism (with substantial contributions from other
American traditions, too, which accounted for Rahv's and Kazin's fasci-
nation with nineteenth-century American literature), was the sometimes
unspoken article of faith of the group. When Barrett wrote of them as
truants from ordinary life, he took leave not alone of his own youth but
of a tradition: how singular that his resignation should be termed conservative. The idea of a modernist aesthetics attempted what appeared
to be the impossible: to fuse the moral and pedagogic function of art
with an absolutist doctrine of its autonomy. Tom Wolfe's later mockery
of "the painted word" isn't stupid: it showed how Greenberg and Rosenberg were (as, of course, was Meyer Schapiro) iconographers. The idea
of a revolutionary politics refracted a hope that America would join (an
imagined version of) world history. The Depression, the Russian Revolution and its sequels, turbulence and fascism in Europe, and the social
movements of New Deal America rendered revolutionary expectation a
good deal more plausible fifty years ago. America, in any event, had not
fully accepted its imperial role. Even if the New York intellectuals rarely
ventured north of Fourteenth Street, they had sensed something about
their country that subsequent generations have either forgotten or will-
fully extirpated from memory—its relentless progressivism.

William Phillips terms the forties the most creative of *Partisan Review*'s decades: it published the first works of new American writers
(whereas in the thirties it had introduced Kafka). The forties, however,
marked the beginning of the end of the distinctiveness of the New York
intellectuals. War and its resultant prosperity and the assumption of an
imperial role by the nation brought about the integration of the ethnic
groups, Irish Catholic and East European Jewish especially; a vast expansion of higher education; an equivalent expansion in cultural consumption, if not at an exalted level: American society, American culture, had
changed. The intellectuals renounced transcendence, the nation renounced large aspects of its own turbulent past to pronounce itself a
fulfilled revolution, and avant-garde culture acquired market value. The
process extended over two decades, and at its end, academics and ideologues replaced the spiritually disheveled bohemians who had given New
York life such charm and excitement.

The New York intellectuals did not join the mainstream—whatever, in our fragmented culture and society, that may be. The mainstream changed, and with it the functions of and publics for art and thought altered. The neoconservatism of many of the survivors of the early period (and of second-generation figures like Norman Podhoretz) was anticipated in the 1952 symposium "Our Country and Our Culture." What has occurred in recent decades is that these figures no longer write for each other alone, but have acquired segments of the (divided) national public. The conflict and confusion of ideologies that exploded in the sixties, the relative deadening of the seventies, and the sterility of the eighties in New York are evidence for the nationalization of its culture—rather than for the Manhattanization of the hinterland. And, with a number of original members of the group venturing to Europe after the war to disburse CIA monies to continental colleagues, the New World set out to redeem the old in ways that mocked the political and spiritual values of earlier (Protestant) notions of the American mission.

We can now see that the distinctiveness of the group was made possible by a historical moment; we can discern the provinciality in their cosmopolitanism; we can acknowledge that their emancipatory project has been discarded. A model remains—to be activated, no doubt, within the next few years by critics, thinkers, writers upon whom the group's survivors will look with stern disapproval and profound, if secret, pathos, not unmixed with envy.

This excursus on the New York intellectuals suggests that the New Deal period generated not only our liberal technocrats. The New York group consisted of generalists, unafraid of large ideas, able to see the connections (and sometimes the contradictions) between art and politics, eager to insert American experience in an international (more specifically, European) context. And its Europe was not the staid Britain of the genteel professors but the Europe of the civil war between left and right, as well as of the modernist artists then hardly acknowledged in our universities.

Of course, the internationalization of American intellectual life was enormously advanced by the arrival on our shores of thousands of intellectual refugees from European fascism. These were, politically, far from a monolithic group. The Frankfurt School came, and left its mark not least on the generalists of New York. The postwar critique of mass culture, which for many substituted for a postwar politics, surely had its origins in the work of the Frankfurt group, however distilled or by whatever channels it was communicated. We touch here on questions of receptivity. There were any number of Europes available for American use in 1939—much depended upon which America was at issue.

Particularly striking was the mixed American destiny of some of the most original figures of the European left. Ernst Bloch and Karl Korsch, remote from the American academy, worked in nearly complete isolation. Brecht did manage to produce some of his works, but was hardly a large cultural figure. Wilhelm Reich's tragedy is too well known to be recounted. Himself cut off from all but a handful of followers, he did influence figures like Mailer, who gave enormous circulation to his ideas—without doing so explicitly or systematically.

Indeed, Reich's political triumph in America was posthumous, in the doctrines of personal liberation that served as a theory of human nature for a substantial element of the New Left. (Marcuse's idea of "surplus repression" presupposed a far more complex and larger view of history.)

Some who came with critical ideas discreetly abandoned them. A talented group of socially critical psychoanalysts (Fenichel and Simmel among them) turned to a more or less pure form of psychoanalytic theory. Psychoanalytic ego theory, originally developed by Reich, was deployed by Hartmann, Kris, and Loewenstein in almost purely psychological terms. Lazarsfeld had originally conceived of public-opinion research as a mode not alone of studying political consciousness but of altering it. His work in the United States, if it touched on politically significant themes, became more and more technical.

Some ideas, some works, did have an immediate impact. Neumann's analysis of Nazism was alone in its class. Whatever implications it might have had for analysis of other societies and elites (even in democratic systems) were never drawn. Fromm's work on character and milieu, rather like Horney's, took root on terrain already cultivated by the Americans working on culture and personality.

Other ideas surfaced only long after their initial American publication. Erikson took ego theory and connected it with American preoccupations about generational continuity and historical location. The geopolitical doctrines of a Strausz-Hupé, initially remote from a moralistic American conception of foreign affairs, in the end struck our policy elites as so congenial that Strausz-Hupé himself was called to government service.

Perhaps the most enduring American success was reserved less for any one figure or specific doctrine than for a perspective derived from Europeans who may be described as despairing liberals. Much influenced by Max Weber's theory of the bureaucratization of the modern world, devoid of or disappointed in the utopianism that was an ineradicable part of the socialist tradition, and frightened of humanity's potential for irrationality and savagery, they assured Americans that they lived in the best of all possible societies. Their work encouraged Americans to believe that theirs was an achieved revolution—safely behind them. It connected, then, with any number of currents in American politics and thought. In particular, it legitimated (if legitimation was needed) one version of the American idea of progress, which saw the Republic as *ex definitione* the bearer or incarnation of progress.

Bureaucratization, in this reading, was not oppressive, but simply an efficient way to conduct society's business, an inducement to impartiality and objectivity and mobility—a positive leveling or evening force.

An American left bitterly critical of the Soviet Revolution took up the theme of bureaucratization for its own purposes, and from time to time emphasized Weber's sense of the inevitability of historical tragedy. Their more conservative countrymen took this last and used it (recall Niebuhr, who knew German thought) to justify an imperial politics. Clearly, the Europeans and their traditions were used for American purposes. The émigré scholars may have thought they were bringing culture to a European province. In fact, they were assisting a new metropolis in its large tasks of transition to world power.

IX

Academy
and Empire

It has taken forty years of empire to bring some American thinkers to the realization that we have one, that its very existence pervades our culture and society, and that these can no longer be described in sovereign terms. For all the autonomy and singularity of our national tradition, we are so inextricably connected to the rest of the world that tradition is in fact the only autonomous and singular thing about us. If some American thinkers see this, many more do not. They persist in treating empire as if it were the result of a political (or even moral) choice—or a not particularly disturbing accident. Moreover, among those who see it, views are acutely divided as to what value to place upon the fact of empire. A considerable disinclination to use the term is due to more than a respectful memory of Wilson's resolution to set right a world askew. It is also due to the fact that the term is in conflict with an indispensable ideological element in the maintenance of American empire, the denial of continuity with other historial regimes. Our film makers and novelists seem, in this respect, to be more honest and perceptive: their work is full of references to Americans abroad. Indeed, they at least conceive of much of the recent past as a *Bildungsreise,* an educational journey, if one far rougher or savage than those we associate with, let us say, Henry James.

The possession of empire has marked American thought. Did not a president of the American Historical Association declare some forty years ago that we would do well to restrain the expression of critical judgment on our past, lest it be used against us? The scholar in question merits our retroactive admiration for his bluntness. Many of his eminent successors at the apex of the academy followed his precept, while denying their departure from standards of scholarly neutrality. What happened was that entire fields, their assumptions and methods, were increasingly dominated by those for whom America's role in the world was morally unproblematical. When imperial power receded, to be sure, the problem they were seized of was how to avert decline.

A large amount of federal and foundation funding (this last often in close collaboration with the agencies staffing empire) from 1946 onward went into fields like area studies, international relations, and what more recently has been termed the study of national (or international) security. A few hours' attendance at a conference in this last field, or a glance at its journals, will suggest that it has been misnamed: national insecurity studies would be a more accurate term. The practitioners of "national security" doctrines need a decent minimum of insecurity to legitimate their claims to indispensability. When Kissinger left the White House, he was asked if he expected new thought on foreign affairs from our universities. No, he replied: since every professor now wanted to be an assistant secretary of defense or state, the academics could hardly be expected to think differently from bureaucrats. For all of the differences among the experts—between Reaganites and relatively rational imperialists at the moment—the experts in international relations have by and large been accomplices of our elites in narrowing national debate. Fixated on immediate possibilities, they have usually been unable or unwilling to raise larger questions that would challenge the national drift, managed by an apparatus of which they have become part. Indeed, the very term "crisis management" so much in favor bespeaks a technocratic servitude of the spirit. Some crises are unmanageable, and the one constituted by the existence of nuclear weapons seems to have dulled, or stunned, the imaginations of its self-appointed academic custodians. It remains to ask whether others can meet different tests of academic responsibility. Instead of offering answers that are part of our elites' efforts to depict the world as safe, we urgently need thinkers who insist on the dangers we are in.

These fields, then, have increasingly recruited subalterns of empire—those for whom academic education (they term it "training," and the word indeed does have the appropriate connotations) is a precondition of a bureaucratic career. Much has been made of the academicization of administration. The ideological influence of empire, however, suggests that the reverse process is much more evident. Whole sectors of the academy have been colonized by our bureaucratic elites. Harvard's president declared recently that the problems posed by nuclear arms were of such gravity that they required systematic attention by his university. (At Oxford, it was generally assumed that if a subject were not taught there, it was not worth knowing. Harvard has its own and fresher variant of this, as befits a relatively young university: when Harvard treats a political problem, it is indeed news.) A group of the president's colleagues proceeded to publish their reflections under the title *Living with Nuclear Weapons*. It is an interesting question whether the Calvinist Harvard of 1856 would have responded to the Dred Scott case and the imminence of civil war with a volume by several hands entitled *Living with Slavery*. The rapprochement of the university and power is not always an unequivocal sign of human progress.

Views of the American university, throughout its history, as an oppositional fortress are false. Indeed, they are often deliberately promulgated by those seeking control of culture and science, that is, the elimination of opposition. No doubt the universities (more so in the twentieth century than before that) have at times provided protection and even sponsorship for oppositional ideas, frequently giving the larger society opportunity and time to shape these to its purposes. This pedagogic function of the academy has been denigrated by its authoritarian detractors.

X

The Politics of Thought

The politics of the American university are not derivable from the political preferences of its teachers but from the social function of higher education. The land-grant establishments of the late nineteenth century presaged what the private universities (not least their elite sector) were to become: centers for the intellectual processing of social problems. One problem was both posed and resolved, to some extent, by higher education itself: it was a system for dealing with social mobility. Mobility was made possible by labor-market transformations that made the education of new types of workers necessary. Four percent of the eligible age group were in higher education at the turn of the century, and the percentage is now nearer fifty than forty. It would be a mistake to depict the change as a triumph of democratization, particularly in light of the exquisite inner differentiation and stratification of our institutions of learning and quasi-learning. Rather, the universities (and colleges) were responding to tasks of preparation and social selection assigned to them (often quite purposefully and with considerable planning) by the larger society.

I have referred, not ironically, to a pedagogic function for higher education. In fact, reflection upon social problems in our universities has constituted so much intellectual experimentation—a reservoir (or, more precisely, a supermarket) of diverse ideas, some never destined to find favor with consumers. As I write, a Nobel Prize in economics has been announced: the laureate is James Buchanan, who would be the first to acknowledge that for years his theory of public choice excited little interest. Buchanan's derivation of politics from the calculation of interests by groups, his denial of the possibility of the existence of a common good, are clearly congenial in an intellectual climate marked by the retrenchment of the welfare state. (As I edit this text, a year later, the Nobel Prize for 1987 has gone to Robert Solow, a humane Keynesian. Wall Street and the financial markets of the rest of the world are falling.) Do we deal, however, solely with something like an intellectual market, in which ideas rise and fall according to laws of ideological supply and demand? We shall see that the internal organization of the universities and the disciplines, the very institutions supposed to guarantee their autonomy, function as mechanisms of integration with the larger society. Briefly, intellectual markets are no freer than other kinds, and are open to the workings of oligopoly, monopoly, and seller dominance poorly masked as consumer sovereignty. Some institutions, moreover— and especially in market societies—may be thought of as too important to be left to the market. They serve, rather, to enable the market to function. The university is best understood as one of these, an aspect of society's infrastructure as well as part of its culture.

To what extent do the direct educational functions of our universities condition their indirect, but no less important, ones? Universities are not (and ought not to be) exclusively concerned with the education of one generation or cohort of students. It is common enough to join this banality to another one—that their primary obligation is the conduct of inquiry. For what and for whom, however, is inquiry intended? An educated public has almost, but not quite, disappeared behind a crowd of clients, groups, and sponsors to whom scholars relate in ways that do not always bespeak a maximum of independence on their part. Moreover, many scholars speak primarily if not exclusively to one another, in the setting of their disciplines.

Max Weber criticized the desiccated narrowness, the absence of spirit, of modern society's intellectual specialists—and that eight decades ago, when specialization was not as advanced (or the destruction of bourgeois culture's claims to wholeness and transparence still in the future, if the near future). The process of intellectual and occupational specialization, its ineluctable and irreversible nature, is a central (indeed, obsessive) theme of modern social thought. It is often joined to an idea of pervasive depoliticization or a notion of the increasing assumption of decision by technocrats—deplored by some, welcomed by others. In fact, in the academic sphere, the virtual omnipresence of specialization is a thoroughly political phenomenon, if one not invariably acknowledged as such.

Let us limit ourselves to the spheres of culture and society. There specialization entails not only an esoteric language spoken by specialists exclusively; the language expresses a structure of concepts, a view of reality, quite deliberately condensed, distorted, or skewed. The contradiction in these terms (I might have added something anodyne like "partially abstracted") reflects the diverse explanations given by academics for specialization. The customary defense is that it is a heuristic device. Another, not incompatible with the last, is that the fact of specialization or the institutionalization of it leaves modern thought no alternative but to accept the logic of the process: there is no knowledge but specialized knowledge.

If so, this leaves our universe with an intellectual black hole at its center. How do systems of specialized knowledge connect with one another? Are there not fundamental assumptions about power and property, authority and legitimation, human proclivity and possibility, incorporated in these systems—but not directly examined? One answer is that specialization serves to cast some general questions, empirical and moral, into the realm of commonly held opinion—ideologies masked as common sense. Specialization, as Weber argued, diminishes our capacities precisely where it is supposed to enhance them—in the intellectual mastery of a complex reality. Insofar as specialized discourse does not exclude important questions but simplifies them (often absurdly so), it represents a regression from the sophisticated use of reason to a new scholasticism, far more primitive than the original. The early scholastics debated essential questions of theology, if at some risk to themselves. The later ones insist on a rigid distinction between science (what they debate) and theology (what they do not), and fall victim to credulity beyond the narrow limits they set for themselves.

We have reached the point, indeed, where there are at our universities and in our intellectual life specialists in matters general. Nothing quite equals the anxiety evoked in many specialists by generalists. It would be reassuring to suppose that we have indeed resurrected the ancient quarrel of faith with reason, the specialists incarnating blind belief, the generalists critical thought. That consolation, alas, is also denied us. The generalists have the virtue of explicating, more or less openly, the ideologies their colleagues implicitly convey.

Many of the theoretic debates in the social sciences since 1945, from this point of view, lose much of their supposed significance. Empiricists and theorists, detached students of society and engaged problem solvers, votaries of systematic analysis and obdurate defenders of historical method, have quarreled interminably at symposia, in the pages of learned journals, and (occasionally) before the public. With apologies to Tolstoy: the social scientists constitute an unhappy family whose members are very much alike. The politics of much of the argument concerns less the larger issues dividing American society than the narrower questions of academic influence and patronage. Where methodological argument has touched upon politics, it has often taken the vulgar form of attributing a maximum of bad faith and unreflectiveness to those criticized, while proclaiming ideological purity (or intellectual sainthood) for the critics. (Alas, here the opponents of the academic left are not alone in their absence of either magnanimity or simple good sense and taste.)

Let us cast the most cursory of glances upon these thematic arguments. Empiricists, argue the theorists, will never penetrate the moving forces of society and will forever lose themselves in detail. Worse yet, they will be increasingly unable to distinguish between historical wheat and momentary chaff. Theorists, retort the empiricists, will invariably encase themselves in their own abstractions, become prisoners of concepts bound to become remote from society. Indeed, some theorists (under this bill of particulars) are appreciably more interested in their ideas than the events they purport to describe. On this terrain, the argument is utterly unresolvable: both parties are right.

There are times when empirical analysis, nay description, can have the clarifying, even disturbing, effect of a brave new theory. In our own experience, the work of the Chicago School on cities, immigrants, and minorities and the Lynds' study of Middletown imposed new content and contours on our national self-understanding. In the state-socialist societies during the years of early de-Stalinization (circa 1956), empirical studies of class undermined the crude stereotypes of the Stalinist epoch. We may remind ourselves, however, that in both cases (in vastly different political contexts) changes in political sensibility accounted for the genesis and reception of the studies in question. The Chicago School was an element in the reformist thought of the Progressive epoch, and the Lynds refracted a bitter American repudiation of the provincial servitude of the American spirit. (De-Stalinization in the social sciences represented an upsurge that we may term the demand for citizenship in the state-socialist bloc—a demand with an alternative view of socialism and of the common life.) Empirical work, then, can hardly be separated from the eruption of intellectual and political discontinuities.

Theory, too, hardly has an extraterrestrial orbit. The prevailing notion in American social science in the years 1945–60 was consensus. If Hartz and Hofstadter reinterpreted our history in these terms, Parsons in his depiction of American society and in his portrayal of the functioning of social systems in general provided a gloss or a rationale for it. The conflicts that mark any set of values' (or ideology's) road to domination were not quite denied, but these receded from the foreground. The recent renaissance of a Marxist tradition in our universities (or its reinvention) has had several sources. One was the obvious disintegration of consensus. Another was the search for a new agency of transformation, which led so many to identify this with a new professional-scientific-technical labor force rather than an older working class. The third was a demand for coherence, for an understanding of a changing context. That a nineteenth- (or early-twentieth-) century theory served—if for a while—is a commentary on the bewilderment induced by contemporary social complexity, and on the thinness of the alternatives. Critics and advocates of our present institutions, alike, are obliged to work with and through the materials of their experience. The idea of the autonomy of theory is chimerical.

It is hardly more chimerical, however, than the belief that problems can be solved "pragmatically," *sine ira et studio*. The use of the term "pragmatic" by technocrats is evidence for their remoteness from our intellectual traditions. John Dewey (and William James) sought to establish an open context in which problem-solving was not a matter of what Popper termed piecemeal social engineering. It was, rather, a deliberate effort at social reconstruction. It involved, in other words, a very large map of society, and entailed sufficient detachment to enable it to be drawn. Keynes's remark on how the common sense of one age was the distillation of the obscure thoughts of an academic scrivener in the previous period are still valid—and no more so than for those (grotesquely complacent) purveyors of fixed ideas who suppose that they have none.

The conflict between those who insist on the systemic properties of society (and who are uneasy with what they think of as historical explanation) and scholars who, in their own view, think historically or temporally is another instance of the disproportion between the intensity of dispute over method in the social sciences and its importance. A model of society that depicts it as self-contained in time is abstracted from historical sequence and its elements.

Quite apart from the fact that those doing the abstracting are intellectual children of their own setting, their very data is taken from a cumulative, historical process. Those who work historically know this, sometimes denying the extent to which they do not just immerse themselves in the stream of events but are selective or are model builders. It is striking that many of the most strident (their stridency the louder with lack of textual rigor) criticisms of Marxism come from those who actually seem to think that history has no structure, who raise accident and happenstance to the status of Fortuna in Renaissance thought. There are, in other terms, different ways of being historical. It is true that the conflict, or uncertain relationship, of history and structure seems central to much of modern thought. Recall the intellectual discontinuities in the work of Freud or Weber, and the troubled labors of Lévi-Strauss and Sartre. One answer is that there may be no immutable relationship. There are times when the weight of the past weighs heavily on our present possibilities, others when we confront configurations that have become autonomous. These insights, as direct intuitions of history or in the more abstract form of theory, occur when circumstances favor them. The kind of social thinking that dominates a period (there are always dissonances and enclaves, eccentric and even free minds) is, in the end, a form of self-reflection by society.

I have used the phrase "in the end," and I must acknowledge that like the drearily familiar words from one version of the Marxist canon "in the last analysis" the phrase may constitute only an epistemological escape hatch, a device both for giving thought its autonomy and for taking it away. The factor of time is important: just how long before the final weight of distant causality bears upon us? Not only is time important; so is the social organization of thought.

We are back at the institutions of American academic and intellectual life. The postwar expansion of the universities rested, to a great extent, on their immediate social utility. The separate disciplines frequently became so large, or at any rate so self-preoccupied, that they cultivated a notion of self-containment. Meanwhile, the urban intellectual and literary groupings that sixty years ago had effective independence of the universities became centers for the coordination of intellectual production—no, for its direction. Their internal organization allowed the simulacrum of artisanlike independence to many who in reality were so many workers in a national putting-out system.

Given not only the expansion of the universities but what we may term the intellectualization (scientization would be an abuse of the term) of administration in public and private sectors, the self-perpetuation of the disciplines is a large feat. We might have expected that the newer sorts of political and social problems, new knowledge of various sorts, new demands in the labor market, would have led to the reorganization of much of the activities regulated by the disciplines. One additional factor might have pointed in this direction. The university system, after all, teaches millions of students only a small proportion of whom intend scholarly careers. Given the fact that most of those who attain doctorates do not teach at major centers of scholarship, devising general degrees to prepare them for their pedagogic duties would have made eminent sense. The various experiments in this direction were not successful. It is true that we have seen the emergence (in direct response to demands from clients, markets, and sponsors) of institutions teaching "public policy." This has had the result of fragmenting the world of knowledge to yet another degree: a graduate of a school of "public policy" may or may not know much about that ill-defined area, but it is almost certain that he or she will be free of an exhausting burden of historical knowledge or philosophical perspective. Even this attempt to rationalize the education of technocrats has had only partial success. The supreme American social technology remains the law, and lawyers to a considerable extent serve as power's technicians. Since technical and intellectual functions are usually quite inseparable, they also serve (with varying degrees of competence and self-consciousness) as thinkers.

What is interesting about legal studies in America is how sublimely the lawyers have assumed the tasks of Plato's philosopher-kings. By insisting (as in constitutional jurisprudence) that their competence is confined to textual interpretation and the reconciliation of interests defined by society itself, they have moved into the vacuum left by the other disciplines. No other field so confidently takes all of society for its province, and does so not by explicitly adhering to abstractions or models but by accepting enormous ranges of data that supposedly speak for themselves. The disparate pieces of the montage that our society increasingly resembles reappear in academic law, as circumstances, constraints, intentions, norms—a total psychology and politics and sociology that do not quite acknowledge their own names, joined to epistemological and ethical analysis. We can hardly ask for more—except, perhaps, for a heightened self-awareness by the lawyers as to what they are doing. The lawyers sometimes appear before their colleagues as interested (even, astonishingly, humble) students. In fact, their very closeness to social process (more exactly, to conflict) obliges them to take a view of the whole. Perhaps the comparison to medicine is useful. Medicine in treating persons draws upon sciences like biochemistry and neurology, which are both far more precise and far less pretentious than the social sciences used by the lawyers. However, in its effort to seize the singularity of persons and to distinguish among interacting chains of causation, medicine itself resembles the law. It is a continuous exercise in interpretation.

For the most part, however, the disciplines continue, serene in the conviction of their practicioners that they indeed have divided up an intelligible universe in intelligible fashion. This conception of the organization of knowledge usually admits only in parentheses the most obvious fact about itself. The ideas found in the disciplines are not their intrinsic possessions; they are versions of general ideas circulating in the society. Their relegation to the background cannot be likened to their being cast into outer or utter darkness; it is, rather, assignment to a zone of chiaroscuro in which our very difficulty in discerning the terrain and what is on it heightens as it obscures their importance. We can (and do) use these imperfectly apprehended elements selectively. They remain constituents of our view of the world, loose enough to give us the illusion of intellectual autonomy when we work with them, tight enough to provide limits beyond which we do not venture. The consonance of a consensual model in sociology, of an interpretation of American history that made of an unquestioned liberalism its central element, of theories of modernization as the *via regis* to understanding contemporary social change, suggests how closely the disciplines work in their root assumptions.

Nevertheless, in both organization and rhetoric they remain distinct. Many practitioners of the several disciplines spend most of their intellectual lives in the hermetic universes these enclose. The disciplines are the essential forms of scholarly community; their processes of initiation and socialization, their systems of discipline and patronage, their hierarchies, can hardly be described as ancillary to thought. They provide thought's social context, legitimize its expressions, confer (or withdraw) authority upon or from their members. That these communities are often the sites of agitated warfare between ideological clans, struggles between metropolitans and provincials, battles over generational succession, is clear The communities are not monolithic and certainly not totalitarian. They allow, even encourage, what we may term a decent modicum of intellectual change. Nevertheless, the very term "discipline" speaks loudly: they are systems of intellectual centralization and not debating or scholarly societies on an early modern model.

Recently, in one of those periodic adumbrations of a banal thought that provide us with the appearance of intellectual movement while enabling us to stand perfectly still, the social sciences have discovered the importance of what are termed networks. These are organized systems of social relationship, all the more effective for clustering around and within formal institutions rather than merging with them. The distinction is perhaps exaggerated: without these informal systems, formal or chartered ones do not work. Still, we can understand disciplines as part communities, part hierarchies, part networks. Their most striking characteristic remains that their members speak mainly with one another. True, the disciplines severally and singly sometimes appoint or delegate spokesmen to each other, to the learned world in general, and to the larger society. How explain, however, the open distress of many in the disciplines at those whom they term popularizers.

Upon examination, the term is used with very different meanings. Sometimes it refers to vulgarizers. More often than not, however, it is used to describe those who through imaginative anticipation of a market for their intellectual goods (and no small literary skill) distill learned debates for a larger public. Should the distillation entail a perspective of a critical kind, popularization may be disparaged as pamphleteering. Should the popularizer address popular concerns given little attention in the disciplines (rather than doing so in accepted scholarly fashion, by hesitant indirection), he or she is on his own. The academics may then affect an indifference that is real: after all, most are convinced that their work is so complex and sophisticated that matters it does not acknowledge do not exist.

We have to do here with something other than the usual human smallness. We face the fact that the disciplines define themselves (as they did nearly one hundred years ago, when they were first organized) in contradistinction to the public. Those who are integrated in the disciplines are professionals; others are amateurs or dilettantes. The new professionals intended to provide certification for work that influential elites could use, and the identical purpose moves their successors.

Not all writing for a general public is suspect. The nearer the writer to a mean of consensus in the field, the more the work is likely to be praised as an effort at civic education. The model of a textbook comes to mind: introductory students are not supposed to have strongly developed capacities to criticize a field, its assumptions, scope, and conclusions. Why should an educated public be treated differently, when it lacks education in the matter at hand? Troubles begin where the writer disregards or attacks assumptions, widens inquiry, and ignores or erases boundaries between scholarly reticence and public passion.

Consider the contrasting fates of the work of C. Wright Mills and David Riesman in sociology. Both wrote for a larger public. Mills situated himself in an American radical tradition, while Riesman adopted a more detached, even ironic, tone toward these enthusiasms. Each drew upon a large range of academic references, but Riesman was more careful of some of the proprieties. That is, he referred more often and more respectfully to academic contemporaries. Each did speak to public anxieties, Mills to the boundless political disorientation that followed the end of the New Deal era, Riesman to the moral and psychological bewilderment of the expanding middle class.

Each served to communicate to the public, with originality and wit, a selective reading of what the academic social scientists thought. Riesman, despite (or perhaps because of) the genteel distance he took in his later work on academic institutions, remained in touch with what was then a fraternity. Mills (with considerable enthusiasm and no less talent for the role) became an outsider. Upon examination, many of the political differences between the two narrow. What influenced the rather different reception of their work in the academy was the acceptance by Riesman, with a good deal of detachment, of the present intellectual division of labor and a relatively modest role for thought. Mills's demands upon his colleagues were more strenuous, if in profound contradiction to the burden of his analysis of the institutional servitude of the academy. It is true, to be sure, that Riesman in a plea for more utopian thinking once said that America's intellectuals were of more use to the nation when they had less use for it. The implications of his work were, however, far more resigned. (Carl Kaysen has said that upon reading Riesman on the uses of utopia, he persuaded the dean of the faculty of arts and sciences at Harvard, McGeorge Bundy, to propose an appointment for Riesman. That is very much to the credit of both Bundy and Kaysen, who shortly thereafter left Harvard for senior posts in the

Kennedy administration—in which utopianism was not the most conspicuous element of their comportment.)

It is not, then, addressing the public that entails a severe break with the academy—else Daniel Boorstin, with his pious version of American history, would have lost his former Chicago chair decades ago. It is the sort of language the writer uses, the conception of thought he or she exemplifies, the ultimate intellectual authority or authorities to which the writer appeals (or rejects.) Erikson kept his connections with academic psychiatry and organized psychoanalysis despite the large public reception of his work. Even in *Childhood and Society,* with its unique and vivid depictions of the interaction of personality and historical milieu, he did not extend what we may describe as the boundaries of the reigning psychoanalytic view of the world. The overdetermined individual, damaged or not, had little choice but to exemplify in biography what culture and nature had conspired, or unintentionally joined, to foreordain. It is quite correct to think of Erikson as an educator on a grand scale. The psyche and the world being the way they are, the awareness he gives us (exactly like an interpretive structure in analysis) at least enables us to practice the autonomy of insight. His student Robert Lifton, per contra, insists in his works on the therapeutic consequences, or personality-altering consequences, of nontherapeutic action, of politics. His works employ historical and literary and philosophical references, introduce new concepts of the psyche, and render the usual categorizations difficult. So much speculation, official psychiatry and psychoanalysis seem to think, may be the privilege of a Freud; we ought to be more modest. Perhaps—but, again, a process of willed deprofessionalization, purposeful construction of an alternative idea of professional discipline, disturbs a discipline's sleep.

If we turn to a somewhat different field, international relations, we may see some of the same processes at work. Enthusiasm for the person and policies of Henry Kissinger may be limited among scholars in the area, but many of them share his world of discourse. Beginning his public career by directly addressing less the public than the elites concerned with arms and foreign and military policy, Kissinger advanced to his present oracular status by an institutional itinerary. The Kissinger honored, at the height of his power, by the academy and the media was not only a supreme American servant of the apparatus: he represented the fusion of apparatus and academy. Hans Morgenthau, per contra, wrote directly for a public and sought to influence the apparatus by educating the public to demand a different sort of foreign policy.

There are analogies in the field of social policy. In the complicated debate on the effects of social and welfare programs, the matter has been made more complex still by the intervention of direct political representatives of the groups seeking benefits from these programs. Of course, ideology intrudes: the conflict between the Catholic bishops and their critics, between Harrington and Levitan on one hand and Gilder and Charles Murray on the other, is primarily political. In fact, the difference in intellectual quality between the protagonists suggests a deeper politicization of debate. The function of cruder figures like Gilder is to prepare the public for new technical or technocratic solutions within altered (which is to say, narrowed) limits of political possibility. It is striking that public legitimation is fought over in this area rather than in foreign and military policy, where a fabricated consensus sets limits to public debate. That said, it is interesting how much of the published matter in the latter area is not intended for consumption by academic specialists, or by the public at large, but is written for bureaucrats and politicians or opinion-forming elites.

Foreign and military policy and the nation's global role; social and welfare policy and the extent to which the nation is prepared to control the workings of the market—these are questions scholars (and the publicists limping intellectually at their heels) often no longer submit to the nation's judgment.

XI

Countermovements
in Thought

The turbulence (not unmixed with imbecilities) of the period 1965–72 in our universities has so scarred (spiritually) some of our colleagues that they cannot quite remember what the argument was about. They depict it as a struggle between the (at least intellectually) unwashed and themselves, self-flatteringly portrayed as the last incarnations of higher culture. Of course, what occurred was rather different.

The academic revolt of the period was not alone the work of students, or of graduate students or teaching assistants. It included larger numbers of younger scholars and no small contingent of older ones. It began not as a revolt at all, but as an expression of solidarity with the civil-rights movement in the South—in effect, as a campaign that allied itself with those in the Kennedy and, later, Johnson administrations who were pressing for reforms. The first phases of the protest of the Vietnam War represented, again, no break with the technocratic liberalism that had dominated the universities for decades; the war was, simply a mistake (if a large one). It was the generalization of opposition to the war to criticism of the culture and society, its mechanisms of power and ideology, that generated the university revolt proper. What had been irritations—the bureaucratic remoteness of administration in the larger universities, the fragmentation of academic work, the aridity of method and technique and the insubstantiality of content in the human and social sciences—underwent startling interpretive transformations. These were no longer inevitable aspects of modern culture, the acceptance of which was a sign of maturity. They were evidence for the servitude of the university to (and the complicity of its managers and proprietors, the established professoriate, in) an omnipresent system of oppression, for the function of the academy as a factory that produced spiritual alienation and ideological toxin nonstop. This was a drastic inversion of judgment of an organization that had been seen as the most civilized, the most liberal, of major American institutions. It had been viewed as a channel for mobility, as proof that America society opened careers to talent. Now it was seen as a place in which ambition was domesticated and simultaneously, criticism stilled, as a preparatory school for access to the privileges of a bureaucratic elite. Its intellectual pluralism was now depicted as little more than a sham—or, at best, an ornamental concession to the disappearing educative and inquiring role of the university. What really counted was a very specific version of public service—to and for the elites with which the professoriate was so closely connected. Academicism, then, was a refuge, and professionalism an oppressive discipline. The entire criticism was most furious when directed at the very apex of the system, the large research universities and the university colleges that clustered around them. (The stratification of the university system was now seen—not, let it be said, without reason—as a reflection of the organization of American society into classes.)

No doubt in the anger of the critics there was an element of unrequited love or unfulfilled longing: the civilizing and reflective influence of the institution to which they had pledged themselves was now seen as disappointingly small. Criticism, however, did not begin with the university and extend to the larger society. A critical view of America as a whole, a negative revaluation of the imperial liberalism or social imperialism of the postwar consensus, concretized in an effort to change the setting in which the critics lived. That it was Herbert Marcuse who had to remind some of them that among American institutions it was still the most liberal and open tells us much about the historical perspective (and lack of political experience) of those he admonished. Still, they were not European survivors of the Weimar Republic but American continentals, who had known little or no history but their own, lived for the most part in extraordinarily protected circumstances. Their parents had known depression and war (and later that curious combination of inner adaptation and outer pressure we knew as McCarthyism). Generational continuity, however, was not a conspicuous feature of the movement: older figures frequently served as totems, not role models (not, more precisely, as repositories of experience).

The problem of the development of a different national politics turned attention away from the university quickly enough. There were enough incentives for a refocusing of attention and energies: the inner fragmentation of the civil-rights movement and the emergence of an angrily autonomous black grouping; the nascent women's movement; the political success of Richard Nixon (and Henry Kissinger); the death of the figures who might have effected an alliance with the main body of the old Democratic coalition, Robert Kennedy and Martin Luther King; the incursion into Cambodia. Perhaps it would be more accurate and generous to say that past political experience seemed to be of little immediate help: the situation was new, the alliances and ideologies in evidence unexpected, the behavior of many surprising (Nixon neither demolished the Great Society nor made war on China and in due course sought détente with the Soviet Union). Major parts of the movement of the middle and late years of the decade 1960–70 entered the Democratic Party. It is customary for those attached to the warfare-welfare–state tradition epitomized by Humphrey to indulge themselves in a curious combination of self-pity and fervid denunciation: if only the party would return to the fixed ideological universe of the recent past, how well it would do. How well it would do, especially, were it to eliminate the blacks, consumerists, environmentalists, feminists, nuclear disarmers, and radical unionists in its ranks. These political Ptolemaicists do not grasp the obvious: the Democrats cannot win with these groups alone, but will surely lose without them. The McGovern campaign saw these groups, if briefly, in possession of the party (or its name, since its structures are so impermanent and changing). The high point of the movement also showed its weakness, its inability to generate an enduring economic and social project and to construct a large coalition on the basis of a new common denominator that would employ traditional values to legitimate a future design—values consonant with the past to legitimate a design for the future. No doubt the thinkers who reflected upon this failure in its wake were (and are) right to suggest that the virtual extirpation (or at least substantial flattening) of the memory of the past is a major barrier to a critical public consciousness. Briefly, a surprised American left found that many of the things it had thought about the difficulties of reform were true.

Some twenty-five years ago, Dwight Macdonald reviewed an anthology of articles from *Dissent* and jested at the contributors as "professors of revolution." The remark was not without its autobiographical roots; at the time, Macdonald was writing about culture (if with his characteristic independence and verve), having withdrawn from politics. The withdrawal was temporary, and the problems of America in the middle of the decade 1960–70 drew him back to questions of class and power. *Dissent's* contributors, of course, were those survivors of the decades 1930–50 (and their younger colleagues) who somehow remained adamantly indifferent to the view that the postwar American consensus united history and reason in a perfect synthesis.

The situation today is similar. The thoroughly politicized and radicalized academic generation of the decade beginning with 1960 is not only a memory. Many of its members have withdrawn from politics to seek satisfaction in work or a private sphere: the line between youthful radicalism and what Lasch terms the consumption of self in the varied forms of the new concern with the psyche is direct. Some have remained politically active or articulate (insofar as there is a difference), but have reversed their earlier opinions. Many have sublimated their radicalism in a striking way. It was Max Weber, after all, who declared that political values were an inextricable element in the selection of problems, the formulation of hypotheses, and (by implication, at least) the construction of categories of analysis. The reemergence of rather neglected themes of social inquiry, the development of entire new areas of research, the persistent if often implicit continuation in academic form of the supersession of the notions of American society institutionalized in the postwar period, may be thought of as a continuation of politics (and of radical politics at that) by other means. For no small number of scholars, the process has been entirely purposeful: they are engaged in an examination of the possibilities of a new American social project. For many more, other purposes serve: they are interested in the causes of their recent defeat, or were sensitized by their experiences to the discontinuities of the American experience. In one sense, these differences of intention are secondary. Intention is, alas, not achievement; those attempting to construct a new social project may for any number of reasons be incapable of doing so. Sometimes sublimation works: Freud's disappointment in the possibilities of liberalizing politics in the Austro-Hungarian Empire led him to seek a far different kind of enlightenment and liberation. Ostensible withdrawal may provide just the distance needed for profound critical activity, even if the critic does not quite acknowledge the implications of what he or she may be saying.

We possess a body of scholarship and thought we could hardly imagine twenty years ago. Perhaps the term "body," with its implication of articulation and purpose, is inappropriate. Let us say that we have a series of works in connected areas of social inquiry that suggest the elements of a new view of American society. These may inspire or inform a new politics, but have as yet to do so. A common social project, a common denominator drawn from our experience and applied to the future, is still missing. Still, the inquiries in question are radical in that they frequently pose, not alone new answers to old (or perennial) questions, but new questions—to which we have, clearly, no answers.

Profound currents flow in the opposite direction. The adaptation of much social inquiry to the presently defined political limits and ends of state action bespeak an unwillingness, a refusal, to enlarge the scope of social thought. In matters concerning our nation's global role, our empire is treated theologically: it is hypostatized. These tendencies are not new. At some future date, the technocrats (or a new generation of them) will alter their assumptions, incorporate other political ends in their work, and as before cultivate a public image of neutrality. For the moment, the technocratic areas of social thought enjoy a curious sort of autonomy, while an ideological battle rages elsewhere.

The depiction of the American university as the world's last outpost of revolution (the Soviet Academy of Science has fallen to the Soviet technocrats, and at the Mao Institute of Marxism-Leninism and Maoist thought in Peking, the virtues of the market monopolize attention) may constitute perceptual madness, but there is method to it. The temporary reign of a neoconservative ideology among publicists requires, in the long run, academic reinforcement. It has had some, but evidently its protagonists consider it insufficient. I see no reason not to acknowledge the correctness of their judgment. Neoconservatism was and is, in any event, a direct derivative of the decomposition of the postwar consensus. That accounts for its reactive, strident character, its compulsive iteration of a few quarter-truths, and its instinctive denial of the possibility of constructing a better future, coupled with its insistence that the nation has diverged from a true path to which its self-appointed intellectual guides will, if given the chance, return it. The compulsive quality of the neoconservative advocacy of optimism (rather reminiscent of criticisms of "unhealthy" negativism in fascism and Stalinism) does not quite conceal a despairing substratum. Neoconservatism rests on a rejection of the idea of progress. The attack on the university radicals, their influence vastly exaggerated, is a holding operation designed to keep the enemy at bay until reinforcements arrive. These, for the incoherent coalition that runs from *Commentary* and the *National Review* to (parts of) the *New Republic* and *The Public Interest,* do not appear to be either on or over the horizon.

The radical party is one mainly in the eyes of its antagonistic beholders. (The Socialist Scholars Conference resembles a class reunion, not least in its demographic characteristics from year to year.) The academic radicals at once overestimate and underestimate themselves. They overestimate the value of good critical intentions, and they underestimate the long-term consequences of ideas. Often in despair because of their isolation from the American mainstream, they fail no less often to see that the mainstream is an ideological fabrication, not a fixed historical datum. Moreover, the university does offer a protected space for thought, in which current definitions of what is central to our history and what is not can be examined. The relative isolation of the critical spirit can lead to sectarian self-pity, but it can also constitute an advantage.

I have said that the radical party in the university exists mainly in the eyes of anxious adversaries. That should be corrected. The radical party in the university exists in that singular alternation of activity and resignation that characterizes radicals outside it. It has no one theme, no single set of categories, no standard version of the national experience. Its diversity, and diffuseness, may also be its strength. Its intellectual energies can flow, more or less freely, without being subjected to the exigencies of a focused ideological struggle. Shifting boundaries now align the radicals with the still large liberal remnant in the university, now provide contact and exchange with conservatives (some of whose themes do bespeak a sense of contemporaneity and immediacy both liberals and radicals lack). A connection to the technocratic scholars so prominent in the universities is useful. They do have experience of politics and society (if of an intentionally narrow kind), and their support, or that of their successors, will have to be won for any serious reform project in the near or distant future.

Let us turn from programmatic intention, historical affiliation, and contextual analysis to our subject matter itself—and to the questions we put to it. Are there new social ideas, what are they worth, and what possible use can we make of them?

CONCLUSION

With so much intelligence, learning, and moral energy evident in critical American social thought, why do its protagonists lack a concrete utopia, a social project, a vision of society? They know what they like; what they do not know is the art of achieving it. Their most obvious deficiency is that of a common denominator. They do indeed speak about the same themes, but they do so in different tongues. They sense that they have raised, if not another Tower of Babel, a house in Carpenter's Gothic style, but continue to work in frenzied unconcern on its lawn. Their ideas of character development and psychic function, of cultural continuity and community, of equality and participation, are assembled (or, rather, juxtaposed) in a not entirely coherent collage. Different kinds of cultural sensibilities, conflicting ideas of historical possibility, and opposing sorts of political aims clash, or coexist uneasily, in their works. They cannot agree on anything but an additive program—for our intellectual institutions and for our nation. Indeed, many of those to whom we are most indebted for new charts of our past and maps of our present, who have given us acute and sometimes profound insights into matters hitherto neglected or obscure, are quite explicitly unprogrammatical. They sense, correctly, that they are engaged in a common venture whose terms are only beginning to be set. They consider that their task is not the formal promulgation of a project but the provision of the substance from which, eventually, it can be drawn. Their hesitation, then, is not tactical but strategic. The martial metaphor is appropriate. They are preparing to do battle—if in some doubt as to with whom, on what fields, and exactly when.

I

Defense and
Its Limits

Confronted by so many immediate threats, do we actually need to look for enemies? Menaces to human health and to nature, an attack on values that cannot be homogenized or sold on the cultural market, restrictions on the most fundamental of democratic rights despite their constitutional protections, the reduction of the living standard of the American labor force (including the middle stratum that has thought itself so privileged), and the possibility of total extirpation in nuclear war do not necessarily call for an elegantly complex politics. It remains to state the obvious, to appeal to the common sense and minimal reflectiveness of our fellow citizens (and their everyday experiences of the arrogance, exploitativeness, and venality of our elites). Installed, with all due modesty, in the vanguard of an aroused citizenry, we may set forth once again to redeem a not quite fallen world. The theological reference is appropriate. We secular thinkers will find ourselves in the midst of those who take their social conscience and, more broadly, their self-definition from ecclesiastical tradition. Indeed, the putative alliance may remind us, particularly but not exclusively those who are Jewish, that we are nearer to our own traditions than we sometimes think. (One of the excrescences of the current situation is to hear Jewish publicists denounce the American churches for not confining themselves to "problems of meaning" and to complain, subsequently, of the rootlessness of the surviving advocates of progress. Were the prophets of the Old Testament first published by Pantheon?)

The difficulty is that the public is adamantly resistant to mobilization on so broad a front. The public-opinion polls are, no doubt, blunt or crude instruments. They do show that most citizens can identify these problems. What the citizenry's own language for phrasing them may be remains largely unknown. The language of the polls is the language of the pollsters, or (worse yet) a language they impute to others. Its themes are almost invariably drawn from the surface of events and almost never from the depths of society. Those who construct polls (with honorable exceptions like Daniel Yankelovich) are not, in their capacity to penetrate the surface, likely to betray descent from Hawthorne, or even Dos Passos or Mailer. They do have a common denominator of conception that they share with the politicians and publicists who claim to register public consciousness—an exceedingly low one. These groups (along, of course, with the institutional advertisers of the private sector) claim to exercise pedagogic functions. The radical party has taken the claim literally and accused them of responsibility for the crudification of consciousness, the ideological deformation of the public mind. That debate is hardly new: large elements of it were in place at the beginning of the Progressive period. For the moment, we can certainly say that public opinion gives every evidence of fragmentation, of incapacity to construct a picture of society as a whole. It is as if most Americans accepted the robust disorientation and hearty stupidity of the creed of the British historian who concluded that history is one damned thing after another.

The condition of opinion is a jagged refraction of the multiplicity of objects glowing dully in the academic firmament. Perhaps there is a systematic connection. With no insistent public demand for a social project pressing upon them, those on the frontiers of knowledge and thought find their own dispersed order perfectly natural. The academic division of labor in its present form will continue as long as the public asks our universities for so very little, least of all for a vision of the whole. Some decades ago, the *New York Times* reported that a resident of Muncie, Indiana (the *Times* having decided to revisit Middletown before Theodore Caplow did), said that his child was about to go to college, and that there was nothing he feared so much as professorial subversion of parental values. One wonders whether he (and more sophisticated purveyors of anxiety still so much with us) need have worried. Our students, as surrogates for the nation, do not seem obsessed by radical ideas. Earlier, I argued that Beard and Dewey did not so much write for a public as call, or recall, one into existence. For the moment, those in the academy who engage in an active politics that is not one of ideological apologetics or technocratic servitude are stuck with a politics of defense. They seek to ward off catastrophes they are obliged to depict as neither quite imminent nor reassuringly distant. The public is receptive to many of the warnings, but has much difficulty in entertaining the idea that our social arrangements as a whole constitute a permanent catastrophe.

Defense, clearly, is not enough. The connection between the several spheres of society is by no means easy to establish, even for those with an untamed will to see things entire. Society, and its spheres, are by no means unchanging: the choice of beginning point requires a historical judgment that may well be out of date by the time its intellectual implications are worked out. If, however, defense is not enough, it still has something to recommend it. It gives us a sense of matters alive, of moral purpose, of the resistance of social organization to reason. As diverse as these derivatives of engagement may be, they do allow us to test our abstractions against several sorts of hardness. Some thinkers will become stuck in immediacy. Others may find the tasks of defense an occasion for, or a stimulus to, a deeper kind of thought.

Consider, as instances of defensive thought, the related problems of the environment and of human health. The newer environmental sensibility has given us a critique of the domination or possession of nature by humans. This has extended to a reconsideration of the idea of unceasing economic growth and a reexamination of the assumptions of industrial civilization. The articulation of an alternative, however, makes for severe difficulties. If growth is curtailed, those who have hitherto benefited from increments in it will be severely affected. These include the impoverished and developing nations. Those strata in our own society most dependent upon the welfare state are bound to suffer: allocations of national income to the more egalitarian ends of social policy have been dependent upon generalized material prosperity, measured in quantitative terms.

We are quite unable, given the inertia of our institutions and ideologies, to conceive of alternatives that would make a basic change in our treatment of the environment possible. (Witness the unresolved conflict over acid rain in the Northeast of our continent.) There exist almost no allocative or ascriptive mechanisms, further, for shifts from harder to softer technologies.

Enormous numbers of Americans camp, fish, hike, and hunt. Still, it is difficult to claim that the environmental critique has taken roots so profound as to produce demands for a different culture. It is one thing to assent to the proposition that polluting industries must be regulated. It is another to imagine a very different economic organization, with extensive and intensive changes in patterns of expenditure, the structure of work, and the use of time—as well as a change in the organization of space. At one level, the environmental question is one of economic structure. At another, connected one it involves an ideology in which uncriticized notions of individual choice and the current form of property have been utterly confounded. It is not surprising, in the circumstances, that a while ago a legal scholar propounded a remedy for pollution subsequently acclaimed as a triumph of administrative imagination: firms would be allowed to purchase, in units, the right to pollute. If the units were expensive enough, they would pollute less.

Ideas of health entail the same intricacies of relationship between ostensibly simple remedial steps and an immovable and pathogenic setting. Much psychic and somatic disorder is induced by economic and social stress outside the reach of the practice of medicine. To be sure, just as the American upper middle class has through fiscal legislation and fringe benefits constructed its privatized version of the welfare state, it conducts its own preventive health programs. Diet and fitness schedules, and the spread (sometimes more imaginary than real) of the values termed postmaterialist may well have improved the health of a part of our nation. Postmaterialism, if we understand it as the search for satisfaction of a qualitative and personalized kind, is a luxury good available to those who already have high levels of material security. The entire matter may be closer to the culture of narcissism than to the distant promise of liberation. The broad dissemination of minimal disciplines toward health would require any number of conflicts (with the food industry, for instance). Moreover, effective popular education as to matters of health may hardly be possible under the surveillance of new or old fundamentalists—as the controversies attendant upon sexual education and AIDS suggest.

In short, questions of environment and health bring us to confront conventionalized notions of autonomy and life space. The immensity of the ideological transformations that could encourage our contemporar-

ies to consider the very possibilities of major institutional and technological transformations has contributed to the shrinkage of social thought.
Something like piecemeal social engineering seems to represent the
outermost limits of possibility, and even that is dismissed by those who
have made of the working of the market not a matter for analysis but
an item of faith. Given the cumulative effects of the threats to our very
existence, limited social engineering itself seems incapable of dealing
with the acceleration of them. Solutions like the cessation of nuclear-
plant construction because of excessive costs engendered by litigation
and regulation provide no models that would avoid future crises. They
seem only to exemplify our historical immobility. The parallel to the
efforts of the arms-control party to limit the nuclear-arms race is evident.
Agreements painfully reached are rendered out-of-date by new inven-
tions. The sources of conflict in social structure remain out of reach and
at times out of mind.

II

Universal and Particular, Community and Polity

We face a situation, then, in which our life spaces, unless redesigned,
will be narrowed still further. Most of our citizens, however, consider
that they have no options but to hold on to terrain they now possess.
They interpret suggestions for change as threats of eviction. We come
to the issue of community, phrased by Harry Boyte and Sara Evans as
the problem of free spaces. With others who identify with our populist
tradition, they seek counterforces to the overcentralization and overor-
ganization of culture and society. They do so not for the sake of an
abstract, empty, or negative idea of liberty, but because of attachment
to the exercise of experiment, the practice of solidarity, the enjoyment
of spontaneity.

Community is as community does. The positive values of community, in fact, have often been far less visible than constriction, oppression, and prejudice. In our own history, a communitarian strain is something other than Jefferson's idyll (or Brook Farm). It has entailed rigidification, and belated mobilization for causes bound to be lost. The defensive reactions of American communities (communities in the sense of groupings sharing culture rather than merely contiguous or the same space) included much undifferentiated hostility to the outside world. That world has been understood (correctly) to promise the termination of their autonomy. Anxiety and rage, however, have not invariably been wise counselors: they have generated a politics of resentment born of the sense of defeat. More defeats, of course, have been incurred by the inability of these communities to contract enduring political alliances with groups unlike themselves. Here again the experience of community has been narrowing.

Analogies drawn from the practice of imperial domination are familiar. Ideas of inner colonialism apply, and remind us that Arendt understood fascism as *inter alia* the treatment of European peoples in the twentieth century as imperial subjects had been treated in the age of empire. No doubt the newer forms of relation between metropolis and province allow more analogies of this sort. Are not the cultural elites of the Third World often loud in their denunciations of linguistic and symbolic occupation? The substitution of penetration by multinational corporations and international banks for the Marines and the Légion Étrangère, equally, has been depicted as no improvement (the more so, presumably, because the Marines and the Légionnaires have not in all cases departed for good).

For our society, at least, the analogy is of very limited usefulness. We are not ruled by a united White Anglo-Saxon Protestant caste—not, at any rate, any longer. Our putative subject peoples do not think of themselves as culturally oppressed. Indeed, they may conceive of themselves as disadvantaged, even exploited, but not as oppressed or dispossessed in their own land. Moreover, insofar as the colonial analogy is used in politics, it is used not by those seeking revolutionary changes but by those who most desperately fear these. It is the fundamentalist right that accuses a supposedly universalist elite of seeking to rob it of its heritage.

In the terrible cacophony of American cultural and political debate, they actually believe what they say. The idea of our elites as bearers of an American version of a *mission civilisatrice* is preposterous. The corporate managers and politicians who direct the nation's affairs (or who desperately seek to stay afloat atop the waves of the epoch) are not conspicuous for their articulation of the premises of the Enlightenment—of which they last heard in a survey course early in college, if then.

Those liberals who have some knowledge of their own tradition, and no small part of the radical party, do seek a new universalism. They are quite unclear as to how best to connect it with our cultural pluralism. Their recourse to older formulations (a universalism of procedure, a framework of rights) partakes of that defensive effort of which I have written. It does not give us a vision that can sustain a redefinition of our politics. The most intelligent of the new conservatives have seized upon this weakness in our position and turned it against us. Do we not espouse the values of community in the abstract? How explain, then, our singular skepticism about community in particular—except, of course, for those assemblages of the like-minded in which we find ourselves? Peter Berger and Richard Neuhaus have insisted on the value of what they term mediating structures, between the larger institutions of society and the individual: church, ethnic group, family, neighborhood. Berger has gone further and proclaimed the naturalness of existing communities, and by implication the artificiality of the promise of the French Revolution and the Enlightenment, the impossibility of a human community as a new and global polis. Walzer is not, I know, usually numbered among the new conservatives. He does employ some old conservative arguments, however, in *Spheres of Justice* and his *Interpretation and Social Criticism.* He, too, insists on existing communities as root social institutions—against the claims of humanity in general, or some hypothetical future organization of the entire race.

The position is a withdrawal of philosophical cathexis from universal aspiration. The retrenchment contains more than a hint of an elegant version of social Darwinism. Suppose that concrete communities are the major forms of social existence, making possible everything from authentic solidarity to effective prophecy. Conflicts between communities (and, of course, nations) are then subject to other, more schematic and thinner rules.

Geertz, most articulately, has argued that there is no monolithic or unilinear modernizing process at work. Other critics of the uses of the idea of modernization have protested that the idea is an apologia for the extension of the capitalist market worldwide (Wallerstein and Eric Wolf can be cited, along with Gendzier). Within the historiography of our own nation, a number of scholars have insisted on the pathos of resistance to domination from the center. Goodwyn and Wiebe, in their defense of the Populist movement and portrayal of the segmentation of our culture, echo earlier themes from the Progressive historians, if with a much more positive view of movements once depicted as opponents of progress.

The conservatives have taken the communitarianism, newfound or not, of the radicals and stood it on its head. Why so much criticism of our society, they ask, for undermining community, when in the eyes of the critics its actual communities merit so little attention? A new radical social project will have to begin by acknowledging that we have yet to find a way to reconcile the claims of the particular and the universal. Marx supposed that the capitalist market would raze, in the sphere of culture, humanity's separate houses. Nothing of the sort has occurred, or occurred in unambiguous form. Within and without our borders, meanwhile, the forms of resistance to a global leveling process are not invariably attached to the morally expansive traditions of the Enlightenment. The available modes of ideological integration of world politics, as well as the forms of countermobilization, are often oppressive, without aesthetic and moral attractiveness.

Notions of a new relationship in our own society between community and polity remain indistinct, partly a result of our difficulty in moving between particular and universal social concepts. In one version of American constitutional jurisprudence, the rights of communities to set their own standards include the authority to ban books. The rights of local governments to prevent firms from closing plants or offices are most definitely not understood as extensions of community autonomy. Legal challenges to book banning have sometimes argued that the boundaries of community dissolve into those of nation, that given the density of communication and the frequency of mobility, no purely local community is isolable. The argument might be thought likely to appeal to those who hold that a national economy requires local disequilibria (like regional unemployment). It does not, allowing us to conclude that for some thinkers the autonomy of local communities and the sovereignty of the market are unconnected items of belief. Alternatively, we may say that these persons do not engage in a process that can be termed thinking: they react to an existing situation in immediate ways, but hardly imagine that it can be much altered.

Perhaps this is another way to declare that we lack a national political culture. We flatter ourselves on our diversity, as contrasted with the uniformity we impute to the Europeans. Suppose, however, that our diversity resembles nothing so much as a modern version of the ways in which empires (even Asiatic ones) once functioned. As long as a ruling court and its servants could exact tribute, village cultures and other enclaves could flourish. Precisely—our national political culture of the moment, as incarnated in our elites, does not have deep roots in the consciousness and existence of ordinary Americans. Many claim to speak for them, but they speak only sporadically for themselves. What seemed authentic, if unpleasantly so, the revival of the Christian Right, now strikes us as in some part the work of ideological entrepreneurs and ecclesiastical racketeers. No doubt tens of millions of Americans believe that the two Testaments compel the maintenance and possibly the use of nuclear weapons, or subventions to the Somocistas. Even these beliefs, if sustained by reinforcement in small communities, hardly connect with the daily lives of those who espouse them. When did they last see a godless Communist? (To be sure, Soviet diplomats or journalists occasionally appear on television. The Christian Right has interpreted this as prima facie evidence for the corruption of the media.) These groups may be speaking most truthfully when they declare themselves at war with our cosmopolitan elites. Did not Bebel remark that anti-Semitism in the nineteenth century was the socialism of fools? Disliking the Columbia Broadcasting System and Harvard University, for many Americans, is the one version of class conflict they permit themselves.

That the industrial democracies, and above all our own, possess social structures that nullify the promise of democracy is one of those truisms that constitute the capital from which so many of us (like aging intellectual rentiers) live. If this is to be of more use than endless rumination on why socialism—or at least a morally improved society—has not yet been achieved, we will have to ask different (and specific) questions. Again, defensive intellectual maneuvers are too likely to absorb our energies. Much has been won, in our own society, by our version of the welfare state, by the unions, by the extension of state protection of citizens' rights to realms hitherto left to their own (often cruel or unjust) devices. What has been done, however, can be undone—and, frequently, with disheartening ease and speed.

The recent reorganization of market and polity in the industrial democracies has resulted in what Peter Glotz terms two-thirds societies, in which a third of the nation struggles with a declining standard of living and hopes denied, while the rest live more rather than less comfortably. It is interesting that this phrase from a German Social Democrat recalls Franklin Roosevelt's second inaugural address, with its explicit avowal of class division. ("I see one-third of a nation ill housed, ill clad, ill nourished. . . .") It is no less interesting that it comes from a society with a very well-developed welfare state, more powerful unions than our own, and a deeply rooted social democratic movement. It is even more interesting that Glotz, in the end, suggests that we need a new idea of the path to change, a new historical bloc—and a rebirth of much older ideas of solidarity.

The very successes of the welfare state may well have precipitated its present difficulties. Providing rather firm guarantees of economic and social advantages to a large section of the labor force, it has split society. Many are covered by one or another segment of a social contract elaborated now in collective bargaining, now in the national budget. The successive integration of the generations in the American welfare state has not created a politically useful memory. Our welfare state has been extended *pari passu* with the national market. The beneficiaries of the struggles of past generations have been induced to ignore their—or their families'—more precarious beginnings. The enormous capacity of American culture in its modern capitalist variant to create new cultural demands is also at work. This is something quite distinct from, even antithetical to, a simple process of integrating groups of the most diverse sort into the system (whatever "the system" may be). The very forms of protest change from brief generation to short-lived cohort, just as expectations change. The task of constructing a continuous historical bloc to achieve a long-range program of social transformation is very, very difficult when the potential constituents of the bloc are themselves continuously changing.

We are unable to flatter the academy by asserting that its attention span, or collective memory, is uniformly longer than that of the more vulgar sectors of the cultural industry. We may certainly place Gilder (alternately denouncing the impoverished for parasitism and thanking wealthy sponsors for supporting his writing) in this last area. Despite an entire literature on the precise ways in which the Great Society's programs were successful (as in the writings of Sar Levitan), massed armies of economists and political scientists, the identical clichés and stereotypes stored in their word processors, have assured us of their "inefficiency." That the alternatives they propose are singularly consonant with crude notions of reducing the responsibility and scope of the government allows us to suppose that these scholars are, in one respect at least, verifying the existence of laws of supply and demand.

It is, surely, not news that an educated public will have to decide for itself among competing and conflicting interpretations of society, and the programs derived from (or giving rise to) them. It is, equally, not news that the academy, especially where it most loudly protests its objectivity, is thoroughly politicized. We can connect these perfectly unexceptionable assertions with a larger problem. Citizenship can hardly be limited to political participation in a narrow sense. It requires a capacity to learn. Culture and education are aspects of politics no less important than direct struggles in the market. Nothing is gained by designating these areas "superstructure." If we still wish to employ the terms "base" and "superstructure," we must acknowledge that the processes they designate are increasingly fused.

The analysis of mass culture that some of us recall from forty years ago retains its cutting edge. No doubt the discussion was for some a flight from the other areas of politics, become so unpromising. For others, it was a way to deplore what American democracy had wrought, while insisting on the ultimate educability of the nation. Its mixed ideological origins apart, the analysis points to problems still very much with us. Some of it came from a long tradition of American social criticism. Some was enriched by the work of Adorno and his colleagues on the cultural industry. A few (Greenberg and Macdonald, for instance) used both currents. Perhaps we now can put the matter in a different way.

Seen solely in terms of the assault on human intelligence and sensibility mounted by the cultural industry, the problem is insoluble. It is true that the media have a preternatural sensitivity to momentary political fluctuations. No major American network would have carried a report from an obscure Beirut weekly of arms sales by the Reagan administration to Iran had the president not previously lost his Senate majority. As I write, the media still show exquisite restraint about the organization and practice of terror by our covert-action agencies. Even when particular crimes and scandals are evoked, the media demonstrate a quite extraordinary capacity to get to the surface of events—and stay there. Many prominent journalists resemble specialists in international relations or microeconomics in their intellectual attainments. That is, they combine abject servility to power and complacent ignorance in equal measure. To expect a serious effort to introduce pluralism into our national politics from those who control the media is very improbable. The fragmented American public has in the recent past shown a strong capacity to resist total indoctrination. It has been unable to formulate a view of economy and society to challenge, in its assumptions, the prefabricated one offered it daily in the guise of information.

Perhaps we should cease to ask, so obsessively, what else can be done to strengthen popular resistance to that permanent intellectual mockery of the public practiced by those who pretend to serve it. There is something more than vaguely patronizing about our assuming the role of new Narodniki. Rather, let us examine the relationship of private lives to the public sphere—or, in a society in which the boundaries between culture and politics are all but erased, let us look at their interpenetration. Resistance, if that is the term (opposition is what we are really after) may be more substantial than we think.

III

Public and Private,
Again

Historians have been especially acute in describing the fate of public space and public life in our nation. In the nineteenth century, the parties served as fulcra of social activity. They gave some substance to the idea and practice of citizenship, while leaving much else to church, family, and neighborhood. Election campaigns served as recurring festivals; an important part of public life was bounded, made concrete and visible. It is quite true that, if many immigrants were gradually included in the process, racism excluded many. It is also true that women did not enter the political realm until after its immediate character was transformed in the twentieth century into something approaching the agitated vacuum that is our present polity. The temptation to look with nostalgia on an (imagined) superior democratic past can be overcome. After all, nineteenth-century American public life witnessed the gradual obliteration of earlier republican doctrines of civic virtue as well as the process termed by Trachtenberg the incorporation of America. Politics also failed, singularly, to solve the question of slavery and its racist sequel.

By dealing with blacks, children, farmers, immigrants, slaves, women, and workers in the last century and this one, the historians have shown us how little of our social life has been rendered public by politics. Yet many of them seem to suppose that a newer and improved America will make room in politics for these groups, or their contemporary descendants. Suppose, however, that despite the growth of the American welfare state, a realm of politics has rather less weight than it once had. Suppose we do not know how to make changes that would enlarge lives.

We come to ordinary lives, beset by economic constraints and psychic complaints, to routine and its mixture of discontent and content. Our fellow citizens are quite unwilling to venture into a public sphere, defined in institutional and political terms. They see no connection between it and their own lives. This is presumably what led a political scientist recently to conclude, gravely, that it was economically rational for most American voters to make choices based on character. Since they are disinterested in issues, by concentrating on character they maximize their returns from their abbreviated sort of political participation. The scholar, who holds that only 5 percent of our population is in any serious way politically engaged, does suggest that older ideas of citizenship are not merely old, they are obsolescent. His is a philosophical *reductio ad absurdum* of a condition of fact. He derides the political philosophers and those who would improve our polity for their illusions. His are, however, not smaller, notably the belief that things being the way they appear, discussion of change is superfluous. Are matters, however, so flat, so simple?

In generations past, when the Chicago School of Sociology was still an honorable presence, we might have looked to sociology to deal with ordinary lives. The Lynds did so from the perspective of their Protestant criticism of our culture when they visited Middletown. Now we have occasional works that inform us of life in the American depths: Jonathan Rieder's study of Canarsie or Kristin Luker's of the antiabortion move-ment stand for others of their kind. The study of larger processes by many American social scientists, however, has taken them away from this sort of vivid confrontation with daily life. It is a pity that their depiction of larger social processes often wrenches them out of historical context. Matters are not improved when we turn to the obsession with the minutiae of interaction, equally out of context. Briefly, if asked to name the interesting American students of lives, we would have to choose among William Gaddis, Jayne Anne Phillips, and John Updike. The anthropologists, for their part, are either programmatically enun-ciating their vocation or practicing it elsewhere. We are obliged, again, to return to the historians (and sometimes, the biographers drawn from the literary disciplines). They have given us portraits in depth of periods that would otherwise be known by their institutions or their political events.

Withal, the moral ethnography of American social science is bifur-cated. Inquiries like the new studies of women tell us how blocked from access to wider possibilities women were (and are). The idea of auton-omy implicit, and often explicit, in these studies is often little else than a quantitative improvement of market position. The full resources of a middle-class culture are, so runs the complaint, denied to substantial numbers on grounds of gender, race, or the more open forms of economic exploitation. Others argue, however, that our middle class in any case does not know what to do with itself, or is in some other way a diminished prisoner of its advantages. In the best of cases, the question of larger changes are raised. Bellah and his colleagues in *Habits of the Heart* did precisely that, asking whether an active practice of citizenship might make the lives they described more ample. Much of the literature, however, suggests how right Lasch was to anathematize the consumption of self. Even, or above all, the discussion of postmaterialist values treats these as values of consumption, the larger society as an impingement, a source of mistakes to be corrected. Ideas of an alternative polity, of a newer sphere of public space, hardly appear.

It is as if history, as an articulated and visible setting for individual lives, had come to a stop. Immigration and industrialization brought deprivation and misery. The unremitting toil of settlement on the land was accompanied by large perils, natural and social. The horrors of the extirpation of the Indians, and of slavery, were so great that vulgar historiography is devoted to denying these. The students of social movements (Eric Foner, Herbert Gutman, David Montgomery, and Nell Irvin Painter) have joined those studying the republican tradition in a common insistence, if in very different phrases, that for much of American history there was countermovement. A sense of connectedness, and no little hope, was achieved by ordinary Americans who participated in these movements, or who engaged themselves in *res publica*. We experienced these things in the period of the New Deal, and during the decade that began in 1960. There are traces of them, it must be said, in the mobilization of the New Right. (To be sure, there is a difference between the compulsive demand for authority and the drive to replace it.)

Now, largely, the connection has been broken. I use the term in a sense more institutional and tangible, perhaps, than intended by Lifton. His analysis of the isolation of the psyche, the attenuation of symbol, nevertheless is both complementary and very telling. The struggle for social survival, to attain or retain a bit of life space in which personalized goals can be pursued, has replaced deeper and grander visions.

Into the ensuing vacuum have flowed, on the surface, the mechanical—even obsessional—vulgarities of slogans. ("America is back" is an assertion that supplies no hint of where, precisely, we went when we were away. As for "America is number one," we may soon be able to verify that, among the industrial nations, in statistics of infant mortality.) It would be wrong to say that social discourse of this sort is tinny: it is the spiritual equivalent of Styrofoam. More importantly, at the depths we have experienced an increase in moral and psychological disorientation, a deeply rooted rootlessness. A flight into an entirely private sphere is but part of the result. The depiction of society as atomized, of humans as monads, has intrinsic appeal when the larger setting offers so little. The recourse to drugs (for the affluent, as it is not of our urban subproletariat of which I now speak) is one consequence. In other social strata, violent accessions of anxiety over AIDS reflect a pervasive dread. No doubt the anxious have problems with their own sexuality, but more is at work. There is, it appears, no substitute for a sustaining public life.

Most of our cineasts and novelists, in their portrayal of contemporary men and women (and children) have gone, indeed, beyond James Joyce. History, said Stephen Dedalus, is a nightmare from which I am trying to awake. Our antiheroes make little distinction between sleeping and waking. They seem convinced that whatever there is of the good life has to be seized within a very, very bad dream. Our social scientists appear to have gotten the message. They usually eschew the question of what, in our institutions, can change. They assume that history is pervasive, but that whatever meaning it may have is irretrievable. They arrive at a condition of resignation no less profound than that conveyed by art, their means being no less intuitive—if decidedly less compelling aesthetically.

At the beginning of this book, I said that most social scientists may suffer from a (largely unacknowledged) sense of loss. They have lost hope, and their attachment to the idea of progress, and even more to its sources in the Enlightenment, has where it is still faintly evident a conventionalized, indeed an aridly ritualized character. The lack of immediacy and (alas) of intellectual originality in much of social science is a consequence. Our disciplines are sicklied over with the pale cast of stale thoughts. I do not wish to slight the empathic or therapeutic party.

They, too, limit their hopes—to personal changes. To what extent these may only amount to slight rises in a landscape of metahistorical flatness, the future must judge. The institutionalists, for their part, write as if that sort of alteration is none of their business.

The nuclear age and its culture have done their work. So has the downward movement of the world economy (and the business cycle)—and the thieving incompetence of our elites. Cultural and social antagonisms, often unavowed, divide what was once the body politic. It is now something between a corpse and a chronic invalid. History for most Americans is simultaneously incomprehensible in its inner structure and all too clear in its consequences for them. They have depersonalized, as best they can, their experience of it—and yet they recognize in it a destructive potential so immense that everything they value is at risk.

IV

A Social Project

We come to the question that perplexes liberals and radicals alike. The liberals worry about achieving a return to citizenship, to republican virtue. The radicals ask when groups exploited, grossly or subtly, will seek to alter their fate. In the end, the questions are inextricable: who will act for the transformation of society, and under what conditions and with what beliefs and motives?

Two recent influences upon American thought present us, initially, with a paradox. From a decaying liberal society, scholars in the Marxist tradition (or struggling with it), insisted upon the cultural prerequisites of a new politics. Edward P. Thompson and Raymond Williams understood culture as a collective creation. It was certainly not a fixed symbolic system, but a continuously rewrought structure of meaning, produced in ways both obvious and not by the tasks of family, community, and work. The British New Left had begun, after all, by asking what would become of British socialism in an epoch of mass culture and prosperity that had eroded many of the presuppositions of the movement. Eugene Genovese's work on the culture of American slaves owed as much to Thompson as to Du Bois. The Port Huron statement reflected a reading, however diffused, of Williams and of the early *New Left Review.*

From another society that had not (and has not yet) achieved liberalism, there came what we can term a liberalizing influence. It was a sophisticated kind of liberalism, not at all empty of historical and social specificity like the dogmatic liberalism current at the same time. Habermas in his ideas of authority-free communication in effect gave us a sociophilosophical basis for the practice of citizenship. It is striking that his recourse to Dewey's educative ideas reached us just as Richard Bernstein and Richard Rorty were turning to Dewey, too. Once, however, we have decided that there is no direct derivation of political response from social setting, what then? Particularly in a matter as complex as the reinvention of citizenship, we cannot expect to start history anew. In an American society we find so fragmented, even atomized, how are changes to be effected by a public which itself needs to be reinvented?

The answer in recent American thought is to look to our tradition of social movements. It is an interesting and unsteady compound of extrapolation, hope, and nostalgia. Perhaps the mixture is unreliable as well. Movements of the most diverse kind (abolitionism, feminism, populism are but some of them) have been studied in careful, loving, and even obsessive detail. They have been interpreted as forms of articulation for new social groups, modes of expressing new needs for established groups. American social movements have drawn their energy and plausibility from intricate conjunctures of constraint and consciousness. Their natural history, as recounted by our social botanists, is a witting parody of the injunction to let one hundred flowers bloom. It makes a largely unexamined political point. It is that we can expect little of citizenship and the political realm if left to their normal course. The left's social movements may in the end turn out to be just another edition of liberalism's pluralistic politics. As I write, I read a newspaper report of a meeting of the Citizens' Action Coalition (Chicago, August 1987). One of its leaders, the experienced and intelligent Heather Booth, has declared that the coalition seeks to unite those who do not have enough, those who have only enough, and those who, having enough, think of others. She has the right idea. Specific social movements have their limitations. They cannot replace the common denominator of a politics.

True enough, but has not historical creativity in our own society and others come from larger social groupings that provided the political energy and ideological passion for changes? True again, but social movements do not necessarily lead to institutional innovation. An important point about our search, sometimes stereotyped, for historical possibility was made recently by Aristide Zolberg. Perhaps, he declared, the modern German case of a class-conscious working class organized in a social democratic party was exceptional. America might be more nearly like the norm of the Western democracies, with electoral politics encompassing (and blunting) the force of class conflict. In brief, there may be no way in which we can reactivate citizenship by a *deus ex machina* termed a social movement. Even an unimaginably broad and radical American movement, in the near or distant future, will have to reckon with the weight of the society from which it will come and to which it will return.

In our present situation, the intellectual development of a new social project may be possible, but it may take a shape we cannot now, in its general cast and finer structure, say much about. For the moment, the academic division of labor is our resigned response to the fragmentation of society. A broader sort of thought (matters are not made more precise by using the term "discourse") is not encouraged by our setting. We face nothing so crude as penalties for general ideas, even for critical general ideas. It is absurdly shallow to attribute neoconservatism to careerism alone. It is unserious to say that works of synthesis do not appear because of a tacit conspiracy by foundations, publishers, reviewers, and tenure committees. Indeed, we have a plethora of new syntheses, most of which upon examination purvey old ideas.

For many of our most interesting contemporaries, the institutional limits of present intellectual life (conventional or standard language, method, and theme) are quite secondary, almost irrelevant, to their attempts to deal with reality, to gain a purchase upon our world. Why not, then, weigh the several burdens of their separate arguments on the same scale? Our contemporary novels are in the main diminutive in their historical or social ambition (which is not to say that they are uncritical).

USA, The Naked and the Dead, and *Gravity's Rainbow* have been succeeded by Gaddis's new Gothicism and Bellow's recent imitations of Boethius. Is there no narrative history of the present to be drawn from the social sciences—the more so as the word "science" can no longer stand for the conventions of the laboratory: we are all interpreters now. Again, it would be trivial to denounce the (imaginary) tyranny of the disciplines. Those free of academic constraints do as poorly as (if not worse than) those who have to fashion some sort of antagonistic co-existence with them.

Ideally, a large community of thought (not necessarily identical with a community of scholars) would supply meaning, a larger plot for the separate stories of individual scribes. (I first used the word "bards"—that was exaggerated.) A community of this kind is in itself not easy to realize; if we had one, some of our troubles would diminish. The ideal haunts us, and for good reason. For those of us who have not given up the idea of an educated republic, a democracy of citizens for whom politics is more than voting periodically, or responding occasionally to a poll, a community of thought is indispensable. Our universities at present produce intellectual goods for specific clients or markets. Too much of the rest of their activity is turned inward, esotericism unrestrained. We do not have to resort to a notion of free spirits freely assembled to conclude that our present institutions narrow thought. The universities, of course, can hardly be regarded as the sole or privileged repositories of thought. In the most creative periods of American intellectual life, they were sometimes silent, sometimes connected to creative currents outside themselves.

In the past, the existence of a public has encouraged and sustained thought. It is excessively artificial to ask for a renewal of public intellectual life for the sake of renewal. It will come when demand in our society evokes a readiness among our scholars and thinkers to move onto different terrain. By confronting its own temporary blindness or obscured vision, thought may find new terms. A hard look at society's unresponsiveness to work we consider important may touch upon resistances mobilized by avarice, anxiety, and resentment. It may at the same time tell us of impulses, needs, and sensibilities in a condition of troubled latency, of a public waiting to be called into activity.

What, then, must thought confront?

The end of the idea of secular transcendence, the decomposition of the idea of progress, affects us all—from the shallowest of ideologues to the most anguished of theologians. Adorno asked if poetry were possible after Auschwitz. The idea of American imperviousness is untenable, and American naïveté is feigned. The history of the rest of humanity has flowed across our borders. Our despair at our own performance, meanwhile, is founded enough. At the beginning of the American Republic, the ideas of the Enlightenment animated our elites. Certainly, the early idea of civic virtue was connected to notions of human autonomy, of the possibility of progress. The crime of slavery may have reduced the Enlightenment in America to one doctrine among many. It is impossible, at any rate, to ignore the arguments of those (like John Diggins) who see in a stringent Calvinism the source of periodic moral renewal in the early history of our nation. Now much of Calvinism has been reduced to a caricature of its former nobility. The shrunken band of believers in progress still finds that its most reliable allies are to be found in the churches, not least the Roman Catholic one.

What is at issue is less a reversal of alliances than an agreement on matters dealt with rather casually in the past, even the recent past. As a nation, we have not been around for very long. Moreover, because of our bewildering pluralism, our culture may require even more of a substratum of hope than others (certainly not less). The expansion of a sector of the cultural industry, selling plastic hopes at discounted prices, bespeaks some kind of underlying demand. Yet, of whatever degree of sophistication, most contemporaries evince huge discomfort at the idea of historical continuity. Avoidance, falsification, trivialization, mark our encounter with past and future. One of the moral strengths of the scholarly group reexamining the American past is in fact its avowal, however implicit, of hope. The rejection of illusion implies a human capacity to endure truth in the present and to act differently in the future.

A new approach to what nearly a half century ago was called the authoritarian personality will have to include the problem of aborted historical awareness. Modern authoritarianism is not subtle, but it is omnipresent. Its new form is not obeisance to human authority alone, but a reification of the present, a refusal to believe that human institutions could be different. So obsessive is the refusal that challenges to it often produce angrily defensive responses. We may suppose that anxiety about the course of human events is overwhelming to egos reduced in strength. Numbing, resignation before the awful facticity of the world, is a result. Egos (or selves) might be stronger were they engaged in a conflict with reality instead of a flight from it. To the argument that reality is in fact menacing, there is no obvious answer. In any event, we may see how far we have come, or how deeply we have descended. The thinkers who proposed the idea of the authoritarian personality, and those who then developed it, supposed that there was something pathological about humans who did not walk upright. Cringing has now become the norm.

The struggle for an educated citizenry is a struggle against spiritual proletarianization. It assumes a great deal. Humans, in addition to control of their destructive impulses (and also their vicarious satisfaction), on these assumptions are supposed to have a very great potential for rationality. Their capacity to suspend immediate and simple judgment, to set aside ethnocentrism, to experience empathy, would have to be very developed if the present division of cultural labor is to be reversed.

Lawrence Kohlberg thought the normal growth of the personality was a record of moral education. If so, a moral population has somehow been implanted in an immoral society. We have learned something of the consonance and conflict of character and society. It is impossible to believe that a new effort at public education (amounting to nothing less than the reinvention of the public) can succeed without change in the deeper levels of millions of psyches. A century after the psychoanalytic revolution, alas, we have to admit that we know very little about how to achieve these alterations in a larger historical setting. John Dewey's proposals for a democratic pedagogy are almost as old; these, too, are far from realization, and we suffer the same perplexity about advancing them.

American pluralism here has a paradoxically uniform result. Our classes, churches, ethnic groups, regions, and races provide distinctive milieux of character formation. Large groups of Americans live in very different, even conflicting, fragments of history. The peripheries are, in effect, free. Somehow, however, their freedom is connected to a tacit bargain: they do not intrude upon the economic and political center. The center's culture may be described as one of technocratic morosity, the characters of its denizens labile.

Our nation and its parts have hardly been colonized in a spiritual sense. Perhaps segmentation still describes the process. Marcuse's idea of repressive desublimation may not be differentiated enough. It implies more functional purposiveness to the society than it may have. Indeed, the idea of a system is increasingly difficult to sustain across all the spheres of our culture and society. In matters economic and political, it is clear that there is one. Total cultural control from a center is not evident, even in as ostensibly homogenized a nation as our own. But homogenization is not very deep. Our society secretes covert oppositions, dissidences, deviations, and huge variations on supposedly agreed cultural themes. No doubt, were they to be joined in a single movement of opposition, our politics would be different. Since some of these groups think there is far too much opposition already, it is very unlikely that they will make common cause with those who think there is not enough. Even a coalition of the economically deprived is difficult to form when many of those afflicted interpret their distress as evidence of their own failing, while others allow themselves anger at the gross inequalities of socially produced fortune.

No wonder, then, that contemporary social thought has been unsuccessful in depicting society as a whole. Decades ago, Talcott Parsons's structural-functionalism was accepted as a canon of analysis by one faction in the academy. His understanding (or, rather, misunderstanding) of the nature of the social sciences has for all practical purposes not survived. The unreflective empiricists look elsewhere for apologies for their work. There is, perhaps, little to lament in the passing of a need to construct vacuously abstract models of society, the more so as these usually entailed banality and tautology in unholy union. What is disturbing is that depictions of what Sweezy once termed the present as history, ideas of our society in movement (however problematical its inner structure), are so unconvincing.

Political economists do employ a market model to describe society. Some thinkers with moral concerns hold images of power as a force or substance rushing to fill the ethical void of our institutions. Something strained characterizes these depictions of the nation, as if they were designed to circumvent the problems of our social complexity rather than work through them. That is why the recent concentration of intellectual energy on the fate of specific social groups, especially those who did not previously write much about their own histories, is so promising. By indirection and refraction, a new descriptive ethnography of our society may afford us insight into how (however tenuously) the nation works. In the end, we may well have to reintegrate familiar categories (class, gender, race, and religion) in an unfamiliar fashion. Rather than seeing these as segmented or separate aspects of our society, we may come to understand them as a connected series of conflict-laden differences.

That, in one of the more remarkable works of recent history, was the point made by Ann Douglas. In her *Feminization of American Culture*, she insisted that the categories of class and gender served as polar nodes of oppression. Her depiction of an excessively spiritualized or depoliticized religion, of the belief by its ministers that the commercialization of America had denuded them of function, was cast in sexual terms. These men thought of themselves as women. They did so not because of immutable differences between the sexes, or unalterable natural categories. They did so because women had been denied access to power, confined to the home and the sphere of culture, of higher matters—or matters removed, at any rate, from the actual business of society. Douglas held that male pastors and the female public were excluded from active roles in politics because late nineteenth-century capitalism would have been much disturbed by the intrusion of (female) feeling and (pastoral) morality.

It is, however, difficult on Douglas's reading to understand how these supposedly emasculated ministers and servile women could, by the turn of the century, produce the Progressive generation. Crunden in *Ministers of Reform* argued that the secularization of Protestantism brought hitherto damned up energies, often in the most creative ways, to the very center of our culture. The Progressive movement had as an accompaniment, to which the attitude of many Progressive males was ambivalent, the nascent American feminist movement. Our difficulties of understanding may dissolve if we recall Lears's analysis of what he called weightlessness. The culture of consumption and passivity anathematized by Douglas in her description of the mid-nineteenth century had by its end encompassed men as well as women. More recently, Montgomery has argued that male workers in the nineteenth and early twentieth centuries were patriarchal in their thought because they defined themselves as men through their mastery of craft, their assertion of their rights through unions. The homogenization of labor, the decline of unionism, has in effect denuded them of a large source of self-respect.

The Progressives no doubt drew upon a Protestant legacy in their demand for the remoralization of public life. They may also have expressed, in class and in culturally specific idiom, a general human demand for limits upon the spiritual havoc wreaked by the new American market.

The examples remind us of how, by questioning the apparent continuity of our categories, our understanding can be deepened. Let us take two very dissimilar contemporary historians, Lasch and Arthur Schlesinger, Jr. Lasch, in his criticism of spurious doctrines of liberation, certainly does not deny the emancipatory ends of politics. He urges, however, that emancipation cannot result from the personalization of politics, just as autonomous selves cannot be purchased like consumer items in the therapeutic marketplace. By criticizing a spurious radicalism, he allows us to envisage the possibility of a more authentic one. Schlesinger, in arguing against the economic analysis of American imperialism, rivals Mills in his depiction of the imperial American state as denuded of all political reason. It is, he asserts, a construction of military and political elites seeking prepetuation of their power. His liberalism, with its attachment to the sovereignty of citizens rather than that of the state, here proves itself to be far more authentic than mere rhetoric. It provides, again, the possibility of common ground between liberals and radicals in the defense (or, rather, reappropriation) of the tradition of the republic. It is a pity that there are so few authentic conservatives around to join us.

The argument moves in spirals. The early American proclamation of citizenship was irreconcilable with the continuation of slavery. It is also incompatible with the sovereignty of the market. The modern quest for the conditions of the self's coherence and freedom leads back to the idea of citizenship. The conditions of citizenship, however, now are immensely complex, so much so that those who are nominally citizens find it very difficult, at times impossible, to achieve the substance of it.

Whether the spiral is in fact ascending or descending, it is too early to tell.

We do know that American social science has, in large measure, abandoned its earlier search for the conditions of citizenship. The idea of progress in knowledge was its bastard substitute for belief in human progress, a substitution all the more fatuous for its origins in a mistaken conception of science. If we are to reenact, in contemporary terms, the early American belief in a republic of virtue, we shall have to find a new philosophical basis for both social inquiry and politics. That is a matter for further reflection.

A Bibliographical Note

Some thirty-six years ago, I had a conversation with two colleagues at Harvard. One was the late Howard Hugo, who was about to teach a new general education course in the humanities. The other was Morton White. Hugo declared that he was in a quandary: he did not know how to name the course. His alternatives, he thought, were either "Fate, God, and Man in the Western Tradition" or "Divine Transcendence and Earthly Tragedy in Western Thought." White, entirely sympathetic, asked what, more precisely, the course was about. "Plato, Aeschylus, Augustine, Dante, Shakespeare, Racine, Goethe, Dostoyevski, Mann, and Joyce" was the answer. "Then," White suggested, "you could term it, 'Reading I've Liked.'" The advice, sound then, is sound now.

There follow some notes on reading I've liked. I do exclude a category from which I've profited greatly—works of imaginative literature. I was encouraged to do so by reading Daniel Bell's remarks on aesthetics in his *Cultural Contradictions of Capitalism.* Bell's excursus on art and the novel remind us how fortunate we are that neither Geoffrey Hartman nor J. Hillis Miller have favored us with labor-market analysis. Additionally, I have left to a later book a consideration of another genre of imaginative literature, frequently more imaginative than the mere works of art it describes: the entire discussion of what is termed postmodernism. The work I do cite comes from the social sciences, broadly understood. I apologize in advance to colleagues who, upon finding their writing unmentioned, may quite justly feel that they were unjustly omitted. Perhaps I may ask for more understanding of the plight of absentminded professors. This Bibliographical Note is being written after a phase of the House-Senate hearings into the not quite aborted coup d'état constituted by the Iran-contra affair. Surely, if cabinet secretaries, White House officials, and assorted bureaucrats and officers can plead forgetfulness with such persuasiveness, we, too, ought to have the benefit of the doubt.

It is difficult to situate my book in a sequence of general treatments of the social sciences. Some are insufficiently critical and some are, perhaps, overly so—and each is critical or not in a different way. Russell Jacoby's *The Last Intellectuals* has the spirited thrust one expects of the author, but he is wrong to dismiss as academic in the pejorative sense (either pedantic or remote) so much of what our contemporaries are doing. Not everyone is Hegel, and work ostensibly specialized often raises important general questions, not despite, but because of its specific focus. Daniel Bell's *Social Sciences Since the Second World War* at first glance appears to accept the assumptions of social-science official-dom—that there is linear development and cumulation in these disciplines, and that they are indeed separate disciplines.

Bell is simply too educated and intelligent to believe this, and when he indulges his systematic doubts, he raises major questions. Karl Deutsch's *Advances in the Social Sciences, 1900–1980* is a highly articulate defense of the idea of progress in the social sciences, described in terms of a uniform model of natural and social science. The book is so bound to the model that it confounds works of authentic insight with those of obscure conventionality. It reminds us of the typical grant application, which insists that nothing is known of the object of inquiry, and that once the grant has been expended, nothing more will need to be known about it, until, of course, an application for renewal is submitted.

Let us go back to 1939, when Robert Lynd published one of the last New Deal theoretic tracts, *Knowledge for What?*, an argument not for an applied social science, but for a politically critical and accessible one. Lynd's direct descendant, in this sense, was C. Wright Mills with his *Sociological Imagination.* Mills's argument was marked by his idiosyncratic synthesis of the great tradition of European sociology and his American radicalism. It was the hypertrophy of social science, a new scholasticism, that excited his opprobrium. Christopher Lasch, on the contrary, in his *New Radicalism in America* examined the indigenous historical sources of the excessive integration of intellect and power in modern America, and made the case that our difficulties did not begin only in 1945. Noam Chomsky's *American Power and the New Manda-*

rins was a reckoning with the cynical manipulativeness and intellectual shallowness of the academic servants of empire. It showed how right Lasch had been to describe the Kennedy administration as a mixture of café society and Route 128 (the Boston peripheral highway alongside which the new centers of managerial and military research were strewn). Chomsky's *Problems of Knowledge and Freedom* suggests the connection between his (ostensibly arcane) views of language and his politics.

This book is certainly exceedingly close in intention and method to the work of my dear departed friend, Alvin Gouldner. I refer not only to his *Coming Crisis of Western Sociology,* but also to his splendid settlement of accounts with Marxism, *The Two Marxisms.* Meanwhile, Robert Alford and Roger Friedland have attempted to synthesize a large body of recent critical inquiry in a book entitled *Powers of Theory: Capitalism, the State, and Democracy.* The book has the virtue of exemplifying the internationalization of discussion among political economists, political scientists, and sociologists. It also shows, if unintendedly, the limits of an analysis of institutions and politics often arbitrarily separated from historical inquiry.

The authors' conclusion merits attention. "No theory seems to be able to adequately comprehend the conditions under which we might live, and no politics seems able to move toward them. In this desperate sense, theory is powerless." It may be said that the kinds of theory cultivated in many of the inquiries they favor is especially powerless to do so. It is the academic left's version of that scientism which has been the property of the technocrats. Had the authors (and the scholars for whom they speak) moved toward history and philosophy, their conclusions might have been different, their despair tempered.

Finally, David Ricci's *Tragedy of Political Science: Politics, Scholarship, and Democracy* is admirable in its independence of spirit and broad scope.

Much can be learned about the institutional nature of American academic social thought by direct examination of its historical origins. I've found three books by historians indispensable. Burton Bledstein, *The Culture of Professionalism,* sets the development of the separate disciplines in larger currents of American middle-class intellect and policies. Thomas Haskell, *The Emergence of Professional Social Science,* is an invaluable description of the transition from genteel amateurism to rigorous professionalization during the secularization of Protestant-ism. (I read these books many years after studying with Talcott Parsons, and I would have understood him better had I been able to read them beforehand.) Laurence Veysey's *Emergence of the American University* covers not the institutional history of the university alone, but considers its ideological conflicts as well. Finally, I'll take the liberty of mentioning a monograph of mine which anticipated the present text, "Students, Professors and Philosopher Kings," in the volume edited by Carl Kaysen for the Carnegie Commission on Higher Education, *Content and Context.* As for the remarks on the social sciences by Allan Bloom in his *Closing of the American Mind,* they suggest that our colleague is not exhaustively burdened with knowledge of these matters although, of course, he does not hesitate to profess unequivocal opinions about them. It would be elegant if I could continue by taking as a point of reference a classical tradition in social science. After all, I did refer to Mills's attachment to the great tradition of European sociology. Mills's version of that tradition was, however, not that of Parsons. Just where tradition resides, and of precisely what it consists, are in the social sciences matters of argument. T. S. Eliot defined a classic in literature as a work which revises our reading of all that has gone before, which changes the canon. The social sciences have, in fact, no one canon, but several antithetical ones.

What follows, then, is an account of postwar thought that constitutes one canon—a canon of critical political and social inquiry. By critical, I understand a perspective which judges our society by other than its own standards. Critical thought seeks possibilities of positive change, and defines these by the values of the Enlightenment. Where these possibilities are not immediately evident, it does not relapse into re-signed acceptance of the world before us as the only thinkable one. Critical thought, moreover, eschews a model of social knowledge drawn mechanically from the natural sciences. It recognizes the historical na-ture of society (which casts much doubt on the effort to establish invariant laws in social science). It accepts, finally, the connection be-tween social science and philosophy, especially the philosophical tradi-tion of interpretation.

I begin with a European thinker who defied the conventional categories. Hannah Arendt's *On Revolution* records her encounter with the tradition of civic virtue developed in the earliest years of our republic.

It is impossible to reread her exposition of the difference between market and polis without being reminded of the curious complacency of Saul Bellow's response to Günter Grass at the 1986 PEN Congress in New York. Bellow, it will be recalled, derided foreigners who did not understand that, for Americans, virtue resided precisely in our pursuit of material goods: did he ever listen to his former University of Chicago colleague?

I continue with Theodor W. Adorno, Max Horkheimer, Elsa Frenkel-Brunswick, Daniel Levinson, and R. Nevitt Sanford, whose *Authoritarian Personality* transposed an earlier analysis of German authoritarianism to American public life. The work, equally, brought the perspectives of the Frankfurt School and of a politically engaged use of psychoanalysis directly to empirical social research. It did so, moreover, at a time when eminent European figures like Paul Lazarsfeld were at pains to depoliticize their own work.

In *Monopoly Capital*, Paul Baran and Paul Sweezy revised the treatment of Marxist political economy developed by Sweezy in his *Theory of Capitalist Development*. It was a revision that took account of the postwar successes (however temporary they may prove in the long run, in the short run they were decisive) of welfare-state capitalism and Keynesian expansionism. The authors also dealt in their own way with what Gramsci had termed "Fordism" (mass consumption) and with the American imperial state. Baran and Sweezy gave Marxist political economy new life at a time when in the analysis of culture and social structure the newer Marxist analyses of ideology, more complex notions of interaction between economy and society, were gaining ground.

The period 1945 through 1970, in constitutional theory and jurisprudence, was singular by comparison with other fields. These disciplines had outstanding thinkers who, if critical of the assumptions and work of their colleagues, did address a larger public receptive to radical social thought. In legal studies, there seemed to be a long interval between the generation of the realists, who wrote in the period up to 1945, and the younger critics who began to write after 1970. The one exception is an ambiguous one. Alexander Bickel, in *The Least Dangerous Branch*, insisted on the necessity of political sensitivity by the judiciary, while warning against too much of what is crudely termed activism. A politically sensitive judiciary, however, is hardly one abdicating before politics: it is one that relies on its political judgment. Later the Critical Legal Studies movement, took Bickel seriously: it asked for a different sort of sensitivity.

From a standpoint that could not be more authentically rooted in native soil, the long experience of movements for black emancipation, Harold Cruse gave us a major work, *The Crisis of the Negro Intellectual.* The book did more than analyze the limited success of black emancipatory movements in our country. By comparing the role of the black intellectuals to that of other cultural elites, it told us much about the general relationship of thought to power in America.

Erik Erikson's *Childhood and Society* took the inheritance of ego psychology (and behind that of the sort of character analysis developed by Wilhelm Reich) and combined it with the work of American anthropologists like Margaret Mead and Edward Sapir. Erikson also profited, if discreetly, from his own earlier exposure to socialism in its Austro-Marxist version and his own participation in the German youth movement. He adapted his experiences to America but did not deny them. Rather like Arendt, he sought continuity in discontinuity and could so retained his creativity.

Franklin Frazier published his *Black Bourgeoisie* first in France. His depiction of the well-situated blacks as both agents of social control for the white majority and potential leaders of voices of renewed black militancy was an entirely accurate anticipation of what was about to occur in the civil-rights movement.

John Kenneth Galbraith's *Affluent Society* seems to me to be a more important book than his subsequent *New Industrial State. The Affluent Society,* published as the Eisenhower years were wearing down, no doubt could be dismissed as a liberal call to repair the (temporarily) defective mechanisms of a managed economy rather than as a radical critique of capitalist society. I recall a conversation with Marcuse at the time in which he insisted on the book's limitations in these terms. Perhaps—but Galbraith's own Calvinist honesty made his brief for repairs a moral indictment. It induced in younger liberals a readiness to consider a more profound criticism of our society—a criticism that was to crystallize, politically, but half a decade later. *The New Industrial State*, for all the lucidity of its formulations, brought to a larger reading public matters not new to readers of Berle and Means, Schumpeter and Weber.

Herbert Marcuse's *Eros and Civilization* strikes me as the critical masterpiece of the Frankfurt School. It had to be written in an America awash (or partially so) in affluence. Marcuse took seriously the enormous development of production under late capitalism and asked what changes in superstructure these would allow. The idea of surplus repression has several dimensions. One, to be sure, entailed instinctual freedoms in the sphere of personal life—freedoms that could be expressed through what Lasch was later to term the consumption of self, and which would leave many structures of domination and exploitation intact. This notion led Marcuse to the idea of repressive desublimation. Another possibility, however, was a profound change in human nature itself, opening the way for a conscious effort by these new humans to alter history. Marcuse remained enough of a historicist to conceive of the process as one of exquisite complexity, with the self-development of freer humans making possible new institutions, and these in turn encouraging alterations in the psyche.

C. Wright Mills, dismissed by the pygmies above whom he towered as a populistic simplifier, was no such thing. He was far more literate, and far more at home in America, than most of his detractors. His project, of which *White Collar* and *The Power Elite* were but two components, sought to find new social protagonists, and new ideas, for a revival of American democracy. As James Miller has just argued, the Port Huron Statement is not the least of his gifts to us. James Miller's *Democracy Is in the Streets* documents the large intellectual indebtedness of the early New Left to the thinkers of the preceding decade.

Mills's rival for the attention of the public was not Parsons, but David Riesman. Riesman's work was saturated with ambiguity. A lawyer, he seemed to enjoy writing briefs for a hypothetical client (the American middle class) who, if he read them carefully, might well wonder whether he was facing not one but two prosecuting attorneys, one disguised as his counsel. It was not surprising that he became an early spiritual patron of the protest movement of the decade beginning with 1960: he could, not without reason, argue that he had been protesting all along, if only his readers had noticed. His essay "The American Crisis" (with Michael

Maccoby) in *Commentary* in 1960 (along with Norman Podhoretz's first editorial) was a challenge to the comfortably limited reformism of the late Eisenhower years—a challenge the Kennedyites were careful to ignore. "Other directedness," for Riesman, in the end was systematically devoid of the benign content his enthusiastic readers initially found in it. Rather, it was an expression of that loss of civic sense, the fragmentation (and obliteration) of the moral imagination, he so deplored in America. Like Mills, he looked—if despairingly—for a revival of our sense of freedom. The autonomous characters he hoped would emerge from the new prosperity would have to win autonomy from social institutions pervaded by bureaucratization and its ideological derivative, technocratic conformity. His elegant iconoclasm in the end won him far fewer friends than he was entitled to—but perhaps he took that as evidence that he was not entirely wrong.

Henry Nash Smith, meanwhile, in *Virgin Land* took a sympathetic distance from the Turner thesis on the frontier. His analysis connected myth and symbol to economic constraint and political power, and gave us an American example of history in depth before more than a handful of scholars began to read *Annales*. He also continued the work of the Americanist generation led by Perry Miller and F. O. Matthiessen and served as an exemplar to so many in the third generation who have made of American studies (with American history) our most rewarding contemporary field.

William Appleman Williams in two major works gave answers to the curious mixture of liberal piety and democratic despair found in both Hartz and Hofstadter. He also challenged the moralizing apologists of empire, from Reinhold Niebuhr to the diplomatic historians and their impoverished intellectual cousins, the professors of international relations. His *Contours of American History* was not a repetition of Progressivist schema. Williams saw no people in perpetual combat with oligarchs since he thought that our democracy had been gradually denuded of substance. His *Tragedy of American Diplomacy* refused reigning notions like the identification of an isolationist strain in our modern history: Williams showed that isolationism was also anti-imperialism by another name. Above all, he offered an alternative definition of national interest—and provided an intellectual basis for what was to become the peace movement, a basis which went far beyond dissent and opposition to another vision of our role in what could become, but most definitely is not yet, a community of nations.

Sheldon Wolin's *Politics and Vision* was a reinterpretation of the history of political thought with a major contemporary point—indeed, with several. Wolin meant by political thought our vision of community and society, and so refused to split the human world into lands of fact and oceans of value. By insisting on the connection between political philosophy and social science, he denied conceptual arbitrariness to philosophy and stripped social science of its systematic amorality. He also (not the least of his achievements) dealt with the intellectual and political defects of what was termed methodological individualism and of the insistence that there were two and only two kinds of liberty (negative and positive). Wolin, then, brought political thought back to life from the darkness to which it had been consigned by those imitating the natural sciences and by those who supposed that the last word in history had been spoken in the Oxford English of one narrowed version of liberalism.

The scholars whose work I have described have given us a considerable legacy. What use have we made of it? I turn to the work of those who in a large sense were this generation's students, and also to our own successors. I acknowledge that the use of the idea of generation in this note is imprecise. Chomsky and Wolin took their degrees after the war and are contemporaries of many whose names follow, but whom they did influence. Hartz and Hofstadter, let it be said, were not appreciably older. There follow notes on a number of thinkers, and on work that in fields like American studies or feminist studies constitutes significant scholarly groupings.

Robert Bellah (who worked on Japan and Islam before turning his attention to the United States) is a sociologist versed in church history and theology, a social theorist who insists that there is nothing by that name which can be separated from moral and political philosophy. Beginning with *Beyond Belief* and continuing with *The Broken Covenant,* he has argued that secularization is no unilinear process, that current arguments over values (or ideologies) draw their substance from religious convictions far from extinguished, if altered by the conditions under which we must live. In *Habits of the Heart,* he and his collaborators examined the present vacuum at the center of the spiritual existence of the American middle class, and ascribe it to the pervasive depoliticization of our nation.

Richard Bernstein's work is exemplary in two respects. He has connected European argument to an American tradition of social thought (returning the compliment paid us by no less a figure than Jürgen Habermas, whose own encounter with Charles Peirce and our tradition has been decisive for his struggle to integrate the German Federal Republic in the West in terms other than those set forth by NATO's military command). He has, equally, refused a reduction of philosophy to the analysis of language or worshipful commentary on the work of natural scientists. In providing a synthetic view of the inseparability of content and method in the human sciences, he has contributed to their present rapprochement and possible reunification. *The Restructuring of Social and Political Theory* and *Beyond Objectivism and Relativism* provide evidence that the inquiries of John Dewey retain their model functions.

(We may say the same of Richard Rorty, who indeed argues that the work of Dewey and William James constitutes an American contribution to Western thought as important as anything that has come from the Europeans. In his *Philosophy and the Mirror of Nature* and his essays, *Consequences of Pragmatism,* Rorty continues the demystification of the natural sciences begun by Kuhn. His value for social scientists is hardly limited to that. He, like Bernstein and Geertz, enables us to situate ourselves in the larger cultural field. He makes sense of the cultural pluralism so desperately resisted by the defenders of traditions whose historical and intellectual foundations have collapsed.)

Walter Dean Burnham is, formally, a political scientist. He is scientist enough, in one use of the term, to employ quantitative methods. His work on American elections and parties, however, is at once historical (which is to say, causal and sequential) and political (he is engaged in a search for the conditions of citizenship). His most recent work, *The Current Crisis in American Politics,* extends the analysis of *Critical Elections and the Mainsprings of American Politics* by showing which of the springs has dried up—the one that's supposed to give us a representative democracy.

Clifford Geertz is an Islamist who has worked in Morocco and Indonesia. More important, he has used these inquiries to develop general notions of cultural structures—and an acute appreciation of the limits of the present interpenetration of cultures. In *The Interpretation of Culture,* he widened the scope of anthropology. In his essays, it moved forward (or back) to the status of a general theory of social nature and its symbolic dimensions. In *Local Knowledge,* Geertz—*inter alia* in a skeptical approach to the universality of law—gives us an anti-imperialist manifesto in the guise of a global ethnography. If knowledge is local in the sense that it must rest on the specificity of the group under examination—a certain kind of generalization is, in effect, an attempt to obliterate that specificity. No more telling obituary for the theory of modernization could be written.

The revival of a radical political economy will be viewed eventually as a far more significant aspect of recent decades than the obsessive iteration of old ideas by new apologists. David Gordon is so central a figure in this revival that his name figures on two of its major works. With Samuel Bowles and Thomas Weisskopf, he wrote *Beyond the Waste Land.* The introduction of the concept of waste into economic analysis breaks with the curious view that it is more scientific to adhere to a flat scale of quantitative measurement. In another book, *Segmented Work, Divided Workers,* he and his coauthors Richard Edwards and Michael Reich provide us with an analytical and historical depiction of the economic dimensions, particularly with respect to the organization of the labor force, of what is usually termed American exceptionalism.

Occasionally, one work illuminates new terrain—more accurately, creates new land. Carol Gilligan's *In A Different Voice* ought not to be categorized as an achievement of feminist scholarship alone. It is an achievement of social science as a whole, if one made possible by a feminist perspective. Gilligan argues that women do feel, and above all, act and think in a different voice, one which reflects their capacity to take the standpoint of the other. For years male philosophers have been ruminating about communication and its preconditions. Gilligan has shown how role-related these are. In a society rent by conflict, it is reassuring that slightly more than half the population may be qualified to exercise a decent minimum of sociability. Gilligan's work promises, by implication, considerable changes in our public life when more women enter it. Barbara Ehrenreich, in *The Hearts of Men,* suggests that in the recent past, the avatars of feminist protest on behalf of more empathic and solidary values were in fact men repelled by the demands made upon them by bureaucratic, corporate, or professional existence. Ehrenreich's argument is reminiscent of that of Lears, and the entire sequence connects with the rather aseptic discussion of postmaterialism in a very different kind of writing. We may also remind ourselves that Gilligan reverses Ann Douglas's depiction of the relegation of empathy and solidarity to a feminine sphere—by removing the negative value put upon the sphere by society. We could also say that this is a case of an older psychic world come to redeem a newer one utterly deracinated or, at least, distorted.

Whatever the specific argument about the nature of femininity and the historical forms this has taken, particular achievements like Gilligan's do rest upon the work of a greatly enlarged number of colleagues concerned with these issues. What is at stake is a great deal more than questions of the female segment of human nature, or women's roles in history. Our general conceptions require revision when feminist scholarship is taken seriously. Nothing, of course, is as disturbing to many of our colleagues as the demand, implicit if not explicit, that they consider that there are more things under heaven and earth than they dreamed of in graduate school: the resistance to feminist thought is a pure instance of the inextricable union of fear of loss of privilege and sloth. Studies of women, clearly, are too important to be left to the social sciences, if these are conceived in the usual disciplinary terms. Contributions from history, literature, and psychology in fact erase the usual boundaries. Not the least of the justifications for women's studies as an institutionalized field is that it enables us to appreciate the limitations of the separate disciplines when these have to deal with new (and continuously changing) objects of inquiry. Jane Gallop on feminine psychology, Sandra Gilbert and Susan Gubar on characterizations of women in literature, and Phyllis Rose on the politics of marriage can hardly be ascribed to specific disciplines. Indeed, the issue is supremely unimportant. What counts is that the new (or relatively new) object, once in place, alters our map of society, our notion of psyche.

On the literature of autobiography, confession, and memoir produced by the New York intellectuals, I am reminded of an anecdote about Isaac Bashevis Singer. At a gathering of Nobel laureates, he listened to a talk by the physicist Steven Weinberg on the first three minutes of the universe. The scientists in attendance responded, until Singer rose to ask, "Professor Weinberg, how can you be so sure that you know what happened in the first three minutes of the universe, when my wife and I never agree on who said what to whom last night?" The memories of the group's survivors increase in contentiousness as their collective past recedes.

Of the autobiographies, Irving Howe's *Margin of Hope* and Alfred Kazin's *New York Jew* demonstrate (if demonstration is needed) their large qualities of character and insight. William Phillips's *Partisan View* is valuable testimony by a major participant. Norman Podhoretz merits our appreciation for his portrait of both milieu and self in *Making It.* One understands why Lionel Trilling urged him not to publish the book. Trilling admired ambition in the personages he found in the pages of Lytton Strachey. It is a pity that he should have found it so disturbing in a student of his own from Brooklyn.

Of the books about the group, the most interesting are one of the first, James Gilbert's *Writers and Partisans,* and an excellent recent one, Alan Wald's *New York Intellectuals.* Mark Schechner's *After the Revolution* can be read with profit along with Mark Krupnick's *Lionel Trilling and the Fate of Cultural Criticism.*

William Barrett's *Truants* is a charming and well-written personal record, but its major point is absurd. Why does he think that the New York intellectuals, at the height of their struggle with our culture, were fleeing reality—whatever that may be? Barrett himself as a young man living in the Village and writing on existentialism was surely not less real than he is as an older professor commuting to Westchester and lamenting our declining standards. As for Barrett's colleagues on and around *Partisan Review,* would William Phillips and Dwight Macdonald have been appreciably closer to reality had they gone, respectively, into the garment industry and Wall Street? Certainly, the ensuing increment to the gross national product would not have been very great. Come to think of it, Macdonald was in Wall Street as a journalist on *Fortune.* That is why he became a radical. One recent source on the New York intellectuals has been ignored: Hannah Arendt in her correspondence with Karl Jaspers displayed brilliant gifts of portraiture as well as an acute sense of the historical constraints upon her new friends, so different from those she knew in the Europe that haunted her (and which, in a different way, haunted the New Yorkers, too).

Interpretations of American history have had to confront a major difference from the European societies. We lack, as a major component of the national experience, a socialist tradition—and its essential component, a class-conscious labor movement. Upon reflection, the supposed intellectual sovereignty of individualism is an insufficient explanation of the uniqueness of our experience. From Congregationalism to Catholicism, from Jacksonism to Populism, from the American socialist movement itself to the social movements that animated the New Deal, our nation does not lack a tradition of collective action. If we have been subjected, recently, to an organized attempt to obliterate the complexity of our past, we also possess, thanks to the determination of scholars who bowed their heads over books and not before power, a newer and more ample vision of it.

So ample is the vision, indeed, that the stereotyped assertion with which I began the paragraph above requires correction. Whatever the vicissitudes of the socialist tradition in America, it has had an important role in twentieth-century history. The present constriction of the labor movement is evident. Nevertheless, we did have class-conscious and combative unions for long periods of time. A renewed effort to understand our history as a whole will now have to take account of the work of a group of labor historians whose thought can hardly be circumscribed by the phrase "labor history." They deal with the organization of local communities, kinship ties, and solidarity within the workplace. They consider the general development of the economy, the impact of expansion and contraction, and the interconnection of market and policy. In effect, they use the experience of workers as a beginning point for a reconsideration of our history in its entirety.

A number of names come to mind in this area, and any number of texts. We do well, however, to begin with the late Herbert Gutman, whose *Work, Culture, and Society in Industrializing America* gave voice to much of what had been accomplished, and impetus to what followed. Gutman's strength resided in his refusing a narrow conception of labor history: the title of his collection of essays attests the equal weight he attached to the several dimensions of the problem of work, workers, and society. Everyday settings, cultural traditions and their continuities and discontinuities (especially in the lives of immigrants and domestic migrants), and the refraction of class conflict in politics and the state constitute for Gutman not separate realms, but elements united, in singular ways in singular situations. Like his colleagues Eric Foner and David Montgomery, he employs a narrative form and fills it with analytic content. Foner's *Free Soil, Free Labor, Free Men* and David Montgomery's recent *Fall of the House of Labor* demonstrate, if demonstration were needed, the identity of labor history with the rest of the inquiry into our social antecedents. Themes of citizenship, participation, and solidarity are juxtaposed with the problems of ethnicity, race, and religion. Our labor historians have shown that the homogenizing process entailed by industrial capitalism was strongly, even fiercely, resisted by successive generations of workers who voiced a republican rhetoric. Their work on the past raises questions about the future that contemporary studies of labor do not often evoke. If past generations of workers interpreted their conflicts with capital as the expression in the labor market of their political rights, an American version of socialism can hardly be deemed eccentric to national tradition. At the least, we are led to inquire into the pervasive segmentation that resulted in a unionism restricted in its politics as the twentieth century wore on.

In any event, we can say that the newer labor history is not written—in the conventional phrase—from the bottom up. It is, rather, a strikingly new version of what is central in our history.

There are some thinkers whose merits lie in the persistence with which they raise issues thought relegated to the past, not least because in doing so, they bespeak intellectual and moral continuities we would be poorer without. By narrowly academic criteria, Michael Harrington fits into no conventional category. Is he a political economist or philosopher, a historian of social movements or a student of contemporary politics, an Americanist or a Europeanist? The answer, of course, is that he is all of these—and analyst and moralist, too.

His *Other America* served by altering awareness as a beginning point for much of the Great Society program. In refusing to depart from socialism (when to have done so might well have opened the way for a different kind of public career) he contributed largely to the renewal of an important American tradition. Harrington has also, by virtue of his work in the Socialist International, brought European thought to America and has taken ours there, if in a rhetoric somewhat different, than, shall we say, the contributors to *Telos*. His *Socialism* and his account of his own work, *Child of the Century*, also suggest that he has another function. Since no one is ever really an ex-Catholic, any more than one is a former Jew, Harrington has also brought to the center of attention of many who would otherwise not quite see it a Catholic contribution to critical American social thought. At any rate, his work inside and outside universities suggests that what Russell Jacoby has termed the public intellectual is still with us.

Another public intellectual is Christopher Lasch. What makes his work so distinctive is his capacity to unite several separate intellectual currents in a single enterprise. He is historian enough to be able to use the past and insist on the uniqueness of the changes we confront in the present. He is Americanist enough to draw upon the crowded and sometimes creative area of American studies for new perspectives on our culture and society. He is attuned to work in psychology, especially psychoanalysis, and so can sense the historical and social point about otherwise abstruse discussions of the theory of character. Lasch is closer to academic work, despite his obvious (and justified) skepticism about much, than is, for instance, John Kenneth Galbraith. We can say that Galbraith brought the demands of the polity, or of the citizenry, to a field (political economy) intellectually resistant to broader thought. Lasch brings to a segment of the educated public matter possibly arcane in its original form, but reworked by himself to touch on common concerns. For his pains, he has been denounced as voicing public prejudice, whereas, in fact, he has been insisting on the continuity between public distress and academic preoccupation.

The Critical Legal Studies group has been discussed in the text. Its indignant critics on law school faculties seem devoid of a historical sense: the group, after all, can claim descent (and even legitimation) from the project we now honor as Legal Realism. The group works in several idioms, some of them contradictory. Some of its members (like David Trubek) owe much to the social-scientific study of law. Others took encouragement and ideas, at least, from the work of legal historians in recent decades (from Willard Hurst to Morton Horwitz). Still others (Duncan Kennedy) tried to revivify jurisprudence by prolonged journeys into territories no American legal scholar had trod since, let us say, Oliver Wendell Holmes: the more arcane regions of European thought. The weightiest of contributions come from two scholars whose intellectual connections to work in social thought and history make their work accessible (and persuasive) to larger publics. Roberto Unger is a social philosopher or social theorist (the distinction is increasingly unclear) who uses law as evidence for general reflection on society and its changes. Mark Tushnet is both a constitutional scholar and a legal historian who uses social thought to examine the workings of our legal institutions. His *Red, White, and Blue* can be used as a summary of the work of the entire group. It is, however, primarily a distinctive contribution to the understanding of our politics and society in their entirety. As always with a serious intellectual movement, boundaries and questions of membership are less important than affinities of purpose, rhetoric, and substance. Neither Abram Chayes nor Frank Michelman can be reckoned members of the group. Their work, on new dimensions of public-law litigation and on the reinvention or recapture of our republican tradition, respectively, extends the liberal jurisprudence of the reformist sector of the Democratic Party in radical ways—especially when we mean, by radical, profound.

The field of American studies presents the happiest of problems, an embarrassment of riches. What might have been causes of weakness, the very fluidity of its boundaries and the changing nature of its objects of inquiry and themes, are in fact its strengths. Once a somewhat uneasy alliance of American historians and students of American literature, it is now open to theoretic novelty (perhaps too much so) and substantive influence from the most diverse sources. Withal, it has retained a continuity of purpose. When, in 1987, Sacvan Bercovitch edited a volume entitled *Reconstructing American Literary History,* he dedicated it to his predecessors, F. O. Matthiessen and Perry Miller. Theirs was an effort to understand the specificity of American culture in the light of its European descent. Fortunately, the newest generation of Americanists is not so enamored of empire that they measure Europe with American eyes. (Some who do so, it has to be said, may be described as equally wanting in their knowledge of both continents.) A continuity of question has been kept. A senior thinker in the area, Leo Marx, serves to connect scholarly generations in ways not always available to colleagues in other disciplines. His *Machine in the Garden* brought the analysis of the frontier to the threshold of the new environmental movement. His most recent set of essays, *The Pilot and the Passenger: Essays on Literature, Technology, and Culture in the United States,* gives content and definition to the often arid and sometimes apologetic discussion of what is sometimes termed a postindustrial society.

Jackson Lears's *No Place of Grace* exemplifies the vitality of American studies. He employs historical reflection on the development of the psyche, but purifies the usual discussion of alienation of its tedious scholasticism. He draws upon a good deal of work on the consolidation of corporate capitalism in our nation and does so with precision and subtlety, making of the omnipresence of the market not an empty abstraction but a complex and contradictory institutional process, a felt human reality. His remarkable sketch of the origins of the modern malaise (which he terms weightlessness, presumably in ironic comment on the pseudo-triumphs of a later technology) locates our experience by showing how continuous it is in its stuff with the European one, how discontinuous in its rhetoric—and social issue.

The work of Robert Lifton has been discussed in the text. A student of Erikson in a larger sense, he has continued the tradition of cultural and historical reflection in psychoanalytic psychology. The integration of psychoanalysis with psychiatry after 1945 resulted in a discernible narrowing of focus. (Russell Jacoby has discussed this in his *Repression of Psychoanalysis.*) It is interesting that much of the interdisciplinary discussion after the war resembled nothing so much as diplomatic negotiations on boundaries or trade treaties. A medicalized psychoanalysis and a consensualized social science united in their insistence that the normal color of human existence was gray. The origins of official ego psychology in the work of that later heretic, Wilhelm Reich, was discreetly ignored. An earlier period of interest in psychoanalysis among social scientists (as with Margaret Mead) was characterized by an interest in the possibilities of characterological change. It would be a caricature to say that the postwar years were more exclusively concerned with the adaptation of characters with fixed structures to the defined tasks of the society we saw around us. Enough of the caricature is true, however, to make us uneasy. No wonder that Marcuse's work so shocked anthropologists, psychoanalysts, and sociologists that they paid it deferential rhetorical respect, and then displayed a convincing inability to deal with it. Norman Brown's *Life Against Death* per contra, was acclaimed—precisely, one suspects, because of his decided deformation of Freud, his rejection of his pedagogic and political aims.

An entire spectrum of psychoanalytic thinkers, of course, deals with the larger issues of culture and history. It is striking how few of them are psychiatrists. Lifton, to be sure, has been joined by medical colleagues like Joel Kovel. Still, historians (and literary scholars) have recently been more likely to be proponents of the extension of psychoanalysis to the context of the psyche. Peter Gay has, like Schorske, situated the psychoanalytic movement in its immediate setting. Steven Marcus, finally, has taken a problem found in the consulting room (a pattern of disorder involving the diffusion of the sense of self, a pervasive absence of psychic definition, as loss of relatedness) and suggested that these alterations in symptomatology may eventually require changes in psychoanalytic theory, changes not quite yet offered us by the analysts themselves.

At some point, a clinical theory may give rise to a revision of psychoanalysis whose dimensions we can only dimly see. However, what we know of the early history of the exceedingly complex relationship of clinical experience, scientific legacy, and cultural perplexity in Freud's own thought renders the probability of so linear a progression small. It is more likely that a new ordering of our view of the unconscious will come from therapeutic demands we do not imagine we can utter—not a new sobriety, or an older resignation clothed as wisdom, but a new sense of possibility. For the moment, our historical awareness and our refusal to abandon a minimum of social criticism combine to make us skeptical of both received notions of psychic inevitability and views that culture is always open. Nowhere is the character of our period as a prolonged cultural and political interregnum more evident. The stridency of those who insist that they hold the keys to portals leading to new realms of felicity, the bitterness of those who hold that the very hope of change is a dangerous illusion, bespeak a brittleness which suggests that some sort of major break lies ahead: we quite literally do not know where to look.

I come to sociology, which has less of a claim to be thought a discipline than the other social sciences, as disjointed or synthetic as these may be. Sociology is a term for widely disparate and even antithetical pursuits. One major end of sociology has been the promulgation of universal laws covering the development and functioning of entire societies—universal in that these laws would hold despite all the accidents and fatalities of history. No one in American sociology has had anything to say on this theme, since 1945, that was not already said (with more depth and nuance) by Weber. Often, in piously repeating dogma from the positivist philosophers of science, the proponents of a scientific sociology seem to go back not to Weber, but to Condorcet (of whom not many have heard and fewer will have read). Thomas Kuhn's work introduces some clarity into the discussion, even if Kuhn himself is skeptical that the social sciences can be inserted in the framework of his thought.

The tiresome reiteration of methodological injunction or the tireless adumbration of categorical schemes are not authentic substitutes for the construction of a science. We can now understand the work of Talcott Parsons, whatever his own intentions, as an aspect of ideological conflict in the period 1945–60. I am aware that he was indefatigable in denying just this.

Another, and perhaps the predominant, end of sociology has been the depiction of the inner movement of a specific historical formation, which we may term either capitalism or industrial society. In America economists like Veblen, historians like Charles Beard, jurists like Roscoe Pound, and philosophers like John Dewey have been more successful at portraying the larger processes of our society than sociologists. That much said, it is certainly true that sociologists have done a large amount of interesting work in the past forty years on American social structure. C. Wright Mills and his successor, Alvin Gouldner, have been discussed. It is curious that when we turn to the theme which condenses much of our understanding of American society, social class, nothing in the form of a commanding new synthesis comes immediately to mind. The inquiries of Digby Baltzell, William Domhoff, Richard Hamilton, Seymour Martin Lipset, and Erik Olin Wright are indispensable, but they seem, at once, very familiar and (despite differences of emphasis) almost interchangeable. The one general view that requires attention is by a Briton, Anthony Giddens, whose treatment of class across the borders of the industrial societies reminds us of Raymond Aron's a generation ago.

Class, it seems, has hardly disappeared or diminished in significance, but precisely what its significance may be and where its boundaries lie are matters of secondary perplexity rather than of fundamental debate.

Daniel Bell, in his portrayal of a postindustrial society, clearly intended to lead us out of bondage to gods not strange but all too familiar: to idolized derivatives of Marxist belief. A reading of his texts suggests that he hardly holds that a postindustrial society is free of classes, conflicts, property, and concentrations of power. These elements, rather, are organized in ways different than in the first half of our century. In his most recent account of the matter, he reverts to an earlier rhetoric. The cultural contradictions of capitalism (by which he means the ideological discontinuities and disjunctions it generates even in an ostensibly postideological age) all bear a family likeness to what was once termed alienation. In the English Revolution, ecclesiastical radicals mocked the reappearance of hierarchy: "New presbyter is but old priest writ large." Is postindustrial society a new social formation, or does it embody the intensification of tendencies already evident much earlier in the century, if not even before? Bell insists that knowledge is the essential instrument of power in our society. Is it, however, the possession of knowledge—or the command of it? The knowledge of which he writes is not that of Greek texts. It is not the moral reflectiveness, the supposed departure of which from our existence he deplores, in suitably lachrymose terms. It is knowledge which lends itself readily to administrative, economic, or political exploitation. Those who know have to work, usually, for those with power and wealth. The scientific and technical component of the labor force has greatly expanded. Some recruited from it have climbed to the lesser ranks of our ruling elites. Domination, exploitation, and hierarchy remain. Bell is too skeptical of the possibility of an educated democracy to argue for alternative institutions. He is too honest to propagate a doctrine of institutional pluralism. Finally, he offers us rather little: complaint about the unmanageable scale of modern society, the assurance that our experience is so fragmented that we cannot grasp it in its entirety. Unenthusiastic about deconstruction in literature and philosophy, his implicit conclusion in sociology is that the best interpretation of society is no interpretation. For his part, the role of sober scribe will do, as long as an appreciative public recognizes the moral force of his sobriety. In fact, Bell remains a prophet, if an antiprophetic one. The new postindustrial society, in the end, is but old capitalism writ on a word processor.

Most sociologists acknowledge that with the internationalization of the economy, national borders no longer demarcate self-contained societies. Most, too, think that class conflict and politics are often fused, that analytical distinctions between political and social institutions are excessively abstract. Finally, however reluctantly, many will recognize that process and structure are one. Put in another way, they cannot defend a sociology that transcends the stuff of history. Having subscribed to so much in theory, a good many sociologists proceed to deny it in practice: their work gives little evidence that they have really learned these ideas. Immanuel Wallerstein, however, takes these precepts seriously. He should, as he has been their most articulate and successful proponent.

If his work on the modern world system were a sustained treatise on the internationalization of class conflict, it would have merit enough. It is more—an effort to develop new categories of analysis that would enable us to rethink the legacy of sociological analysis. Core and periphery are rather different, as concepts, from metropolis and province: the newer ideas enable us to situate the older ones—more precisely, to deepen and enlarge their historical referents. Like many of our contemporaries, Wallerstein's point of departure is the limited achievement of the Western socialist movement. His search for explanations takes us very far beyond the usual excursuses on imperialism, labor aristocracies, and the counterpolitics of capitalism. It connects in one way with the work of historians like Hobsbawm (who, with Wallerstein, may be understood as an ally of Braudel). It connects, equally, with questions raised by Arendt in her *Origins of Totalitarianism* (the analysis of colonialism) if we interpret her as a radical critic of Western society.

Wallerstein did write on the protest movement of two decades ago, and on the university revolt. At first reading, it is difficult to connect his work with the confused immediacy of our own national history. A bit more thought suggests its use. If American history is to be treated as part of the history of a world system, we cannot settle for anodyne accounts of immigration, or the international aspects of our economic growth. The American frontier, as part of a world system, assumes a significance that makes our history seem somewhat less exceptional, and at once more European and more tragic. Here Wallerstein's work touches on themes recently salient in American studies. Slotkin's *Fatal Environment* is a superb synthesis of the history of class conflict in America with the problems of continental expansion, racism, and the specificity of our ideology. It is with work like his that ideas of a Western society take content, if not the content read into it by the chroniclers of a supposed ascent of liberalism. American studies, begun by scholars who were part of the movement of social criticism of the first third of the century, have come back to Perry Miller's intentions.

These were not to depict an America free of domination and exploitation, a nation which had expunged old Europe from its new being. Miller, rather, sought to uncover the European origins of American culture and society. He invariably recurred to the continuity of our experience with that of the Europeans. The articulation of the idea of a world system makes some of the structural connections at issue manifest, and so frees our historians of culture to concentrate on the analysis, rather than the fabrication, of American myth.

Bibliography

Aaron, Daniel. *Writers on the Left: Episodes in American Literary Communism.* Harcourt, New York, 1961.

Ackerman, Bruce A. *Reconstructing American Law.* Harvard University Press, Cambridge, Mass., 1984.

Adorno, T.W.; Elsa Frenkel-Brunswick; Daniel Levinson; and R. Nevitt Sanford. *The Authoritarian Personality.* Harper, New York, 1950.

Albert, Judith Clavir, and Stewart Edward Albert. *The Sixties Papers: Documents of a Rebellious Decade.* Praeger, New York, 1984.

Alexander, Jeffrey C. *Theoretical Logic in Sociology* [Vol. 1: *Positivism, Presuppositions, and Current Controversies;* Vol. 2: *The Antinomies of Classical Thought: Marx and Durkheim;* Vol. 3: *The Attempt at Theoretical Synthesis: Max Weber;* Vol. 4: *The Modern Reconstruction of Classical Thought: Talcott Parsons*]. University of California Press, Berkeley, 1982–83.

Alford, Robert R., and Roger Friedland. *Powers of Theory: Capitalism, the State, and Democracy.* Cambridge University Press, New York, 1985.

Alperovitz, Gar. *Atomic Diplomacy: Hiroshima and Potsdam; the Use of the Atomic Bomb and the American Confrontation with Soviet Power.* Simon and Schuster, New York, 1965.

Alperovitz, Gar, and Jeff Faux. *Rebuilding America: A Blueprint for the New Economy.* Pantheon, New York, 1984.

Amin, Samir; Giovanni Arrighi; André Gunder Frank; and Immanuel Wallerstein. *Dynamics of Global Crisis.* Monthly Review, New York, 1982.

Anderson, Perry. *Considerations on Western Marxism.* New Left Books, London, 1976.

Anderson, Perry. *In the Tracks of Historical Materialism.* University of Chicago Press, Chicago, 1984.

Anderson, Quentin. *The Imperial Self: An Essay in American Literary and Cultural History.* Knopf, New York, 1971.

Anderson, Walter Truett, ed. *Rethinking Liberalism.* Avon, New York, 1983.

Arendt, Hannah. *The Origins of Totalitarianism.* Harcourt, New York, 1951.

Arendt, Hannah. *The Human Condition.* University of Chicago Press, Chicago, 1958.

Arendt, Hannah. *On Revolution.* Viking, New York, 1963.

Arendt, Hannah, and Karl Jaspers *Briefwechsel: 1926–1969,* edited by Lotte Koehler and Hans Saner. Piper, Munich, 1985.

Arnove, Robert F., ed. *Philanthropy and Cultural Imperialism: The Foundations at Home and Abroad.* Hall, Boston, 1980.

Aron, Raymond. *Dix-Huit Leçons sur la Société Industrielle.* Gallimard, Paris, 1962; *Industrial Society,* tr. M. K. Bottomore. Praeger, New York, 1967.

Aronowitz, Stanley. *False Promises: The Shaping of American Working Class Consciousness.* McGraw-Hill, New York, 1973.

Arrow, Kenneth J. *Social Choice and Individual Values.* Wiley, New York, 1951.

Attewell, Paul A. *Radical Political Economy Since the Sixties: A Sociology of Knowledge Analysis.* Rutgers University Press, New Brunswick, N.J., 1984.

Bailyn, Bernard. *The Ideological Origins of the American Revolution.* Belknap, Harvard University Press, Cambridge, Mass., 1967.

Baltzell, E. Digby. *The Protestant Establishment: Aristocracy and Caste in America.* Random House, New York, 1964.

Baran, Paul A., and Paul M. Sweezy. *Monopoly Capital: An Essay on the American Economic and Social Order.* Monthly Review, New York, 1966.

Barber, Benjamin R. *Strong Democracy: Participatory Politics for a New Age.* University of California Press, Berkeley, 1984.

Baritz, Loren. *The Servants of Power: A History of the Use of Social Science in American Industry.* Wesleyan University Press, Middletown, Conn., 1960.

Barnet, Richard J. *Intervention and Revolution: The United States in the Third World.* World, New York, 1968.

Barnet, Richard J. *Roots of War.* Atheneum, New York, 1972.

Barnet, Richard J.; and Ronald E. Müller. *Global Reach: The Power of the Multinational Corporations.* Simon and Schuster, New York, 1974.

Barney, Gerald O. Study Director. *The Global 2000 Report to the President of the U.S., Entering the 21st Century: A Report,* prepared by the Council on Environmental Quality and the Department of State. Pergamon, New York, 1980.

Barrett, William. *The Truants: Adventures Among the Intellectuals.* Anchor, Garden City, N.Y., 1982.

Bateson, Gregory. *Mind and Nature: A Necessary Unity.* Dutton, New York, 1979.

Becker, Gary S. *The Economics of Discrimination.* University of Chicago Press, Chicago, 1957.

Becker, Gary S. *Human Capital and the Personal Distribution of Income: An Analytical Approach.* Institute of Public Administration, Ann Arbor, Mich., 1967.

Bell, Daniel. *The End of Ideology: On the Exhaustion of Political Ideas in the Fifties.* Free Press, Glencoe, Ill, 1960.

Bell, Daniel. *The Coming of Post-Industrial Society: A Venture in Social Forecasting.* Basic Books, New York, 1973.

Bell, Daniel. *The Cultural Contradictions of Capitalism.* Basic Books, New York, 1976.

Bell, Daniel. *The Winding Passage: Essays and Sociological Journeys, 1960–1980.* Abt, Cambridge, Mass., 1980.

Bell, Daniel. *The Social Sciences Since the Second World War.* Transaction, New Brunswick, N.J., 1982.

Bell, Derrick. *And We Are Not Saved: The Exclusive Quest for Racial Reform.* Basic Books, New York, 1987.

Bellah, Robert N. *Beyond Belief: Essays on Religion in a Post-Traditional World.* Harper, New York, 1970.

Bellah, Robert N. *The Broken Covenant: American Civil Religion in a Time of Trial.* Seabury, New York, 1975.

Bellah, Robert N.; Richard Madsen; William M. Sullivan; Ann Swidler; and Steven M. Tipton. *Habits of the Heart: Individualism and Commitment in American Life.* University of California Press, Berkeley, 1985.

Bellow, Saul. *Mr. Sammler's Planet.* Viking, New York, 1970.

Bellow, Saul. *The Dean's December: A Novel.* Harper, New York, 1982.

Bender, Thomas. *New York Intellect: A History of Intellectual Life in New York City, From 1790 to the Beginnings of Our Own Time.* Knopf, New York, 1987.

Bendix, Reinhard. *Nation-Building and Citizenship: Studies of Our Changing Social Order.* Wiley, New York, 1964.

Bendix, Reinhard, and Seymour Martin Lipset, eds. *Class, Status, and Power: A Reader in Social Stratification.* Free Press, Glencoe, Ill., 1953.

Bercovitch, Sacvan. *The Puritan Origins of the American Self.* Yale University Press, New Haven, Conn., 1975.

Bercovitch, Sacvan, ed. *Reconstructing American Literary History.* Harvard University Press, Cambridge, Mass., 1986.

Berelson, Bernard R.; Paul F. Lazarsfeld; and William N. McPhee. *Voting: A Study of Opinion Formation in a Presidential Campaign.* University of Chicago Press, Chicago, 1954.

Berger, Peter L. *Pyramids of Sacrifice: Political Ethics and Social Change.* Basic Books, New York, 1975.

Berger, Peter L. "Democracy for Everybody?" *Commentary*, vol. 78, no. 3 (September 1983), pp. 31–36.

Berger, Peter L., and Thomas Luckmann. *The Social Construction of Reality: A Treatise in the Sociology of Knowledge*. Doubleday, Garden City, N.Y., 1966.

Berger, Peter L., and Richard John Neuhaus. *To Empower People: The Role of Mediating Structures in Public Policy*. American Enterprise Institute for Public Policy Research, Washington, D.C., 1977.

Berle, Adolf A., and Gardiner C. Means, *The Modern Corporation and Private Property*. Macmillan, New York, 1933.

Berlin, Isaiah. *Two Concepts of Liberty: An Inaugural Lecture Delivered Before the University of Oxford on 31 December 1958*. Clarendon Press, Oxford, 1958.

Berman, Marshall. *All That Is Solid Melts into Air: The Experience of Modernity*. Simon and Schuster, New York, 1982.

Bernheimer, Charles, and Claire Kahane, eds. *In Dora's Case: Freud-Hysteria-Feminism*. Columbia University Press, New York, 1985.

Bernstein, Barton J., ed. *Towards a New Past: Dissenting Essays in American History*. Pantheon, New York, 1968.

Bernstein, Richard J. *The Restructuring of Social and Political Theory*. Harcourt, New York, 1976.

Bernstein, Richard J. *Beyond Objectivism and Relativism: Science, Hermeneutics, and Praxis*. University of Pennsylvania, Philadelphia, 1983.

Berthoff, Warner. *A Literature Without Qualities: American Writing Since 1945*. University of California Press, Berkeley, 1979.

Bledstein, Burton J. *The Culture of Professionalism: The Middle Class and the Development of Higher Education in America*. Norton, New York, 1976.

Bickel, Alexander. *The Least Dangerous Branch: The Supreme Court at the Bar of Politics*. Bobbs-Merrill, Indianapolis, 1962.

Birnbaum, Norman. *The Crisis of Industrial Society*. Oxford University Press, New York, 1969.

Birnbaum, Norman. *Toward A Critical Sociology*. Oxford University Press, New York, 1971.

Black, C. E. *The Dynamics of Modernization: A Study in Comparative History*. Harper, New York, 1966.

Bloch, Ernst. *A Philosophy of the Future*, translated by John Cummings. Herder, New York, 1970.

Bloom, Alexander. *Prodigal Sons: The New York Intellectuals and Their World*. Oxford University Press, New York, 1986.

Bloom, Allan. *The Closing of the American Mind.* Simon and Schuster, New York, 1987.

Bloom, Harold. *A Map of Misreading.* Oxford University Press, New York, 1975.

Bluestone, Barry, and Bennett Harrison. *The Deindustrialization of America: Plant Closings, Community Abandonment, and the Dismantling of Basic Industry.* Basic Books, New York, 1982.

Blumenthal, Sidney. *The Rise of the Counter-Establishment: From Conservative Ideology to Political Power.* Times Books, New York, 1986.

Bookchin, Murray. *Post-Scarcity Anarchism.* Ramparts, Berkeley, Calif., 1971.

Bowles, Samuel. and Herbert Gintis. *Democracy and Capitalism: Property, Community, and the Contradictions of Modern Social Thought.* Basic Books, New York, 1986.

Bowles, Samuel; David M. Gordon; and Thomas E. Weisskopf. *Beyond the Waste Land: A Democratic Alternative to Economic Decline.* Anchor, Garden City, N.Y., 1983.

Boyer, Paul. *Urban Masses and Moral Order in America, 1820–1920.* Harvard University Press, Cambridge, Mass., 1978.

Boyers, Robert, and Peggy Boyers, eds. *The Salmagundi Reader.* Indiana University Press, Bloomington, 1983.

Boyte, Harry C. *The Backyard Revolution: Understanding the New Citizens' Movement.* Temple University Press, Philadelphia, 1980.

Braverman, Harry. *Labor and Monopoly Capital: The Degradation of Work in the Twentieth Century.* Monthly Review, New York, 1975.

Breyer, Stephen. *Administrative Law and Regulatory Policy.* Little, Brown, Boston, 1979.

Brooks, Peter. *Reading for the Plot: Design and Intention in Narrative.* Knopf, New York, 1984.

Brown, Norman Oliver. *Life Against Death: The Psychoanalytical Meaning of History.* Wesleyan University Press, Middletown, Conn., 1959.

Bruce-Briggs, B. ed., *The New Class?* Transaction, New Brunswick, N.J., 1979.

Bruner, Jerome S. *Toward a Theory of Instruction.* Belknap, Harvard University Press, Cambridge, Mass., 1966.

Buchanan, James M. *The Demand and Supply of Public Goods.* Rand McNally, Chicago, 1968.

Buchanan, James M. *What Should Economists Do?* Liberty Press, Indianapolis, 1979.

Burke, Kenneth. *Permanence and Change: An Anatomy of Purpose.* New Republic, New York, 1935.

Burkert, Walter; Rene Girard; and Jonathan Z. Smith. *Violent Origins: Ritual Killing and Cultural Formation*, ed. Robert G. Hammerton-Kelly. Stanford University Press, Stanford, Calif., 1987.

Burnham, James. *The Managerial Revolution: What Is Happening in the World*. John Day, New York, 1941.

Burnham, Walter Dean. *Critical Elections and the Mainsprings of American Politics*. Norton, New York, 1970.

Burnham, Walter Dean. *The Current Crisis in American Politics*. Oxford University Press, New York, 1982.

Burns, E. Bradford. *At War in Nicaragua: The Reagan Doctrine and the Politics of Nostalgia*. Harper, New York, 1987.

Caplow, Theodore; Howard M. Bahr; Bruce A. Chadwick; Reuben Hill; and Margaret Holmes Williamson. *Middletown Families: Fifty Years of Change and Continuity*. University of Minnesota Press, Minneapolis, 1982.

Carnoy, Martin, and Derek Shearer. *Economic Democracy: The Challenge of the 1980s*. Sharpe, White Plains, N.Y., 1980.

Carnoy, Martin; Derek Shearer; and Russell Rumberger. *A New Social Contract: The Economy and Government After Reagan*. Harper, New York, 1983.

Castelli, Jim. *The Bishops and the Bomb: Waging Peace in a Nuclear Age*. Image, Garden City, N.Y., 1983.

Chayes, Abram. "The Role of the Judge in Public Law Litigation," *Harvard Law Review*, vol. 89, no. 7 (May 1976), pp. 1281–1316.

Chayes, Abram. "The Supreme Court, 1981 Term. Foreword: Public Law Litigation and the Burger Court," *Harvard Law Review*, vol. 96, no. 4 (November 1982), pp. 4–60.

Chomsky, Noam. *American Power and the New Mandarins*. Pantheon, New York, 1969.

Chomsky, Noam. *Problems of Knowledge and Freedom*. Pantheon, New York, 1971.

Chomsky, Noam. *Reflections on Language*. Pantheon, New York, 1975.

Chomsky, Noam; and Edward S. Herman. *The Political Economy of Human Rights* [Vol. I: *After the Cataclysm: Postwar Indochina and the Construction of Imperial Ideology;* Vol. II: *The Washington Connection and Third World Fascism*]. South End, Boston, 1979.

Christie, Richard, and Marie Jahoda, eds. *Studies in the Scope and Method of "The Authoritarian Personality."* Free Press, Glencoe, Ill., 1954. (Esp. Edward Shils, "Authoritarianism: 'Right' and 'Left.'")

Clayton, Bruce. *Forgotten Prophet: The Life of Randolph Bourne.* Louisiana State University Press, Baton Rouge, 1984.

Clecak, Peter. *America's Quest for the Ideal Self: Dissent and Fulfillment in the Sixties and Seventies.* Oxford University Press, New York, 1983.

Coleman, John A. *An American Strategic Theology.* Paulist Press, New York, 1982.

Cooper, David. *The Death of the Family.* Pantheon, New York, 1971.

Cooper, John Milton, Jr., *The Warrior and the Priest: Woodrow Wilson and Theodore Roosevelt.* Belknap, Harvard University Press, Cambridge, Mass., 1983.

Coser, Lewis A. *The Functions of Social Conflict.* Free Press, Glencoe, Ill., 1956.

Coser, Lewis A. *Men of Ideas: A Sociologist's View.* Free Press, New York, 1965.

Coser, Lewis A. *Refugee Scholars in America: Their Impact and Their Experiences.* Yale University Press, New Haven, 1984.

Cox, Harvey. *Religion in the Secular City: Toward a Postmodern Theology.* Simon and Schuster, New York, 1984.

Cox, Harvey Gallagher. *The Secular City: Secularization and Urbanization in Theological Perspective.* Macmillan, New York, 1965.

Crawford, Alan. *Thunder on the Right: The "New Right" and the Politics of Resentment.* Pantheon, New York, 1980.

Crews, Frederick. *Out of My System: Psychoanalysis, Ideology, and Critical Method.* Oxford University Press, New York, 1975.

Crews, Frederick. "In the Big House of Theory." *New York Review of Books* vol. 33, no. 9 (May 29, 1986), pp. 36–42.

"Critical Legal Studies Symposium." *Stanford Law Review,* vol. 36, nos. 1 and 2 (January 1984).

Crozier, Michel; Samuel P. Huntington; and Joji Watanuki. *The Crisis of Democracy: Report on the Governability of Democracies to the Trilateral Commission.* New York University Press, New York, 1975.

Crunden, Robert M. *Ministers of Reform: The Progressives' Achievement in American Civilization, 1889–1920.* Basic Books, New York, 1982.

Cruse, Harold. *The Crisis of the Negro Intellectual.* Morrow, New York, 1967.

Cruse, Harold. *Plural but Equal: A Critical Study of Blacks and Minorities in America's Plural Society.* Morrow, New York, 1987.

Dahl, Robert A. *A Preface to Democratic Theory.* University of Chicago Press, Chicago, 1956.

Dahl, Robert A. *A Preface to Economic Democracy.* University of California Press, Berkeley, 1985.

Dallek, Robert. *The American Style of Foreign Policy: Cultural Politics and Foreign Affairs.* Knopf, New York, 1983.

Danziger, Sheldon H., and Daniel H. Weinberg, eds. *Fighting Poverty: What Works and What Doesn't.* Harvard University Press, Cambridge, Mass., 1986.

Davidson, Donald. *Inquiries into Truth and Interpretation.* Oxford University Press, New York, 1984.

Davis, David Brion. *The Problem of Slavery in the Age of Revolution, 1770–1823.* Cornell University Press, Ithaca, N.Y., 1975.

Davis, Mike. *Prisoners of the American Dream: Politics and Economy in the History of the U.S. Working Class.* Verso, London, 1986.

Degler, Carl N. *At Odds: Women and the Family in America from the Revolution to the Present.* Oxford University Press, New York, 1980.

Demerath, N. J., and Richard A. Peterson, eds. *System, Change, and Conflict: A Reader on Contemporary Sociological Theory and the Debate over Functionalism.* Free Press, New York, 1967.

Deutsch, Karl W.; Andrei S. Markovits; and John Platt, eds. *Advances in the Social Sciences, 1900–1980: What, Who, Where, How?* Abt, Cambridge, Mass., 1986.

Dickstein, Morris. *Gates of Eden: American Culture in the Sixties.* Basic Books, New York, 1977.

Diggins, John Patrick. *The Lost Soul of American Politics: Virtue, Self Interest, and the Foundations of Liberalism.* Basic Books, New York, 1984.

Domhoff, G. William. *The Higher Circles: The Governing Class in America.* Random House, New York, 1970.

Douglas, Ann. *The Feminization of American Culture.* Knopf, New York, 1977.

DuBois, W. E. B. *The Souls of Black Folk: Essays and Sketches.* McClurg, Chicago, 1903.

Dworkin, Ronald. *Taking Rights Seriously.* Harvard University Press, Cambridge, Mass., 1977.

Dworkin, Ronald. *A Matter of Principle.* Harvard University Press, Cambridge, Mass., 1985.

Easton, David. *The Political System.* University of Chicago Press, Chicago, 1971.

Edelman, Marian Wright. *Families in Peril: An Agenda for Social Change.* Harvard University Press, Cambridge, Mass., 1986.

Edsall, Thomas. *The New Politics of Inequality.* Norton, New York, 1984.

Edwards, Richard. *Contested Terrain: The Transformation of the Workplace in the Twentieth Century.* Basic Books, New York, 1979.

Ehrenreich, Barbara. *The Hearts of Men: American Dreams and the Flight from Commitment.* Anchor, Garden City, N.Y., 1983.

Ely, John Hart. *Democracy and Distrust: A Theory of Judicial Review.* Harvard University Press, Cambridge, Mass., 1980.

Erikson, Erik H. *Childhood and Society.* Norton, New York, 1950.

Erikson, Erik H. *A Way of Looking at Things: Selected Papers from 1930 to 1980,* ed. Stephen Schlein. Norton, New York, 1987.

Erikson, Kai T. *Everything in Its Path: Destruction of Community in the Buffalo Creek Flood.* Simon and Schuster, New York, 1976.

Evans, Sara. *Personal Politics: The Roots of Women's Liberation in the Civil Rights Movement and the New Left.* Knopf, New York, 1979.

Evans, Sara M. and Harry C. Boyte. *Free Spaces: The Sources of Democratic Change in America.* Harper, New York, 1986.

Falk, Candice. *Love, Anarchy, and Emma Goldman.* Holt, New York, 1984.

Falk, Richard A. *A Study of Future Worlds.* Free Press, New York, 1975.

Falk, Richard A., and Saul H. Mendlovitz, eds. *The Strategy of World Order.* World Law Fund, New York, 1966.

Fausto-Sterling, Anne. *Myths of Gender: Biological Theories About Women and Men.* Basic Books, New York, 1985.

Feinstein, Howard M. *Becoming William James.* Cornell University Press, Ithaca, N.Y., 1984.

Ferguson, Thomas, and Joel Rogers, eds. *The Hidden Election: Politics and Economics in the 1980 Presidential Campaign.* Pantheon, New York, 1981.

Ferguson, Thomas, and Joel Rogers, eds. *The Political Economy: Readings in the Politics and Economics of American Public Policy.* Sharpe, Armonk, N.Y., 1984.

Ferguson, Thomas, and Joel Rogers. *Right Turn: The Decline of the Democrats and the Future of American Politics.* Hill and Wang, New York, 1986.

Finkelstein, Barbara. *Regulated Children/Liberated Children: Education in Psychohistorical Perspective.* Psychohistory, New York, 1979.

Fischer, George, ed. *The Revival of American Socialism: Selected Papers of the Socialist Scholars Conference.* Oxford University Press, New York, 1971.

Fiske, Donald W., and Richard A. Shweder. *Metatheory in Social Science: Pluralisms and Subjectivities.* University of Chicago Press, Chicago, 1986.

FitzGerald, Frances. *America Revised: History Schoolbooks in the Twentieth Century.* Little, Brown, Boston, 1979.

233

Flacks, Richard. *Youth and Social Change*. Markham, Chicago, 1971.

Flacks, Richard. "Making History vs. Making Life: Dilemmas of an American Left." *Sociological Inquiry*, vol. 46, nos. 3–4 (1976), pp. 263–80.

Fleming, Donald, and Bernard Bailyn, eds. *The Intellectual Migration: Europe and America, 1930–1960*. Belknap, Harvard University Press, Cambridge, Mass., 1969.

Fogel, Robert William, and Stanley L. Engerman. *Time on the Cross: The Economics of American Negro Slavery*. Little, Brown, Boston, 1974.

Foner, Eric. *Free Soil, Free Labor, Free Men: The Ideology of the Republican Party Before the Civil War*. Oxford University Press, New York, 1970.

Foster, John Bellamy, and Henryk Szlajfer, eds. *The Faltering Economy: The Problem of Accumulation Under Monopoly Capitalism*. Monthly Review, New York, 1984.

Foucault, Michel. *L'Archéologie de Savoir*. Gallimard, Paris, 1969. *The Archaeology of Knowledge*, tr. A. M. Sheridan-Smith. Pantheon, New York, 1972.

Fox, Richard Wightman. *Reinhold Niebuhr: A Biography*. Pantheon, New York, 1985.

Fox, Richard Wightman, and T. J. Jackson Lears, eds. *The Culture of Consumption: Critical Essays in American History, 1880–1980*. Pantheon, New York, 1983.

Fox-Genovese, Elizabeth, and Eugene D. Genovese. *Fruits of Merchant Capital: Slavery and Bourgeois Property in the Rise and Expansion of Capitalism*. Oxford University Press, New York, 1983.

Frank, André Gunder. *World Accumulation, 1492–1789*. Monthly Review, New York, 1978.

Frank, Jerome. *Law and the Modern Mind*. Brentano's, New York, 1930.

Frazier, Franklin. *Bourgeoisie Noire*. Plon, Paris, 1955; *Black Bourgeoisie*. Free Press, Glencoe, Ill., 1957.

Fredrickson, George M. *White Supremacy: A Comparative Study in American and South African History*. Oxford University Press, New York, 1981.

Freeman, Richard B., and James L. Medoff. *What Do Unions Do?* Basic Books, New York, 1984.

Friedrich, Carl J., and Zbigniew K. Brzezinski. *Totalitarian Dictatorship and Autocracy*. Harvard University Press, Cambridge, Mass., 1956.

Fromm, Erich. *Escape from Freedom*. Farrar and Rinehart, New York, 1941.

Fuchs, Victor R. *How We Live: An Economic Perspective on Americans from Birth to Death*. Harvard University Press, Cambridge, Mass., 1983.

Fulbright, William. *The Arrogance of Power*. Random House, New York, 1966.

Gaddis, John Lewis. *The United States and the Origins of the Cold War, 1941–47.* Oxford University Press, New York, 1972.

Gaddis, John Lewis. *Strategies of Containment: A Critical Appraisal of Postwar American National Security Policy.* Oxford University Press, New York, 1982.

Gaddis, William. *JR.* Knopf, New York, 1975.

Gaddis, William. *Carpenter's Gothic.* Viking, New York, 1985.

Galbraith, John Kenneth. *American Capitalism: The Concept of Countervailing Power.* Houghton and Mifflin, Boston, 1952.

Galbraith, John Kenneth. *The Affluent Society.* Houghton Mifflin, Boston, 1958.

Galbraith, John Kenneth. *The New Industrial State.* Houghton Mifflin, Boston, 1967.

Galbraith, John Kenneth. *A Life in Our Times: Memoirs.* Houghton Mifflin, Boston, 1981.

Galbraith, John Kenneth. *Economics in Perspective: A Critical History.* Houghton Mifflin, Boston, 1987.

Gallop, Jane. *The Daughter's Seduction: Feminism and Psychoanalysis.* Cornell University Press, Ithaca, N.Y., 1982.

Gannon, Thomas M., ed. *The Catholic Challenge to the American Economy: Reflections on the U.S. Bishops' Pastoral Letter on Catholic Social Teaching and the U.S. Economy.* Macmillan, New York, 1987.

Gardner, Howard. *The Mind's New Science: A History of the Cognitive Revolution.* Basic Books, New York, 1985.

Gates, Henry Louis, Jr., ed. *"Race," Writing, and Difference.* University of Chicago Press, Chicago, 1986.

Geertz, Clifford. *The Interpretation of Cultures: Selected Essays.* Basic Books, New York, 1973.

Geertz, Clifford. *Local Knowledge: Further Essays in Interpretive Anthropology.* Basic Books, New York, 1983.

Gendzier, Irene. *Managing Political Change: Social Scientists and the Third World.* Westview, Boulder, Colo., 1985.

Genovese, Eugene D. *The Political Economy of Slavery: Studies in the Economy and Society of the Slave South.* Pantheon, New York, 1965.

Genovese, Eugene D. *Roll, Jordan, Roll: The World the Slaves Made.* Pantheon, New York, 1974.

Gerson, Kathleen, *Hard Choices: How Women Decide About Work, Career, and Motherhood.* University of California Press, Berkeley, 1985.

"Getting on the List: 150 Who Make a Difference." *National Journal,* vol. 18, no. 24 (June 14, 1986).

Giddens, Anthony. *The Class Structure of the Advanced Societies.* Hutchinson, London, 1973.

Giddens, Anthony. *New Rules of Sociological Method: A Positive Critique of Interpretive Sociologies.* Basic Books, New York, 1976.

Gilbert, James Burkhart. *Writers and Partisans: A History of Literary Radicalism in America.* Wiley, New York, 1968.

Gilbert, Sandra M., and Susan Gubar, *The Madwoman in the Attic: The Woman Writer and the Nineteenth-Century Literary Imagination.* Yale University Press, New Haven, 1979.

Gilder, George. *Wealth and Poverty.* Basic Books, New York, 1981.

Gillies, Archibald L.; Jeff Faux; Jerry W. Sanders; Sherle R. Schwenninger; and Paul F. Walker. *Post-Reagan America.* World Policy Institute, New York, 1987.

Gilligan, Carol. *In a Different Voice: Psychological Theory and Women's Development.* Harvard University Press, Cambridge, Mass., 1982.

Gitlin, Todd. *The Whole World Is Watching: Mass Media in the Making and Unmaking of the New Left.* University of California Press, Berkeley, 1980.

Gitlin, Todd. *The Sixties: Years of Hope, Days of Rage.* Bantam, New York, 1987.

Gitlin, Todd, ed. *Watching Television: A Pantheon Guide to Popular Culture.* Pantheon, New York, 1987.

Glazer, Nathan. *Remembering the Answers: Essays on the American Student Revolt.* Basic Books, New York, 1970.

Glazer, Nathan. *Affirmative Discrimination: Ethnic Inequality and Public Policy.* Basic Books, New York, 1975.

Glazer, Nathan. *Ethnic Dilemmas 1964–1982.* Harvard University Press, Cambridge, Mass., 1983.

Glotz, Peter. "Forward to Europe: A Declaration for a New European Left." *Dissent,* vol. 33, no. 3 (1986), pp. 327–39.

Goffman, Erving. *The Presentation of Self in Everyday Life.* University of Edinburgh, Social Sciences Research Center, Edinburgh, 1956; Doubleday, Garden City, N.Y., 1959.

Goffman, Erving. *Asylums: Essays on the Social Situation of Mental Patients and Other Inmates.* Anchor, Garden City, N.Y., 1961.

Goldthorpe, John H., ed. *Order and Conflict in Contemporary Capitalism.* Oxford University Press, New York, 1984.

Goodman, Paul. *Growing Up Absurd: Problems of Youth in the Organized System.* Random House, New York, 1960.

Goodwyn, Lawrence. *Democratic Promise: The Populist Movement in America.* Oxford University Press, New York, 1976.

Gordon, David M.; Richard Edwards; Michael Reich. *Segmented Work, Divided Workers: The Historical Transformation of Labor in the United States.* Cambridge University Press, New York, 1982.

Gouldner, Alvin W. *The Coming Crisis of Western Sociology.* Basic Books, New York, 1970.

Gouldner, Alvin W. *The Future of Intellectuals and the Rise of the New Class: A Frame of Reference, Theses, Conjectures, Arguments, and an Historical Perspective on the Role of Intellectuals and Intelligentsia in the International Class Contest of the Modern Era.* Seabury, New York, 1979.

Gouldner, Alvin W. *The Two Marxisms: Contradictions and Anomalies in the Development of Theory.* Seabury, New York, 1980.

Graff, Gerald. *Literature Against Itself: Literary Ideas in Modern Society.* University of Chicago Press, Chicago, 1979.

Green, James R. *The World of the Worker: Labor in Twentieth-Century America.* Hill and Wang, New York, 1980.

Green, James R., ed., *Workers' Struggles, Past and Present: A "Radical America" Reader.* Temple University Press, Philadelphia, 1983.

Green, Mark. *Winning Back America.* Bantam, New York, 1982.

Green, Philip. *The Pursuit of Inequality.* Pantheon, New York, 1981.

Green, Philip, and Sanford Levinson, eds. *Power and Community: Dissenting Essays in Political Science.* Pantheon, New York, 1969.

Greenberg, Clement. *The Collected Essays and Criticism* [Vol. 1: *Perceptions and Judgments, 1939–1944;* Vol. 2: *Arrogant Purpose, 1945–1949*], edited by John O'Brian. University of Chicago Press, Chicago, 1986.

Gross, Bertram. *Friendly Fascism: The New Face of Power in America.* Evans, New York, 1980.

Gutman, Herbert G. *Slavery and the Numbers Game: A Critique of "Time on the Cross."* University of Illinois Press, Urbana, 1975.

Gutman, Herbert G. *The Black Family in Slavery and Freedom, 1750–1925.* Pantheon, New York, 1976.

Gutman, Herbert G. *Work, Culture, and Society in Industrializing America: Essays in American Working-Class and Social History.* Knopf, New York, 1976.

Habermas, Jürgen. *Erkenntnis und Interesse.* Suhrkamp, Frankfurt am Main, 1968; *Knowledge and Human Interests,* tr Jeremy J Shapiro. Beacon Press, Boston, 1971.

Habermas, Jürgen. *Legitimationsprobleme im Spätkapitalismus,* Suhrkamp, Frankfurt am Main, 1973; *Legitimation Crisis,* tr. Thomas McCarthy. Beacon Press, Boston, 1975.

Hacker, Andrew. *The End of the American Era.* Atheneum, New York, 1970.

Hahn, Steven, and Jonathan Prude, eds. *The Countryside in the Age of Capitalist Transformation: Essays in the Social History of Rural America.* University of North Carolina Press, Chapel Hill, 1985.

Hamilton, Richard F. *Class and Politics in the United States.* Wiley, New York, 1972.

Hamilton, Richard F. *Restraining Myths: Critical Studies of United States Social Structure and Politics.* Sage, Beverly Hills, Calif., 1975.

Handler, Joel F. *Social Movements and the Legal System: A Theory of Law Reform and Social Change.* Academic Press, New York, 1978.

Hareven, Tamara. *Family Time and Industrial Time: The Relationship Between the Family and Work in a New England Industrial Community.* Cambridge University Press, New York, 1982.

Harrington, Michael. *The Other America: Poverty in the United States.* Macmillan, New York, 1962.

Harrington, Michael. *Socialism.* Saturday Review, New York, 1972.

Harrington, Michael. *Fragments of the Century.* Saturday Review, New York, 1973.

Harrington, Mona. *The Dream of Deliverance in American Politics.* Knopf, New York, 1986.

Hartmann, Heinz. *Essays on Ego Psychology: Selected Problems in Psychoanalytic Theory.* International Universities Press, New York, 1964.

Hartmann, Heinz; Ernst Kris; and Rudolph M. Loewenstein. *Papers on Psychoanalytic Psychology.* International Universities Press, New York, 1964.

Hartz, Louis. *The Liberal Tradition in America: An Interpretation of American Political Thought Since the Revolution.* Harcourt, New York, 1955.

Harvard Nuclear Study Group. *Living with Nuclear Weapons.* Harvard University Press, Cambridge, Mass., 1983.

Haskell, Thomas L. *The Emergence of Professional Social Science: The American Social Science Association and the Nineteenth Century Crisis of Authority.* University of Illinois Press, Urbana, 1977.

Havens, Leston. *Making Contact: Uses of Language in Psychotherapy.* Harvard University Press, Cambridge, Mass., 1986.

Hayden, Tom. *The American Future: New Visions Beyond the Reagan Administration.* Washington Square, New York, 1980.

Hayek, F. A. *The Counter-Revolution of Science: Studies on the Abuse of Reason.* Free Press, Glencoe, Ill., 1952.

Heilbroner, Robert L. *The Future as History: The Historic Currents of Our Time and the Direction in Which They Are Taking America.* Harper, New York, 1960.

Heilbroner, Robert L. *An Inquiry into the Human Prospect.* Norton, New York, 1974.

Hennesey, James J. *American Catholics: A History of the Roman Catholic Community in the United States.* Oxford University Press, New York, 1981.

Higham, John, ed. *The Reconstruction of American History.* Humanities, New York, 1962.

Hirschman, Albert O. *The Passions and the Interests: Political Arguments for Capitalism Before Its Triumph.* Princeton University Press, Princeton, 1977.

Hochschild, Arlie Russell. *The Managed Heart: Commercialization of Human Feeling.* University of California Press, Berkeley, 1983.

Hodgson, Godfrey. *America in Our Time: From World War II to Nixon, What Happened and Why.* Doubleday, Garden City, N.Y., 1976.

Hoffman, Stanley. *Primacy or World Order: American Foreign Policy Since the Cold War.* McGraw-Hill, New York, 1978.

Hofstadter, Richard. *Social Darwinism in American Thought, 1860–1915.* University of Pennsylvania Press, Philadelphia, 1944.

Hofstadter, Richard. *The American Political Tradition and the Men Who Made It.* Knopf, New York, 1948.

Hofstadter, Richard. *The Age of Reform: From Bryan to FDR.* Knopf, New York, 1955.

Hofstadter, Richard. *Anti-Intellectualism in American Life.* Knopf, New York, 1963.

Hofstadter, Richard. *The Paranoid Style in American Politics, and Other Essays.* Knopf, New York, 1965.

Hofstadter, Richard. *The Progressive Historians: Turner, Beard, Parrington.* Knopf, New York, 1968.

Hofstadter, Richard, and Seymour Martin Lipset, eds. *Turner and the Sociology of the Frontier.* Basic Books, New York, 1968.

Hofstadter, Richard, and Walter P. Metzger. *The Development of Academic Freedom in the United States.* Columbia University Press, New York, 1955.

Hook, Sidney. *From Hegel to Marx: Studies in the Intellectual Development of Karl Marx.* Reynal and Hitchcock, New York, 1936.

Hook, Sidney. "Education in Defense of a Free Society." *Commentary,* vol. 78, no. 1 (July 1984), pp. 17–22.

Horney, Karen. *The Neurotic Personality of Our Time.* Norton, New York, 1937.

Horwitz, Morton J. *The Transformation of American Law, 1780–1860.* Harvard University Press, Cambridge, Mass., 1977.

Howe, Irving. *Politics and the Novel.* Horizon, New York, 1957.

Howe, Irving, with the assistance of Kenneth Libo. *World of Our Fathers.* Harcourt, New York, 1976.

Howe, Irving, ed. *Twenty-Five Years of Dissent: An American Tradition.* Methuen, New York, 1979.

Howe, Irving. *A Margin of Hope: An Intellectual Autobiography.* Harcourt, San Diego, 1982.

Howe, Irving. *Socialism and America.* Harcourt, San Diego, 1985.

Hughes, H. Stuart. *Consciousness and Society: The Reorientation of European Social Thought, 1890–1930.* Knopf, New York, 1958.

Hughes, H. Stuart. *The Sea Change: The Migration of Social Thought, 1930–1965.* Harper, New York, 1975.

Hunt, Michael H. *Ideology and U.S. Foreign Policy.* Yale University Press, New Haven, 1987.

Huntington, Samuel P. "Bases of Accommodation." *Foreign Affairs,* vol. 46 (July 1968), pp. 642–56.

Hurst, Willard. *Law and the Conditions of Freedom in the Nineteenth-Century United States.* University of Wisconsin Press, Madison, 1956.

Huyssen, Andreas. *After the Great Divide: Modernism, Mass Culture, Postmodernism.* Indiana University Press, Bloomington, 1986.

Hyman, Harold M., and William M. Wiecek. *Equal Justice Under Law: Constitutional Development, 1835–1875.* Harper, New York, 1982.

Inglehart, Ronald. *The Silent Revolution: Changing Values and Political Styles Among Western Publics.* Princeton University Press, Princeton, 1977.

Inkeles, Alex, and David H. Smith. *Becoming Modern: Individual Change in Six Developing Countries.* Harvard University Press, Cambridge, Mass., 1974.

International Association of Machinists and Aerospace Workers. *Let's Rebuild America.* Washington, D.C., revised 1981.

Isserman, Maurice. *If I Had a Hammer: The Death of the Old Left and the Birth of the New Left.* Basic Books, New York, 1987.

Jackson, Kenneth T. *Crabgrass Frontier: The Suburbanization of the United States.* Oxford University Press, New York, 1985.

Jacoby, Russell. *The Repression of Psychoanalysis: Otto Fenichel and the Political Freudians.* Basic Books, New York, 1983.

Jacoby, Russell. *The Last Intellectuals: American Culture in the Age of Academe.* Basic Books, New York, 1987.

Janowitz, Morris. *The Last Half-Century: Societal Change and Politics in America.* University of Chicago Press, Chicago, 1978.

Jay, Martin. *The Dialectical Imagination: A History of the Frankfurt School and the Institute of Social Research, 1923–1950.* Little, Brown, Boston, 1973.

Jencks, Christopher, and David Riesman. *The Academic Revolution.* Doubleday, Garden City, N.Y., 1968.

Jordan, Winthrop D. *White Over Black: American Attitudes Toward the Negro, 1550–1812.* Institute of Early American History and Culture, University of North Carolina Press, Chapel Hill, 1968.

Kadushin, Charles. *The American Intellectual Elite.* Little, Brown, Boston, 1974.

Kairys, David, ed., *The Politics of Law: A Progressive Critique.* Pantheon, New York, 1982.

Kammen, Michael, ed. *The Past Before Us: Contemporary Historical Writing in the United States.* Cornell University Press, Ithaca, N.Y., 1980.

Kateb, George. *Utopia and Its Enemies.* Free Press, New York, 1963.

Kateb, George. *Hannah Arendt: Politics, Conscience, Evil.* Rowman and Allanheld, Totowa, N.J., 1984.

Katznelson, Ira, and Aristide R. Zolberg, eds. *Working Class Formation: Nineteenth-Century Patterns in Western Europe and the United States.* Princeton University Press, Princeton, N.J., 1986.

Kaysen, Carl, ed. *Content and Context: Essays on College Education.* McGraw-Hill, New York, 1973. (Esp. Norman Birnbaum, "Students, Professors, and Philosopher Kings.")

Kazin, Alfred. *On Native Grounds: An Interpretation of Modern American Prose Literature.* Reynal and Hitchcock, New York, 1942.

Kazin, Alfred. *New York Jew.* Knopf, New York, 1978.

Kazin, Alfred. *An American Procession.* Knopf, New York, 1984.

Kennan, George F. *Memoirs* [Vol. 1: *1925–1950;* vol. 2: *1950–1963*]. Little, Brown, Boston, 1967–72.

Kennedy, Eugene. *The Now and Future Church: The Psychology of Being an American Catholic.* Doubleday, Garden City, N.Y., 1984.

Kerber, Linda K. *Women of the Republic: Intellect and Ideology in Revolutionary America.* Institute of Early American History and Culture, University of North Carolina Press, Chapel Hill, 1980.

Kern, Stephen. *The Culture of Time and Space 1880–1918.* Harvard University Press, Cambridge, Mass., 1983.

Kernberg, Otto F. *Borderline Conditions and Pathological Narcissism.* Aronson, New York, 1975.

Keyssar, Alexander. *Out of Work: The First Century of Unemployment in Massachusetts.* Cambridge University Press, New York, 1986.

Kissinger, Henry. *A World Restored: Metternich, Castlereagh, and the Problems of Peace, 1812–22.* Houghton Mifflin, Boston, 1957.

Kissinger, Henry. *White House Years.* Little, Brown, Boston, 1979.

Kissinger, Henry. *Years of Upheaval.* Little, Brown, Boston, 1982.

Kohlberg, Lawrence. *The Psychology of Moral Development: The Nature and Validity of Moral Stages.* Harper, San Francisco, 1984.

Kohut, Heinz. *The Analysis of the Self: A Systematic Approach to the Psychoanalytic Treatment of Narcissistic Personality Disorders.* International Universities Press, New York, 1971.

Kolko, Gabriel. *The Triumph of Conservatism: A Re-Interpretation of American History, 1900–1916.* Free Press, New York, 1963.

Kolko, Gabriel. *Anatomy of a War: Vietnam, the United States, and the Modern Historical Experience.* Pantheon, New York, 1985.

Kornhauser, William. *The Politics of Mass Society.* Free Press, Glencoe, Ill., 1959.

Korsch, Karl. *Marxism and Philosophy,* tr. Fred Halliday. Monthly Review, New York, 1972.

Kovel, Joel. *The Age of Desire: Reflections of a Radical Psychoanalyst.* Pantheon, New York, 1981.

Kovel, Joel. *Against the State of Nuclear Terror.* South End Press, Boston, 1984.

Kris, Ernst. *Psychoanalytic Explorations in Art.* International Universities Press, New York, 1952.

Kristol, Irving. *Two Cheers for Capitalism.* Basic Books, New York, 1978.

Kroeber, Alfred E. ed. *Anthropology Today.* University of Chicago Press, Chicago, 1953.

Krupnick, Mark. *Lionel Trilling and the Fate of Cultural Criticism.* Northwestern University Press, Evanston, Ill., 1986.

Kuhn, Thomas S. *The Structure of Scientific Revolutions.* University of Chicago Press, Chicago, 1962.

Kuklick, Bruce. *The Rise of American Philosophy: Cambridge, Massachusetts, 1860–1930.* Yale University Press, New Haven, 1977.

Kuklick, Bruce. *Churchmen and Philosophers: From Jonathan Edwards to John Dewey.* Yale University Press, New Haven, 1985.

Kuttner, Robert. *The Economic Illusion: False Choices Between Prosperity and Social Justice.* Houghton Mifflin, Boston, 1984.

Kuttner, Robert. *The Life of the Party: Democratic Prospects in 1988 and Beyond.* Viking Press, New York, 1987.

Ladd, Everett Carll, Jr. *Ideology in America: Change and Response in a City, a Suburb, and a Small Town.* Cornell University Press, Ithaca, N.Y., 1969.

Ladd, Everett Carll, Jr., and Seymour Martin Lipset. *The Divided Academy: Professors and Politics.* McGraw-Hill, New York, 1975.

LaFeber, Walter. *The New Empire: An Interpretation of American Expansion:*

1860–1898. American Historical Association, Cornell University Press, Ithaca, N.Y., 1963.

LaFeber, Walter. *Inevitable Revolutions: The United States in Central America.* Norton, New York, 1983.

LaFeber, Walter. *America, Russia, and the Cold War, 1945–1984,* 5th ed. Knopf, New York, 1985.

Laing, Ronald D. *The Politics of Experience.* Pantheon, New York, 1967.

Langer, Elinor. *Josephine Herbst.* Little, Brown, Boston, 1984.

Lasch, Christopher. *The New Radicalism in America, 1889–1963: The Intellectual as a Social Type.* Knopf, New York, 1965.

Lasch, Christopher. *The Agony of the American Left.* Knopf, New York, 1969.

Lasch, Christopher. *Haven in a Heartless World: The Family Besieged.* Basic Books, New York, 1977.

Lasch, Christopher. *The Culture of Narcissism: American Life in an Age of Diminishing Expectations.* Norton, New York, 1978.

Laslett, John H. M., and Seymour Martin Lipset, eds. *Failure of a Dream? Essays in the History of American Socialism.* Anchor, Garden City, N.Y., 1974.

Lasswell, Harold. *Politics: Who Gets What, When, and How.* McGraw-Hill, New York, 1936.

Lasswell, Harold, and Myres McDougall. "Legal Education and Public Policy: Professional Training in the Public Interest," *Yale Law Journal,* vol. 52, no. 2 (March 1943), pp. 203–95.

Leab, Daniel J., ed. *The Labor History Reader.* University of Illinois Press, Urbana, 1985.

Lears, T. J. Jackson. *No Place of Grace: Antimodernism and the Transformation of American Culture, 1880–1920.* Pantheon, New York, 1981.

Lederer, Emil. *State of the Masses: The Threat of a Classless Society.* Norton, New York, 1940.

Lefebvre, Henri. *La Vie Quotidienne dans le Monde Modern.* Gallimard, Paris, 1968. *Everyday Life in the Modern World,* tr. G. Huppert. Harper and Row, New York, 1971.

Lekachman, Robert. *Visions and Nightmares: America After Reagan.* Macmillan, New York, 1987.

Lenz, Gunter H., and Kurt L. Shell, eds. *The Crisis of Modernity: Recent Critical Theories of Culture and Society in the United States and West Germany.* Westview, Boulder, Colo., 1986.

Lerner, Gerda. *The Creation of Patriarchy.* Oxford University Press, New York, 1986.

Lerner, Michael. *Surplus Powerlessness.* Institute of Labor and Mental Health, Oakland, Calif., 1986.

Leuchtenburg, William E., *Franklin D. Roosevelt and the New Deal, 1932–1940.* Harper and Row, New York, 1963.

Lévi-Strauss, Claude. *Tristes Tropiques.* Plon, Paris, 1955. *Tristes Tropiques,* tr. J. Russell. Atheneum, New York, 1961.

Levitan, Sar A., and Robert Taggart. *The Promise of Greatness.* Harvard University Press, Cambridge, Mass., 1976.

Lewis, Oscar. *La Vida: A Puerto Rican Familiy in the Culture of Poverty, San Juan and New York.* Random House, New York, 1966..

Lichtenberg, Joseph D., and Samuel Kaplan, eds. *Reflections on Self Psychology.* Analytic Press, Hillsdale, N.J., 1983.

Lichtheim, George. *Marxism: An Historical and Critical Study.* Praeger, New York, 1961.

Lieberson, Stanley. *A Piece of the Pie: Blacks and White Immigrants Since 1880.* University of California Press, Berkeley, 1980.

Lifton, Robert Jay. *Death in Life: Survivors of Hiroshima.* Random House, New York, 1968.

Lifton, Robert Jay. *The Life of the Self: Toward a New Psychology.* Simon and Schuster, New York, 1976.

Lifton, Robert Jay. *The Broken Connection: On Death and the Continuity of Life.* Simon and Schuster, New York, 1979.

Lifton, Robert Jay. *The Nazi Doctors: Medical Killing and the Psychology of Genocide.* Basic Books, New York, 1986.

Lifton, Robert Jay. *The Future of Immortality and Other Essays for a Nuclear Age.* Basic Books, New York, 1987.

Lifton, Robert Jay, and Richard Falk. *Indefensible Weapons: The Political and Psychological Case Against Nuclearism.* Basic Books, New York, 1982.

Lindblom, Charles E. *Politics and Markets: The World's Political Economic Systems.* Basic Books, New York, 1977.

Lipset, Seymour Martin. *Political Man: The Social Bases of Politics.* Doubleday, Garden City, N.Y., 1960.

Lipset, Seymour Martin. *The First New Nation: The United States in Historical and Comparative Perspective.* Basic Books, New York, 1963.

Lipset, Seymour Martin, and Reinhard Bendix. *Social Mobility in Industrial Society.* University of California Press, Berkeley, 1959.

Lipset, Seymour Martin, and William Schneider. *The Confidence Gap: Business, Labor, and Government in the Public Mind.* Free Press, New York, 1983.

Lipset, Seymour Martin, and Neil J. Smelser, eds. *Sociology, the Progress of a Decade: A Collection of Articles.* Prentice-Hall, Englewood Cliffs, N.J., 1961.

Litwack, Leon F. *North of Slavery: The Negro in the Free States, 1790–1860.* University of Chicago Press, Chicago, 1961.

Loewenberg, Peter. *Decoding the Past: The Psychohistorical Approach.* Knopf, New York, 1983.

Lowi, Theodore. *The End of Liberalism.* Norton, New York, 1969.

Luker, Kristen. *Abortion and the Politics of Motherhood.* University of California, Berkeley, 1984.

Lustig, R. Jeffrey. *Corporate Liberalism: The Origins of Modern American Political Theory, 1890–1920.* University of California Press, Berkeley, 1982.

Lynd, Robert S. *Knowledge for What? The Place of Social Science in American Culture.* Princeton University Press, Princeton, 1939.

Lynd, Staughton. *The Ideological Origins of American Radicalism.* Pantheon, New York, 1968.

McCarthy, Mary. *The Writing on the Wall, and Other Literary Essays.* Harcourt, New York, 1970.

McCaughey, Robert A. *International Studies and Academic Enterprise: A Chapter in the Enclosure of American Learning.* Columbia University Press, New York, 1984.

McCloskey, Donald N. *The Rhetoric of Economics.* University of Wisconsin Press, Madison, 1985.

McClosky, Herbert, and John Zaller. *The American Ethos: Public Attitudes Toward Capitalism and Democracy.* Harvard University Press, Cambridge, Mass., 1984.

Macdonald, Dwight. *Memoirs of a Revolutionist: Essays in Political Criticism.* Farrar, Straus, New York, 1957.

Macdonald, Dwight. *The Responsibility of Peoples, and Other Essays in Political Criticism.* Gollancz, London, 1957; Greenwood Press, Westport, Conn., 1974.

Macdonald, Dwight. *Against the American Grain.* Random House, New York, 1962.

Macdonald, Dwight. *Discriminations: Essays and Afterthoughts, 1938–1974.* Grossman, New York, 1974.

MacIntyre, Alasdair. *After Virtue: A Study in Moral History.* University of Notre Dame Press, Notre Dame, Ind., 1981.

Mackenzie, Norman, ed. *Conviction.* MacGibbon and Kee, London, 1958; Monthly Review, New York, 1959.

McNamara, Robert S. *Blundering into Disaster: Surviving the First Century of the Nuclear Age*. Pantheon, New York, 1986.

Magaziner, Ira C., and Robert B. Reich. *Minding America's Business: The Decline and Rise of the American Economy*. Harcourt, New York, 1982.

Magdoff, Harry, and Paul M. Sweezy. *Stagnation and the Financial Explosion*. Monthly Review, New York, 1987.

Mahler, Margaret S.; Fred Pine; and Anni Bergman. *The Psychological Birth of the Human Infant: Symbiosis and Individuation*. Basic, New York, 1975.

Mailer, Norman. *The White Negro*. City Lights, San Francisco, 1957.

Mannheim, Karl. *Ideologie und Utopie*. F. Cohen, Bonn, 1929; *Ideology and Utopia: An Introduction to the Sociology of Knowledge*, tr. Louis Wirth and Edward Shils. Harcourt, New York, 1936.

Mansbridge, Jane J. *Beyond Adversary Democracy*. Basic, New York, 1980.

Marcus, George E., and Michael M. J. Fischer. *Anthropology as Cultural Critique: An Experimental Moment in the Human Sciences*. University of Chicago Press, Chicago, 1986.

Marcus, Steven. *Engels, Manchester, and the Working Class*. Random House, New York, 1974.

Marcus, Steven. *Representations: Essays on Literature and Society*. Random House, New York, 1975.

Marcus, Steven. *Freud and the Culture of Psychoanalysis: Studies in the Transition from Victorian Humanism to Modernity*. Allen and Unwin, Winchester, Mass., 1984.

Marcuse, Herbert. *Reason and Revolution: Hegel and the Rise of Social Theory*. Oxford University Press, New York, 1941.

Marcuse, Herbert. *Eros and Civilization: A Philosophical Inquiry into Freud*. Beacon, Boston, 1955.

Marcuse, Herbert. *Soviet Marxism: A Critical Analysis*. Columbia University Press, New York, 1958.

Marcuse, Herbert. *One-Dimensional Man: Studies in the Ideology of Advanced Industrial Society*. Beacon, Boston, 1964.

Marglin, Stephen A. "What Do Bosses Do? The Origins and Functions of Hierarchy in Capitalist Production." *The Review of Radical Political Economics*, vol. 6, no. 2, (Summer 1974), pp. 60–112.

MARHO—The Radical Historians Organization. *Visions of History*, ed. Henry Abelove et al. Pantheon, New York, 1983.

Marty, Martin E. *Righteous Empire: The Protestant Experience in America*. Dial, New York, 1970.

Marty, Martin E. *Religion and Republic: The American Circumstance*. Beacon, Boston, 1987.

Marx, Karl, and Frederick Engels. *Letters to Americans, 1848–1895: A Selection*, tr. Leonard E. Mins. International, New York, 1953.

Marx, Leo. *The Machine in the Garden: Technology and the Pastoral Ideal in America*. Oxford University Press, New York, 1964.

Marx, Leo. *The Pilot and the Passenger: Essays on Literature, Technology, and Culture in the United States*. Oxford University Press, New York, 1987.

Mason, Edward. *The Corporation in Modern Society*. Harvard University Press, Cambridge, 1982.

Matthiessen, F. O. *American Renaissance: Art and Expression in the Age of Emerson and Whitman*. Oxford University Press, New York, 1941.

Matthiessen, F. O. *The James Family: Including Selections from the Writings of Henry James, Senior, William, Henry, and Alice James*. Knopf, New York, 1947.

Matusow, Allen J. *The Unraveling of America: A History of Liberalism in the 1960s*. Harper & Row, New York, 1984.

May, Ernest R. *"Lessons" of the Past: The Use and Misuse of History in American Foreign Policy*. Oxford University Press, New York, 1973.

Mead, Margaret. *Culture and Commitment: A Study of the Generation Gap*. Natural History Press, Garden City, N.Y., 1970.

Melman, Seymour. *Pentagon Capitalism: The Political Economy of War*. McGraw-Hill, New York, 1970.

Merton, Robert King. *Social Theory and Social Structure: Toward the Codification of Theory and Research*. Free Press, Glencoe, Ill., 1949.

Mason, Edward. *The Corporation in Modern Society*. Harvard University Press, Cambridge, 1982.

Michelman, Frank I. "The Supreme Court, 1985 Term. Foreword." *Harvard Law Review*, vol. 100, no. 1 (Nov. 1986), pp. 4–77.

Miles, Michael W. *The Radical Probe: The Logic of Student Rebellion*. Atheneum, New York, 1971.

Milgram, Stanley. *Obedience to Authority: An Experimental View*. Harper, New York, 1974.

Miller, James. *Democracy Is in the Streets: From Point Huron to the Siege of Chicago*. Simon and Schuster, New York, 1987.

Miller, Jean Baker. *Toward a New Psychology of Women*. Beacon, Boston, 1976.

Miller, Perry. *The New England Mind: The Seventeenth Century*. Macmillan, New York, 1939.

Miller, Perry. *The New England Mind: From Colony to Province*. Harvard University Press, Cambridge, Mass., 1953.

Miller, S. M., and Pamela A. Roby. *The Future of Inequality*. Basic Books, New York, 1970.

Miller, S. M., and Donald Tomaskovic-Devey. *Recapitalizing America: Alternatives to the Corporate Distortion of National Policy.* Routledge and Kegan Paul, Boston, 1983.

Mills, C. Wright. *White Collar: The American Middle Classes.* Oxford University Press, New York, 1951.

Mills, C. Wright. *The Power Elite.* Oxford University Press, New York, 1956.

Mills, C. Wright. *The Causes of World War Three.* Simon and Schuster, New York, 1958.

Mills, C. Wright. *The Sociological Imagination.* Oxford University Press, New York, 1959.

Mitchell, Juliet. *Psychoanalysis and Feminism.* Pantheon, New York, 1974.

Mitchell, Juliet, and Ann Oakley, eds. *What Is Feminism?* Pantheon, New York, 1986.

Montgomery, David. *Workers' Control in America: Studies in the History of Work, Technology, and Labor Struggles.* Cambridge University Press, New York, 1979.

Montgomery, David. *The Fall of the House of Labor: The Workplace, the State, and American Labor Activism, 1865–1925.* Cambridge University Press, New York, 1987.

Moore, Barrington, Jr. *Social Origins of Dictatorship and Democracy: Lord and Peasant in the Making of the Modern World.* Beacon, Boston, 1966.

Moore, Barrington, Jr. *Reflections on the Causes of Human Misery and Upon Certain Proposals to Eliminate Them.* Beacon, Boston, 1972.

Moore, Barrington, Jr. *Injustice: The Social Bases of Obedience and Revolt.* Sharpe, White Plains, N.Y., 1978.

Morgan, Edmund S. *American Slavery, American Freedom: The Ordeal of Colonial Virginia.* Norton, New York, 1975.

Morgenthau, Hans Joachim, *Politics Among Nations: The Struggle for Power and Peace.* Knopf, New York, 1948.

Moynihan, Daniel P. *The Politics of a Guaranteed Income: The Nixon Administration and the Family Assistance Plan.* Random House, New York, 1973.

Murphy, Paul L. *The Constitution in Crisis Times, 1918–1969.* Harper, New York, 1971.

Murray, John Courtney. *We Hold These Truths: Catholic Reflections on the American Proposition.* Sheed and Ward, New York, 1960.

Nash, George H. *The Conservative Intellectual Movement in America Since 1945.* Basic Books, New York, 1976.

National Academy of Sciences, Behavioral and Social Sciences Committee. *The Behavioral and Social Sciences: Outlook and Needs; A Report.* Prentice-Hall, Englewood Cliffs, N.J., 1969.

National Conference of Catholic Bishops. *Economic Justice for All: Pastoral Letters in Catholic Social Teaching and the United States Economy.* Washington, D.C., 1980.

Neuhaus, Richard John. *The Naked Public Square: Religion and Democracy in America.* Eerdmans, Grand Rapids, Mich., 1984.

Neuman, W. Russell. *The Paradox of Mass Politics: Knowledge and Opinion in the American Electorate.* Harvard University Press, Cambridge, Mass., 1986.

Neumann, Franz. *Behemoth: The Structure and Practice of National Socialism.* Oxford University Press, New York, 1942.

Neumann, Franz. *The Democratic and the Authoritarian State: Essays in Political and Legal Theory,* ed. Herbert Marcuse. Free Press, Glencoe, Ill., 1957.

Newman, Charles. *The Post Modern Aura: The Act of Fiction in an Age of Inflation.* Northwestern University Press, Evanston, Ill., 1985.

Niebuhr, H. Richard. *The Social Sources of Denominationalism.* Holt, New York, 1929.

Niebuhr, H. Richard. *The Kingdom of God in America.* Willett, Clark, New York, 1937.

Neibuhr, Reinhold. *Moral Man and Immoral Society: A Study in Ethics and Politics.* Scribner's, New York, 1932.

Noble, David F. *America by Design: Science, Technology, and the Rise of Corporate Capitalism.* Knopf, New York, 1977.

Noble, David F. *Forces of Production: A Social History of Industrial Automation.* Knopf, New York, 1984.

Noble, David W. *Historians Against History: The Frontier Thesis and the National Covenant in American Historical Writing Since 1830.* University of Minnesota Press, Minneapolis, 1965.

Norton, Mary Beth. *Liberty's Daughters: The Revolutionary Experience of American Women, 1750–1800.* Little, Brown, Boston, 1980.

Nozick, Robert. *Anarchy, State, and Utopia.* Basic Books, New York, 1974.

Nozick, Robert. *Philosophical Explanations.* Harvard University Press, Cambridge, Mass., 1981.

Oates, Stephen B. *Let the Trumpet Sound: The Life of Martin Luther King, Jr.* Harper, New York, 1982.

Obey, David R., and Paul Sarbanes, eds. *The Changing American Economy: Papers from the Fortieth Anniversary Symposium of the Joint Economic Committee of the United States Congress.* Blackwell, New York, 1986.

O'Connor, James. *The Fiscal Crisis of the State.* St. Martin's, New York, 1973.

O'Connor, James. *Accumulation Crisis.* Blackwell, New York, 1984.

Offe, Claus. *Contradictions of the Welfare State,* ed. John Keane. MIT Press, Cambridge, Mass., 1984.

Okun, Arthur. *Equity and Efficiency: The Big Tradeoff.* Brookings Institution, Washington, D.C., 1975.

Ollman, Bertell, and Edward Vernoff, eds. *The Left Academy: Marxist Scholarship on American Campuses* [Vols. 1, 2, and 3]. McGraw-Hill, New York, 1982–86.

Olson, Mancur. *The Logic of Collective Action: Public Goods and the Theory of Groups.* Harvard University Press, Cambridge, Mass., 1965.

Olson, Mancur. *The Rise and Decline of Nations: Economic Growth, Stagflation, and Social Rigidities.* Yale University Press, New Haven, 1982.

Oppenheimer, Martin. *White Collar Politics.* Monthly Review, New York, 1985.

Ortner, Sherry B. "Theory in Anthropology Since the Sixties." *Comparative Studies in Society and History,* vol. 26, no. 1 (1984), pp. 126–66.

Page, Benjamin I. *Choices and Echoes in Presidential Elections: Rational Man and Electoral Democracy.* University of Chicago Press, Chicago, 1978.

Page, Benjamin I. *Who Gets What from Government.* University of California Press, Berkeley, 1983.

Palmer, John L., and Isabel V. Sawhill, eds. *The Reagan Experiment: An Examination of Economic and Social Policies Under the Reagan Administration.* Urban Institute Press, Washington, D.C., 1982.

Palmer, John L., and Isabel V. Sawhill, eds. *The Reagan Record: An Assessment of America's Changing Domestic Priorities.* Ballinger, Cambridge, Mass., 1984.

Parsons, Talcott. *The Social System.* Free Press, Glencoe, Ill., 1951.

Parsons, Talcott, and Edward Shils, eds., *Towards a General Theory of Action.* Harvard University Press, Cambridge, Mass., 1951.

Pechman, Joseph A. *Who Paid the Taxes, 1966–85.* Brookings Institution, Washington, D.C., 1985.

Peele, Gillian. *Revival and Reaction: The Right in Contemporary America.* Oxford University Press, New York, 1984.

Pells, Richard H. *The Liberal Mind in a Conservative Age: American Intellectuals in the 1940s and 1950s.* Harper, New York, 1985.

Pertschuk, Michael. *Revolt Against Regulation: The Rise and Pause of the Consumer Movement.* University of California Press, Berkeley, 1982.

Pertschuk, Michael. *Giant Killers.* Norton, New York, 1986.

Peters, Charles, and Phillip Keisling, eds. *A New Road for America: The Neoliberal Movement.* Madison, Lanham, Md., 1985.

Phillips, Jayne Anne. *Machine Dreams.* Dutton, New York, 1984.

Phillips, William. *A Partisan View: Five Decades of the Literary Life.* Stein and Day, New York, 1983.

Phillips, William. ed. *Partisan Review: The 50th Anniversary Edition.* Stein and Day, New York, 1985.

Phillips, William, et al. "Our Country and Our Culture." *Partisan Review,* vol. 19, nos. 3–5 (May–Oct., 1952).

Phillips, William, and Philip Rahv, eds. *The Partisan Reader: Ten Years of Partisan Review, 1934–1944: An Anthology.* Dial, New York, 1946.

Phillips, William, and Philip Rahv, eds. *The New Partisan Reader, 1945–1953.* Harcourt, New York, 1953.

Phillips, William, and Philip Rahv, eds. *The Partisan Review Anthology.* Holt, New York, 1962.

Piore, Michael J., and Charles F. Sabel. *The Second Industrial Divide: Possibilities for Prosperity.* Basic Books, New York, 1984.

Piven, Frances Fox, and Richard A. Cloward. *Poor People's Movements: Why They Succeed, How They Fail.* Pantheon, New York, 1977.

Pocock, J. G. A. *The Machiavellian Moment: Florentine Political Thought and the Atlantic Republican Tradition.* Princeton University Press, Princeton, N.J., 1975.

Podhoretz, Norman. "The Issue." *Commentary,* vol. 29, no. 2 (February 1960), pp. A and 182–84.

Podhoretz, Norman, ed. *The Commentary Reader: Two Decades of Articles and Stories.* Atheneum, New York, 1966.

Podhoretz, Norman. *Making It.* Random House, New York, 1967.

Podhoretz, Norman. *Breaking Ranks: A Political Memoir.* Harper, New York, 1979.

Podhoretz, Norman, et al. "How Has the United States Met Its Challenge Since 1945?" *Commentary,* vol. 80, no. 5 (November 1985).

Poirier, Richard. *The Performing Self: Compositions and Decompositions in the Languages of Contemporary Life.* Oxford University Press, New York, 1971.

Popper, Karl. *The Open Society and Its Enemies.* Routledge, London, 1945; rev. ed., Princeton University Press, Princeton, N.J., 1950.

Posner, Richard A. *Economic Analysis of Law.* Little, Brown, Boston, 1972.

Prins, Gwyn, ed. *The Nuclear Crisis Reader.* Vintage, New York, 1984.

Purcell, Edward A., Jr. *The Crisis of Democratic Theory: Scientific Naturalism and the Problem of Value.* University of Kentucky Press, Lexington, 1973.

Rader, Benjamin G. *The Academic Mind and Reform: The Influence of Richard T. Ely in American Life.* University of Kentucky Press, Lexington, 1966.

Rahv, Philip. *Image and Idea: Fourteen Essays on Literary Themes.* New Directions, New York, 1949.

Rahv, Philip. *Literature and the Sixth Sense.* Houghton Mifflin, Boston, 1969.

Rahv, Philip. *Essays on Literature and Politics, 1932–72,* ed. Arabel J. Porter and Andrew J. Dvosin. Houghton Mifflin, Boston, 1978.

Rainwater, Lee, and William L. Yancey. *The Moynihan Report and the Politics of Controversy.* MIT Press, Cambridge, Mass., 1967.

Rajchman, John, and Cornel West, eds. *Post-Analytic Philosophy.* Columbia University Press, New York, 1985.

Raskin, Marcus G. *The Politics of National Security.* Transaction, New Brunswick, N.J., 1979.

Raskin, Marcus G. *The Common Good: Its Politics, Policies, and Philosophy.* Routledge and Kegan Paul, New York, 1986.

Raskin, Marcus G., and Herbert J. Bernstein. *New Ways of Knowing: The Sciences, Society, and Reconstructive Knowledge.* Rowman and Allanheld, Totowa, N.J., 1987.

Ravetz, Jerome R. *Scientific Knowledge and Its Social Problems.* Clarendon, Oxford, 1971.

Rawls, John. *A Theory of Justice.* Belknap, Harvard University Press, Cambridge, Mass., 1971.

Reagan, Michael D. *Regulation: The Politics of Policy.* Little, Brown, Boston, 1987.

Reich, Charles. "The New Property." *Yale Law Journal,* vol. 73, no. 5 (April 1964), pp. 733–87.

Reich, Michael. *Racial Inequality: A Political-Economic Analysis.* Princeton University Press, Princeton, N.J., 1981.

Reich, Robert B. *The Next American Frontier.* Times, New York, 1983.

Reich, Robert B. *Tales of a New America.* Times, New York, 1987.

Reichley, A. James. *Religion in American Public Life.* Brookings Institution, Washington, D.C., 1985.

Remini, Robert V., ed. *The Age of Jackson.* Harper, New York, 1972.

Renner, Karl. *Die Rechtsinstitute des Privatrechts und Ihre Soziale Funktion: Ein Beitrag zur Kritik des Bürgerlichen Rechts.* Mohr, Tübingen, 1929; *The Institutions of Private Law and Their Social Functions,* Ed. O. Kahn-Freund; tr. Agnes Schwartzschild. Routledge and Kegan Paul, London, 1949.

Report by the AFL-CIO Committee on the Evolution of Work. *The Future of Work.* August 1983.

Report by the AFL-CIO Committee on the Evolution of Work. *The Changing Situation of Workers and the Unions.* February 1985.

Report of the President's Commission. *A National Agenda for the Eighties.* Government Printing Office, Washington, D.C., 1980.

Report of Special Task Force to the Secretary, Department of Health, Education, and Welfare. *Work in America.* MIT Press, Cambridge, Mass., 1972.

Ricci, David M. *The Tragedy of Political Science: Politics, Scholarship, and Democracy.* Yale University Press, New Haven, 1984.

Rieder, Jonathan. *Canarsie: The Jews and Italians of Brooklyn Against Liberalism.* Harvard University Press, Cambridge, Mass., 1985.

Rieff, Philip. *Freud: The Mind of the Moralist.* Viking, New York, 1959.

Rieff, Philip, ed. *On Intellectuals: Theoretical Studies, Case Studies.* Doubleday, Garden City, N.Y., 1969.

Riesman, David. *Individualism Reconsidered, and Other Essays.* Free Press, Glencoe, Ill., 1954.

Riesman, David. *Abundance for What?, and Other Essays.* Doubleday, Garden City, N.Y., 1964.

Riesman, David, with Reuel Denney and Nathan Glazer. *The Lonely Crowd: A Study of the Changing American Character.* Yale University Press, New Haven, 1950.

Riesman, David, and Michael Maccoby. "The American Crisis: Political Idealism and the Cold War." *Commentary,* vol. 29, no. 6 (June 1960), pp. 61–74.

Rodell, Fred. *Woe Unto You, Lawyers.* Reynal and Hitchock, New York, 1939.

Rorty, Amélie Oksenberg, ed. *The Identities of Persons.* University of California Press, Berkeley, 1976. (Esp. Charles Taylor, "The Self in Question.")

Rorty, Richard. *Philosophy and the Mirror of Nature.* Princeton University Press, Princeton, N.J., 1979.

Rorty, Richard. *Consequences of Pragmatism: Essays, 1972–80.* University of Minnesota Press, Minneapolis, 1982.

Rosaldo, Michelle Z. *Knowledge and Passion: Ilongot Notions of Self and Social Life.* Cambridge University Press, New York, 1980.

Rose, Phyllis. *Woman of Letters: A Life of Virginia Woolf.* Oxford University Press, New York, 1978.

Rose, Phyllis. *Parallel Lives: Five Victorian Marriages.* Knopf, New York, 1983.

Rosenberg, Bernard, and Ernest Goldstein, eds. *Creators and Disturbers: Reminiscences by Jewish Intellectuals of New York.* Columbia University Press, New York, 1982.

Rosenberg, Bernard, and David Manning White, eds. *Mass Culture: The Popular Arts in America.* Free Press, Glencoe, Ill., 1957.

Rosenberg, Harold. *The Tradition of the New.* Horizon, New York, 1959.

Rosenberg, Harold. *Discovering the Present: Three Decades in Art, Culture, and Politics.* University of Chicago Press, Chicago, 1973.

Rosenberg, Rosalind. *Beyond Separate Spheres: Intellectual Roots of Modern Feminism.* Yale University Press, New Haven, 1982.

Ross, Dorothy. "Socialism and American Liberalism: Academic Social Thought in the 1880's." *Perspectives in American History,* vol. 11 (1977–78), pp. 5–79.

Rostow, Walt. *Stages of Economic Growth: A Non-Communist Manifesto.* Cambridge University Press, New York, 1960.

Roszak, Theodore. ed. *The Dissenting Academy.* Pantheon, New York, 1968.

Rozenzweig, Roy. *Eight Hours for What We Will: Workers and Leisure in an Industrial City, 1870–1920.* Cambridge University Press, New York, 1983.

Rumble, Wilfred. *American Legal Realism: Skepticism, Reform, and the Judicial Process.* Cornell University Press, Ithaca, 1968.

Sabel, Charles F. *Work and Politics: The Division of Labor in Industry.* Cambridge University Press, New York, 1982.

Sahlins, Marshall. *Islands of History.* University of Chicago Press, Chicago, 1985.

Said, Edward W. *Orientalism.* Pantheon, New York, 1978.

Salvatore, Nick. *Eugene V. Debs: Citizen and Socialist.* University of Illinois Press, Urbana, 1982.

Sandel, Michael J. *Liberalism and the Limits of Justice.* Cambridge University Press, New York, 1982.

Sandel, Michael J., ed. *Liberalism and Its Critics.* New York University Press, New York, 1984.

Sapir, Edward. *Selected Writing of Edward Sapir in Language, Culture, and Personality,* ed. Daniel Mandelbaum. University of California Press, Berkeley, 1949.

Sartre, Jean-Paul. *Questions de Méthode.* Gallimard, Paris, 1960. *Search for a Method,* tr. H. Barnes. Knopf, New York, 1963.

Schachtel, Ernest G. *Metamorphosis: On the Development of Affect, Perception, Attention, and Memory.* Basic Books, New York, 1959.

Schafer, Roy. *A New Language for Psychoanalysis.* Yale University Press, New Haven, 1976.

Schapiro, Meyer. *Modern Art: 19th and 20th Centuries.* Braziller, New York, 1979.

Schlesinger, Arthur M., Jr. *The Vital Center: The Politics of Freedom.* Houghton Mifflin, Boston, 1949.

Schlesinger, Arthur M., Jr. *A Thousand Days: John F. Kennedy in the White House.* Houghton Mifflin, Boston, 1965.

Schlesinger, Arthur M., Jr. *The Imperial Presidency.* Houghton Mifflin, Boston, 1973.

Schlesinger, Arthur M., Jr. *The Cycles of American History.* Houghton Mifflin, Boston, 1986.

Schorske, Carl. *Fin-de-Siècle Vienna: Politics and Culture.* Knopf, New York, 1979. (Esp. "Politics and Parricide in Freud's Interpretation of Dreams.")

Schrecker, Ellen W. *No Ivory Tower: McCarthyism and the Universities.* Oxford University Press, New York, 1986.

Schroyer, Trent. *The Critique of Domination: The Origins and Development of Critical Theory.* Braziller, New York, 1973.

Schuck, Peter. *Suing Government: Citizens' Remedies for Official Wrongs.* Yale University Press, New Haven, 1983.

Schumpeter, Joseph. *Capitalism, Socialism, and Democracy.* Harper, New York, 1942.

Schwarz, John E. *America's Hidden Success: A Reassessment of Twenty Years of Public Policy.* Norton, New York, 1983.

Schwartz, Herman, ed. *The Burger Years: Rights and Wrongs in the Supreme Court, 1969–1986.* Sifton, Viking, New York, 1987.

Scott, Joan. "Gender: A Useful Category of Historical Analysis." *American Historical Review,* vol. 91, no. 5 (December 1986), pp. 1053–75.

Selznick, Philip. *TVA and the Grass Roots: A Study in the Sociology of Formal Organization.* University of California Press, Berkeley, 1949.

Sennett, Richard. *The Fall of Public Man.* Knopf, New York, 1977.

Sennett, Richard, and Jonathan Cobb. *The Hidden Injuries of Class.* Knopf, New York, 1972.

Shaiken, Harley. *Work Transformed: Automation and Labor in the Computer Age.* Holt, New York, 1985.

Shechner, Mark. *After the Revolution: Studies in the Contemporary Jewish American Imagination.* Indiana University Press, Bloomington, 1987.

Sherwin, Martin. *A World Destroyed: The Atomic Bomb and the Grand Alliance.* Knopf, New York, 1975.

Shils, Edward. *The Intellectuals and the Powers, and Other Essays.* University of Chicago Press, Chicago, 1972.

Shils, Edward. *Center and Periphery: Essays in Macrosociology.* University of Chicago Press, Chicago, 1975.

Shils, Edward. *The Calling of Sociology and Other Essays on the Pursuit of Learning.* University of Chicago Press, Chicago, 1980.

Shils, Edward. *Tradition.* University of Chicago Press, Chicago, 1981.

Shils, Edward. *The Constitution of Society.* University of Chicago Press, Chicago, 1982.

Shorris, Earl. *Jews Without Mercy: A Lament.* Anchor, Garden City, N.J., 1982.

Shoup, Laurence H., and William Minter. *The Imperial Brain Trust: The Council on Foreign Relations and United States Foreign Policy.* Monthly Review, New York, 1977.

Sica, Alan. "Parsons Jr." *American Journal of Sociology,* vol. 89, no. 1 (July 1983), pp. 200–219.

Skinner, Quentin. *The Foundations of Modern Political Thought* [Vol. I: *The Renaissance;* Vol. II: *The Age of Reformation*]. Cambridge University Press, New York, 1978.

Skinner, Quentin, ed. *The Return of Grand Theory in the Human Sciences.* Cambridge University Press, New York, 1985.

Skocpol, Theda. *States and Social Revolutions: A Comparative Analysis of France, Russia, and China.* Cambridge University Press, New York, 1979.

Slotkin, Richard. *The Fatal Environment: The Myth of the Frontier in the Age of Industrialization, 1800–1890.* Atheneum, New York, 1985.

Smith, Henry Nash. *Virgin Land: The American West as Symbol and Myth.* Harvard University Press, Cambridge, Mass., 1950.

Smith-Rosenberg, Carroll, *Disorderly Conduct: Visions of Gender in Victorian America.* Knopf, New York, 1985.

Sontag, Susan. *Against Interpretation, and Other Essays.* Farrar, Straus, New York, 1966.

Sontag, Susan. *Styles of Radical Will.* Farrar, Straus, New York, 1969.

Sorin, Gerald. *The Prophetic Minority: American Jewish Immigrant Radicals, 1880–1920.* Indiana University Press, Bloomington, 1985.

Stafford, Right Reverend J. Francis. *This Home of Freedom.* Pastoral Letter to the Archdiocese of Denver, May 28, 1981.

Steinfels, Peter. *The Neoconservatives: The Men Who Are Changing America's Politics.* Simon and Schuster, New York, 1979.

Strausz-Hupé, Robert. *Geopolitics: The Struggle for Space and Power.* Putnam, New York, 1942.

Strout, Cushing. *The New Heavens and New Earth: Political Religion in America.* Harper, New York, 1973.

Stuckey, Sterling. *Slave Culture: Nationalist Theory and the Foundations of Black America.* Oxford University Press, New York, 1987.

Sullivan, William M. *Reconstructing Public Philosophy.* University of California Press, Berkeley, 1982.

Sulloway, Frank. *Freud, Biologist of the Mind: Beyond the Psychoanalytic Legend.* Basic Books, New York, 1979.

Sundquist, James L. *Dynamics of the Party System: Alignment and Realignment of Political Parties in the United States.* Brookings Institution, Washington, D.C., 1973.

Susman, Warren I. *Culture as History: The Transformation of American Society in the Twentieth Century.* Pantheon, New York, 1984.

Sweezy, Paul. *The Theory of Capitalist Development: Principles of Marxian Political Economy.* Oxford University Press, New York, 1942.

Sweezy, Paul. *The Present as History: Essays and Reviews on Capitalism and Socialism.* Monthly Review, New York, 1953.

"Symposium: Judicial Review and the Constitution: The Text and Beyond." *University of Dayton Law Review,* vol. 8 (Summer 1983). (Esp. Mark V. Tushnet, "Legal Realism, Structural Review and Prophecy," pp. 809–31.)

Taylor, Charles. *The Explanation of Behavior.* Humanities Press, New York, 1964.

Teodori, Massimo, ed. *The New Left: A Documentary History.* Bobbs-Merrill, Indianapolis, 1969.

Terkel, Studs. *Working.* Pantheon, New York, 1974.

Thompson, Edward, et al. *Exterminism and Cold War,* ed. *New Left Review.* New Left, New York, 1982.

Thompson, E. P., ed. *Out of Apathy.* Stevens, London, 1960.

Thompson, E. P. *The Making of the English Working Class.* Pantheon, New York, 1964.

Thompson, E. P. *The Poverty of Theory, and Other Essays.* Monthly Review, New York, 1978.

Thurow, Lester C. *Dangerous Currents: The State of Economics.* Random House, New York, 1983.

Tillich, Paul. *The Protestant Era.* University of Chicago Press, Chicago, 1948.

Tomlins, Christopher L. *The State and the Unions: Labor Relations, Law, and the Organized Labor Movement in America, 1880–1960.* Cambridge University Press, New York, 1985.

Touraine, Alain. *La Société Post-Industrielle.* Denoël, Paris, 1969; *The Post-Industrial Society; Tomorrow's Social History: Classes, Conflicts, and Culture in the Programmed Society,* tr. Leonard F. X. Mayhew. Random House, New York, 1971.

Touraine, Alain. *Production de la Société.* Seuil, Paris, 1973; *The Self-Production of Society,* tr. Derek Coltman. University of Chicago Press, Chicago, 1977.

Trachtenberg, Alan. *The Incorporation of America: Culture and Society in the Gilded Age.* Hill and Wang, New York, 1982.

Tribe, Laurence H. *Constitutional Choices.* Harvard University Press, Cambridge, Mass., 1985.

Trilling, Lionel. *The Liberal Imagination: Essays on Literature and Society.* Viking, New York, 1950.

Trilling, Lionel. *Beyond Culture: Essays on Literature and Learning.* Viking, New York, 1965.

Trilling, Lionel. *Sincerity and Authenticity.* Harvard University Press, Cambridge, Mass., 1972.

Tsongas, Paul. *The Road from Here: Liberalism and Realities in the 1980s.* Knopf, New York, 1981.

Tufte, Edward R. *Political Control of the Economy.* Princeton University Press, Princeton, N.J., 1978.

Turner, James. *Without God, Without Creed: The Origins of Unbelief in America.* Johns Hopkins University Press, Baltimore, 1985.

Turner, Victor W. *The Ritual Process: Structure and Anti-Structure.* Aldine, Chicago, 1969.

Tushnet, Mark V. *Red, White, and Blue: A Critical Analysis of Constitutional Law.* Harvard University Press, Cambridge, Mass., 1988.

"Twenty Years After, 1965–1985: Twentieth Anniversary Issue." *Public Interest,* no. 81 (Fall 1985).

Ungar, Sanford J., ed. *Estrangement: America and the World.* Oxford University Press, New York, 1985.

Unger, Roberto Mangabeira. *The Critical Legal Studies Movement.* Harvard University Press, Cambridge, Mass., 1986.

Unger, Robert Mangabeira. *Politics: A Work in Constructive Social Theory* [Part 1: *False Necessity: Anti-Necessitarian Social Theory in the Service of Radical Democracy*]. Cambridge University Press, New York, 1987.

Unger, Roberto Mangabeira. *Social Theory, Its Situation and Its Task* (A Critical Introduction to *Politics, a Work in Constructive Social Theory*]. Cambridge University Press, New York, 1987.

Unger, Roberto Mangabeira. *Plasticity into Power: Comparative-Historical Studies of the Institutional Conditions of Economic and Military Success* [Variations on Themes of *Politics, a Work in Constructive Social Theory*]. Cambridge University Press, New York, 1987.

Verba, Sidney, and Gary R. Orren. *Equality in America: The View from the Top.* Harvard University Press, Cambridge, Mass., 1985.

Vernon, Raymond. *Sovereignty at Bay: The Multinational Spread of U.S. Enterprises.* Basic Books, New York, 1971.

Veysey, Laurence R. *The Emergence of the American University.* University of Chicago Press, Chicago, 1965.

Wald, Alan M. *The New York Intellectuals: The Rise and Decline of the Anti-Stalinist Left from the 1930s to the 1980s.* University of North Carolina Press, Chapel Hill, 1987.

Wallace, Anthony F. C. *Rockdale: The Growth of an American Village in the Early Industrial Revolution.* Knopf, New York, 1978.

Wallerstein, Immanuel. *The Modern World-System: Capitalist Agriculture and the Origins of the European World-Economy in the Sixteenth Century.* Academic Press, New York, 1974.

Wallerstein, Immanuel. *The Capitalist World-Economy: Essays.* Cambridge University Press, New York, 1979.

Wallerstein, Immanuel, and Paul Starr, eds. *The University Crisis Reader.* Random House, New York, 1971.

Walzer, Michael. *Spheres of Justice: A Defense of Pluralism and Equality.* Basic Books, New York, 1983.

Walzer, Michael. *Interpretation and Social Criticism.* Harvard University Press, Cambridge, Mass., 1987.

Ward, John William. *Red, White, and Blue: Men, Books, and Ideas in American Culture.* Oxford University Press, New York, 1969.

Weber, Max. *From Max Weber: Essays in Sociology,* tr., ed., and intro., H. H. Gerth and C. Wright Mills. Oxford University Press, New York, 1946.

Weinstein, James. *The Decline of Socialism in America, 1912–1925.* Monthly Review, New York, 1967.

Weinstein, James. *The Corporate Ideal in the Liberal State, 1900–1918.* Beacon, Boston, 1968.

Weinstein, James, and David W. Eakins, eds. *For a New America: Essays in History and Politics from Studies on the Left, 1959–1967.* Random House, New York, 1970.

Weitzman, Martin L. *The Share Economy: Conquering Stagflation.* Harvard University Press, Cambridge, Mass., 1984.

White, Morton Gabriel. *Social Thought in America: The Revolt Against Formalism.* Viking, New York, 1949.

White, Morton Gabriel. *The Philosophy of the American Revolution.* Oxford University Press, New York, 1978.

White, Morton, and Lucia White. *The Intellectual Versus the City: From Thomas Jefferson to Frank Lloyd Wright.* Harvard University Press, Cambridge, Mass., 1962.

Whitfield, Stephen J. *A Critical American: The Politics of Dwight Macdonald.* Archon Books, Hamden, Conn., 1984.

Wiebe, Robert H. *The Search for Order, 1877–1920.* Hill and Wang, New York, 1967.

Wiebe, Robert H. *The Segmented Society: An Introduction to the Meaning of America.* Oxford University Press, New York, 1975.

Williams, Raymond. *Culture and Society, 1780–1950.* Columbia University Press, New York, 1958.

Williams, William Appleman. *The Tragedy of American Diplomacy,* World, Cleveland, 1959.

Williams, William Appleman. *The Contours of American History.* World, Cleveland, 1961.

Williams, William Appleman. *Empire as a Way of Life: An Essay on the Causes and Character of America's Present Predicament, Along with a Few Thoughts About an Alternative.* Oxford University Press, New York, 1980.

Wills, Garry. *Reagan's America: Innocents at Home.* Doubleday, Garden City, N.Y., 1987.

Wilson, Edmund. *Axel's Castle: A Study in the Imaginative Literature of 1870– 1930.* Scribner, New York, 1931.

Wilson, Edmund. *To the Finland Station: A Study in the Writing and Acting of History.* Harcourt, New York, 1940.

Wilson, Edmund. *The Shores of Light: A Literary Chronicle of the Twenties and Thirties.* Farrar, Straus, New York, 1952.

Wilson, Edmund. *Apologies to the Iroquois.* Farrar, Straus, New York, 1960.

Wilson, Edmund. *Patriotic Gore: Studies in the Literature of the American Civil War.* Oxford University Press, New York, 1962.

Wilson, Edmund. *Upstate: Records and Recollections of Northern New York.* Farrar, Straus, New York, 1971.

Wilson, William Julius. *The Declining Significance of Race: Blacks and Changing American Institutions.* University of Chicago Press, Chicago, 1978.

Wilson, William Julius. *The Truly Disadvantaged: The Inner City, the Underclass, and Public Policy.* University of Chicago Press, Chicago, 1987.

Winnicott, D. W. *Holding and Interpretation.* Hogarth, London, 1986; Grove, New York, 1987.

Wofsy, Leon, ed. *Before the Point of No Return: An Exchange of Views on the Cold War, the Reagan Doctrine, and What Is to Come.* Monthly Review, New York, 1986.

Wolf, Eric R. *Peasant Wars of the Twentieth Century.* Harper, New York, 1969.

Wolfe, Alan. *The Limits of Legitimacy: Political Contradictions of Contemporary Capitalism.* Free Press, New York, 1977.

Wolfe, Alan. *America's Impasse: The Rise and Fall of the Politics of Growth.* Pantheon, New York, 1981.

Wolff, Robert Paul. *The Poverty of Liberalism.* Beacon, Boston, 1968.

Wolff, Robert Paul; Barrington Moore, Jr.; and Herbert Marcuse. *A Critique of Pure Tolerance.* Beacon, Boston, 1965.

Wolin, Sheldon S. *Politics and Vision: Continuity and Innovation in Western Political Thought.* Little, Brown, Boston, 1960.

Wood, Gordon S. *The Creation of the American Republic, 1776–1787.* Institute of Early American History and Culture, University of North Carolina Press, Chapel Hill, 1969.

Woodward, C. Vann. *Origins of the New South, 1877–1913.* Louisiana State University Press, Baton Rouge, 1951.

Woodward, C. Vann. *Reunion and Reaction: The Compromise of 1877 and the End of Reconstruction.* Little, Brown, Boston, 1951.

Woodward, C. Vann. *The Strange Career of Jim Crow.* Oxford University Press, New York, 1955.

Woodward, C. Vann. *Thinking Back: The Perils of Writing History.* Louisiana State University Press, Baton Rouge, 1986.

Wright, Erik Olin. *Class, Crisis, and the State.* New Left, London, 1978.

Wright, Gavin. *Old South, New South: Revolutions in the Southern Economy Since the Civil War.* Basic Books, New York, 1986.

Wright, Louis Booker. *The Cultural Life of the American Colonies, 1607–1763.* Harper, New York, 1957.

Wrong, Dennis H. *Power: Its Forms, Bases, and Uses.* Harper, New York, 1979.

Wyman, David S. *The Abandonment of the Jews: America and the Holocaust, 1941–1945.* Pantheon, New York, 1984.

Yankelovich, Daniel. *New Rules: Searching for Self-Fulfillment in a World Turned Upside Down.* Random House, New York, 1981.

Yerushalmi, Yosef Hayim. *Zakhor: Jewish History and Jewish Memory.* University of Washington Press, Seattle, 1982.

Young-Bruehl, Elisabeth. *Hannah Arendt: For Love of the World.* Yale University Press, New Haven, 1982.

Zeitlin, Maurice, ed. *American Society, Inc.: Studies of the Social Structure and Political Economy of the United States.* Markham, Chicago, 1970.

Zieger, Robert H. *American Workers, American Unions, 1920–1985.* Johns Hopkins University Press, Baltimore, 1986.

Zinn, Howard. *A People's History of the United States.* Harper, New York, 1980.

Zunz, Olivier. ed. *Reliving the Past: The Worlds of Social History.* University of North Carolina Press, Chapel Hill, 1985.

Index

Norman Birnbaum was born in New York in 1926, and studied at Williams College and Harvard University. He has taught sociology at Amherst College, the Graduate Faculty of the New School for Social Research, the London School of Economics and Political Science, Oxford University, and the University of Strasbourg. He was a founding editor of *New Left Review* and on the board of *Partisan Review*. He is presently on the boards of the *Nation* and *Praxis*. His previous books include *The Crisis of Industrial Society* and *Toward a Critical Sociology*. He is University Professor at Georgetown University Law Center. Professor Birnbaum is an adviser to political parties, unions, and the peace movement in Western Europe. In this country he has participated in the presidential campaigns of Edward Kennedy and Jesse Jackson, served as adviser to a number of members of the House and Senate, and worked with public-interest groups and unions.

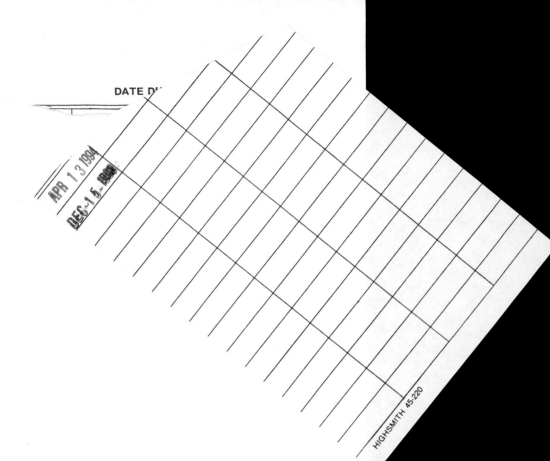